Multistate Corporate Tax Course

2009 EDITION

JOHN C. HEALY
MICHAEL S. SCHADEWALD

.CCH
a Wolters Kluwer business

Contributors

Editor	Cindy Hangartner, JD, LL.M
Contributing Editors	John C. Healy, MST, CPA
	Michael S Schadewald, PhD, CPA
Technical Review	Sharon Brooks
Production Coordinator	Hilary Rawk
Production	Lynn J. Brown
Layout & Design	Laila Gaidulis

This publication is designed to provide accurate and authoritative information in regard to the subject matter covered. It is sold with the understanding that the publisher is not engaged in rendering legal, accounting, or other professional service. If legal advice or other expert assistance is required, the services of a competent professional person should be sought.

ISBN: 978-0-8080-1918-3

Printed in the United States of America

MULTISTATE CORPORATE TAX COURSE (2009 EDITION)
Introduction

This Course is the top quality tax review and analysis that every state tax practitioner needs to keep a step ahead.

Among the topics covered in the Course are:

- Basic Principles of Multistate Corporate Income Taxation
- Combined Unitary Reporting
- Pass-Through Entities
- Nexus
- Sales and Use Tax Base
- Pre-Audit Strategies and Opportunities
- Construction Contractors and Manufacturers

Throughout the Course you will find comments that are vital to understanding a particular strategy or idea, Examples to illustrate the topics covered, and Study Questions to help you test your knowledge. Answers to the Study Questions, with feedback on both correct and incorrect responses are provided in a special section beginning on page 197.

To assist you in your later reference and research, a detailed topical index has been included for this Course beginning on page 219.

This Course is divided into two Modules. Take your time and review each Course Module. When you feel confident that you thoroughly understand the material, turn to the CPE Quizzer. Complete one or all Module Quizzers for Continuing Professional Education credit. You can complete and return the Quizzers to CCH for grading at an additional charge. If you receive a grade of 70 percent or higher on the Quizzers, you will receive CPE credit for the Modules graded. Further information is provided in the CPE Quizzer instructions on page 231.

October 2008

COURSE OBJECTIVES

This Course was prepared to provide you with an overview of multistate tax issues. Upon Course completion, you will be able to:

- Define the basic principles of multistate corporate income taxation—including nexus, apportionment, combined and consolidated reporting, and tax-planning strategies
- Define the concept of a unitary business and distinguish the difference between combined unitary reporting and consolidated returns
- Discuss how states tax the income of S corporations, partnerships, and limited liability companies (LLCs)
- Describe which activities performed by a taxpayer in a particular state will cause the taxpayer to have income tax and/or sales and use tax nexus with that state
- Define the imposition of sales and use taxes—including rates, items and transactions that are subject to sales and use taxes, and the broad category of exemptions
- Apply strategies and recognize opportunities that could reduce audit exposure when a taxpayer is preparing for a sales and use tax audit
- Describe how manufacturers and construction contractors' varying roles can affect their sales and use tax liability

CCH'S PLEDGE TO QUALITY

Thank you for choosing this CCH Continuing Education product. We will continue to produce high quality products that challenge your intellect and give you the best option for your Continuing Education requirements. Should you have a concern about this or any other CCH CPE product, please call our Customer Service Department at 1-800-248-3248.

NEW ONLINE GRADING gives you immediate 24/7 grading with instant results and no Express Grading Fee.

The **CCH Testing Center** website gives you and others in your firm easy, free access to CCH print Courses and allows you to complete your CPE Quizzers online for immediate results. Plus, the **My Courses** feature provides convenient storage for your CPE Course Certificates and completed Quizzers.

Go to **www.cchtestingcenter.com** to complete your Quizzer online.

One **complimentary copy** of this Course is provided with copies of selected CCH Tax titles . Additional copies of this Course may be ordered for $29.00 each by calling 1-800-248-3248 (ask for product 0-0981-200).

MULTISTATE CORPORATE TAX COURSE (2009 EDITION)

Contents

MODULE 1: STATE CORPORATE INCOME TAXES

1 Basic Principles of Multistate Corporate Income Taxation
Learning Objectives 1
Introduction 1
Nexus 2
Computation of State Taxable Income 5
Apportionment Formulas 10
Consolidated Returns and Combined Unitary Reporting 16
Concept of a Unitary Business Group 19
Basic Multistate Tax-Planning Strategies 22

2 Combined Unitary Reporting
Learning Objectives 29
Overview 29
Combined Reporting Versus Consolidated Returns 30
Mandatory Versus Discretionary Combined Reporting 32
Worldwide Versus Water's-Edge Combined Reporting 33
Concept of a Unitary Business 36

3 Pass-Through Entities
Learning Objectives 51
S Corporations 51
Partnerships 59
Limited Liability Companies 69
Fiscal-Year Elections: Partnerships, S Corporations,
and Personal Service Corporations 76

MODULE 2: SALES AND USE TAXES

4 Nexus
Learning Objectives 79
Overview 79
Constitutional Nexus 81
Physical Presence Requirement 82
Meaning of Solicitation [*Wrigley* (1992)] 85
Unprotected Activities 90
Protected Activities 91
Affiliate Nexus 94
Agency and Affiliate Nexus 99

P.L. 86-272 and Independent Agents 100
Other Applications of Agency Nexus Principle 101
Economic Nexus 105
Other Nexus Issues 109

 Sales and Use Tax Base
Learning Objectives 119
Overview 119
Items Subject to Sales Tax 121
Transactions Subject to Sales And Use Taxes 125
Determination of Sales Price 133

Pre-Audit Strategies and Opportunities
Learning Objectives 137
Initial Audit Contact and the Audit Tone 137
Confirmation Letter from Auditor 149
Waiver of Statute of Limitations 151
Performing Self-Audits 154
Reverse audits and refund reviews 159
Record Retention Issues 167
Responding to Audit and Nexus Questionnaires 169
Contacting Taxpayers Suspected of
    Engaging in Nexus-Creating Activities 172

Construction Contractors and Manufacturers
Learning Objectives 177
Treatment of Construction Contractors 177
Treatment of Manufacturers 182

Answers to Study Questions 197
Index 219
CPE Quizzer Instructions 231
CPE Quizzer: Module 1 233
CPE Quizzer: Module 2 241
Module 1: Answer Sheet 251
Module 2: Answer Sheet 255
Evaluation Form 259

MODULE 1: STATE CORPORATE INCOME TAXES — CHAPTER 1

Basic Principles of Multistate Corporate Income Taxation

This chapter discusses the basic principles involved in multistate corporate income taxation, including nexus, apportionment, combined and consolidated reporting, and tax-planning strategies.

LEARNING OBJECTIVES

Upon completing this chapter, the student will:

- Understand which activities of a multistate corporation can create nexus
- Understand how state taxable income is generally calculated
- Be familiar with apportionment formulas and how they vary by states
- Be able to contrast the difference between consolidated returns and unitary reporting
- Understand how the states stand on the issue of consolidated returns and unitary reporting
- Be familiar with multistate tax-planning strategies

INTRODUCTION

Forty-six states and the District of Columbia impose some type of income-based tax on corporations. Nevada, South Dakota, Washington, and Wyoming do *not* levy a corporate income tax.

The corporate income taxes of California, Florida, New York, and a number of other states are formally franchise taxes imposed on, for example, the privilege of doing business in the state. Because the value of the franchise tax is measured by the income derived from that privilege, the tax is computed in essentially the same manner as a direct income tax.

Although many states closely link their corporate tax to the federal income tax, some states impose other types of corporate taxes in lieu of a net income tax.

EXAMPLE

The State of Washington does not have a corporate income tax, but it does impose a gross receipts tax called the *business and occupations tax*.

From 2005 to 2009, Ohio is phasing in a gross receipts tax, called the *commercial activity tax*, as a replacement for its corporate franchise tax on income or net worth.

In 2007, Texas replaced its corporate franchise tax on capital and earned surplus with a tax on gross margin, called the *margin tax*.

Likewise, Michigan recently repealed its *single business tax* (a type of value-added tax), and replaced it with a net income tax and a modified gross receipts tax which takes effect in 2008.

NEXUS

Constitutional Nexus

A threshold issue for any corporation operating in more than one state is determining the states in which it must file returns and pay income tax. A state has jurisdiction to tax a corporation organized in another state *only* if the out-of-state corporation's contacts with the state are sufficient to create nexus.

Historically, states have asserted that virtually any type of in-state business activity creates nexus for an out-of-state corporation. This approach reflects the reality that it is politically more appealing to collect taxes from out-of-state corporations than to raise taxes on in-state business interests. The desire of state lawmakers and tax officials to, in effect, export the local tax burden is counterbalanced by the Due Process Clause and Commerce Clause of the U.S. Constitution, both of which limit a state's ability to impose a tax obligation on an out-of-state corporation.

The most recent landmark case regarding constitutional nexus is *Quill Corp. v. North Dakota* [504 US 298 (1992)]. Quill was a mail-order vendor of office supplies that solicited sales through catalogs mailed to potential customers in North Dakota and that made deliveries through common carriers. Quill was incorporated in Delaware and had facilities in California, Georgia, and Illinois.

Quill did not have an office, warehouse, retail outlet, or other facility in North Dakota, nor were any of its employees or representatives physically present in North Dakota. During the years in question, Quill made sales to roughly 3,000 North Dakota customers and was the sixth largest office supply vendor in the state. Under North Dakota law, Quill was required to collect North Dakota sales tax on its mail-order sales to North Dakota residents. Quill challenged the constitutionality of this tax obligation.

The Supreme Court held that Quill's economic presence in North Dakota was sufficient to satisfy the Due Process Clause's "minimal connection" requirement. On the other hand, the Court ruled that an economic presence was not, by itself, sufficient to satisfy the Commerce Clause's "substantial nexus" requirement.

Consistent with its ruling 25 years earlier in *National Bellas Hess, Inc. v. Department of Revenue* [386 US 753 (1967)], the Court ruled that a substantial nexus exists *only* if a corporation has a nontrivial physical presence in a state. In other words, the Court ruled that a physical presence is an essential prerequisite to establishing constitutional nexus, at least for sales tax purposes.

The Court did not address the issue of whether the physical presence test also applied for income tax purposes. Many states assert that a physical presence is not a requirement for income tax nexus, and that a significant economic presence is sufficient to create income tax nexus. This "economic nexus" issue has been the subject of extensive litigation, and state courts have issued conflicting rulings.

The highest courts in several states have ruled that the *Bellas Hess* physical presence test does *not* apply to income taxes [e.g., *Geoffrey, Inc. v. South Carolina Tax Commission*, 437 S.E.2d 13 (S.C. 1993); and *Lanco, Inc. v. Division of Taxation*, 908 A.2d 176 (N.J. 2006)]. However, appellate courts in several other states have come to the opposite conclusion.

Public Law 86-272

Congress enacted Public Law (P.L.) 86-272 in 1959 to provide multistate corporations with a limited safe harbor from the imposition of state income taxes.

Specifically, P.L. 86-272 *prohibits* a state from imposing a "net income tax" on a corporation organized in another state if the corporation's only in-state activity is:

1. Solicitation of orders by company representatives
2. The sale of tangible personal property
3. Orders sent outside the state for approval or rejection, if approved
4. Filled by shipment or delivery from a point outside the state

Although P.L. 86-272 can provide significant protections for a multistate business, it has several important limitations:

1. It applies *only* to a net income tax and, therefore, provides no protection against the imposition of a sales tax collection obligation, gross receipts taxes (e.g., Washington business and occupations tax or Ohio commercial activity tax), or state franchise taxes imposed on a base other than income (e.g., Pennsylvania capital stock tax).
2. It protects only the *sale* of tangible personal property. It does not protect activities such as leasing tangible personal property, selling services, selling or leasing real estate, or selling or licensing intangibles.
3. For businesses that send employees into other states to sell tangible personal property, P.L. 86-272 applies only if those employees limit their in-state activities to the solicitation of orders that are sent outside the state for approval and, if approved, are filled by shipment or delivery from a point outside the state.

> **EXAMPLE**
>
> If a salesperson exercises the authority to approve orders within a state, the company does *not* qualify for protection under P.L. 86-272.
>
> Likewise, P.L. 86-272 does *not* protect the presence of a salesperson who performs non-solicitation activities, such as repairs, customer training or technical assistance, within a state.

Although P.L. 86-272 does not define the phrase "solicitation of orders," the meaning of the phrase was addressed by the Supreme Court in *Wisconsin Department of Revenue v. William Wrigley, Jr., Co.* [505 US 214 (1992)].

In this case, the Court defined solicitation of orders as encompassing "requests for purchases" as well as "those activities that are entirely ancillary to requests for purchases—those that serve no independent business function apart from their connection to the soliciting of orders."

Examples of activities that might serve an independent business function, apart from the solicitation of orders, include:

- Installation and start-up
- Customer training
- Engineering and design assistance
- Technical assistance
- Warranty maintenance and repair
- Credit and collection activities

STUDY QUESTIONS

1. Which of the following states do *not* impose some type of income-based tax on corporations?

    a. Alabama
    b. California
    c. Florida
    d. South Dakota

2. Which of the following is *not* a limitation of P.L. 86-272?

    a. It applies only to a net income tax.
    b. It protects only sales of tangible personal property.
    c. For businesses that send employees into other states to sell tangible personal property, P.L. 86-272 applies only if those employees limit their in-state activities to the solicitation of orders that are approved out-of-state and are filled by shipment or delivery from a point outside the state.
    d. None of the above.

COMPUTATION OF STATE TAXABLE INCOME

Most states that impose a corporate income tax use either the corporation's federal taxable income before the net operating loss and special deductions (federal Form 1120, Line 28), or the corporation's net federal taxable income (federal Form 1120, Line 30) as the starting place for computing state taxable income.

The states that impose income taxes but do not tie the computation of state taxable income directly to a corporation's federal tax return typically adopt the majority of the federal provisions governing items of gross income and deduction in defining the state tax base.

A corporation's state income tax liability generally is computed using the following steps:

1. Compute the state tax base:

   Federal taxable income (Line 28   +/-   State addition/subtraction
   or Line 30 of the federal corporate   modifications
   income tax return, Form 1120)

2. If applicable, compute the total apportionable income (loss):

   State tax base   +/-   Net amount of allocable nonbusiness income
                            (loss)

3. Determine the income (loss) apportioned to the state:.

   Total apportionable income (loss)   x   State's apportionment percentage

4. If applicable, compute the state taxable income (loss):

   Net amount of nonbusiness income   +/-   Income apportioned to the state
   (loss) allocated to the state

5. Determine the state tax liability before credits:

   State taxable income   x   State tax rate

6. Compute the net income tax liability for the state:

   State tax liability   -   State's tax credits

The use of the federal tax base as the starting point for computing state taxable income is referred to as *piggybacking*. Conformity with federal provisions simplifies tax compliance for multistate corporations, but complete conformity with the federal tax laws would effectively cede control over state tax policy to the federal government. States also must be wary of the effects of federal tax law changes on state tax revenues.

Therefore, although federal taxable income generally is used as the starting point in computing state taxable income, numerous state modifications are required to reflect differences in federal and state policy objectives. The modifications to federal taxable income vary significantly among the states.

Common state modifications include the following:
- Interest income received on state and municipal debt obligations
- State income taxes
- Federal net operating loss carryforward deductions
- Federal dividends-received deductions
- Federal bonus depreciation under Internal Revenue Code ("the Code") Sec. 168(k)
- Royalties and interest expenses paid to related parties
- Expenses related to state tax credits
- Federal domestic production activities deduction under Code Sec. 199
- Expenses related to income that is exempt for state tax purposes

Common subtraction modifications include the following:
- Interest income received on federal debt obligations
- State net operating loss deductions
- State dividends-received deductions
- Expenses related to federal tax credits
- Federal Subpart F and Code Sec. 78 gross-up income with respect to foreign subsidiaries

Distinction Between Business and Nonbusiness Income

In 1957, the National Conference of Commissioners on Uniform State Laws promulgated the Uniform Division of Income for Tax Purposes Act (UDITPA), which is a model law for dividing the income of a multistate corporation among the states for tax purposes. The purpose of UDITPA is to promote uniformity in state allocation and apportionment rules. UDITPA has been adopted, at least in part, by most states.

UDITPA distinguishes between income derived from a corporation's regular trade or business activities (*business income*) and income derived from any activities that are unrelated to that trade or business (*nonbusiness income*). Under the UDITPA approach, a taxpayer apportions a percentage of its business income to each state in which it has nexus, but the taxpayer specifically allocates the *entire* amount of any *non*business income to a single state [UDITPA §§4 and 9].

Therefore, the principal consequence of classifying an item as nonbusiness income is that the income is excluded from the tax base of every nexus state *except* the state in which the nonbusiness income is taxable in full (e.g., the state of commercial domicile). Because the classification of an item as nonbusiness income can effectively remove the income from the tax base of one or more nexus states, the business versus nonbusiness income distinction has historically been an area of significant controversy between taxpayers and state tax authorities.

The distinction between business and nonbusiness income is related to the constitutional restrictions on the ability of a state to tax an out-of-state corporation. Based on these constitutional protections, taxpayers have challenged the ability of nexus states to tax an item of income that, according to the taxpayer, has no relationship to the business activity conducted in the state.

As the Supreme Court stated in *Allied-Signal, Inc. v. Division of Taxation* [504 US 768 (1992)], "the principle that a State may not tax value earned outside its borders rests on the fundamental requirement of both the Due Process and Commerce Clauses that there be 'some definite link, some minimum connection, between a state and the person, property or transaction it seeks to tax.' *Miller Bros. Co. v. Maryland* 347 US 340, 344-345 (1954)."

EXAMPLE

The taxpayer in *Mobil Oil Corp. v. Commissioner of Taxes* [445 US 425 (1980)] was an integrated petroleum company that was incorporated and commercially domiciled in New York. Mobil challenged Vermont's ability to tax the dividends that it received from its foreign subsidiaries.

The essence of Mobil's argument that Vermont could *not* constitutionally tax the foreign dividends was that the activities of the foreign subsidiaries were unrelated to Mobil's business activities in Vermont, which were limited to marketing petroleum products. Stating that "the linchpin of apportionability in the field of state income taxation is the unitary business principle," the Supreme Court ruled that Vermont could tax an apportioned percentage of the dividends Mobil received from its foreign subsidiaries, because those subsidiaries were part of the same integrated petroleum enterprise as its distribution activities in Vermont. In other words, because they were received from unitary subsidiaries, the dividends were includible in Mobil's apportionable business income.

The Court also indicated that if the business activities of the foreign subsidiaries had "nothing to do with the activities of the recipient in the taxing state, due process considerations might well preclude apportionability, because there would be no underlying unitary business."

In *Allied-Signal*, a Delaware corporation that had nexus in New Jersey and was commercially domiciled in Michigan realized a $211.5 million capital gain from the sale of 20.6 percent of the stock of ASARCO. During the tax year in question, New Jersey was a so-called "full apportionment" state--that is, New Jersey took the position that all income of a corporation that had nexus in New Jersey was apportionable business income.

Under this approach, New Jersey was entitled to tax an apportioned percentage of the capital gain. The Supreme Court held that New Jersey could not include the gain in apportionable business income, because the taxpayer and ASARCO were "unrelated business enterprises whose activities had nothing to do with the other." Furthermore, the taxpayer's ownership of the ASARCO stock did not serve an "operational rather than an investment function" in the taxpayer's business.

Thus, in *Allied-Signal*, the Supreme Court reaffirmed the principle that income derived from unitary subsidiaries is business in nature. In addition, the Court appeared to create a second category of business income, that is, income derived from a nonunitary payer where the asset serves an operational rather than investment function.

On April 15, 2008, the U.S. Supreme Court handed down its ruling in ***MeadWestvaco Corporation v. Illinois Department of Revenue*** [U.S. Supreme Court, Dkt. 06-1413, 553 U.S. ___ (2008)]. The issue in this case was whether Illinois could tax an apportioned share of a $1 billion gain realized by an Ohio corporation when it sold its investment in one of its business divisions. An Illinois appeals court ruled that the gain did qualify as apportionable business income because the division served an operational function in the taxpayer's business.

However, the Supreme Court vacated the Illinois appeals court decision on the grounds that it misinterpreted the Court's references to "operational function" in *Allied-Signal* as modifying the unitary business principle to add a new basis for apportionment. The Court explained that the operational function concept described in *Allied-Signal* merely recognizes the reality that an asset can be part of a taxpayer's unitary business even if there is no unitary relationship between the payee (taxpayer) and payer (asset).

Each state is free to adopt its own definitions of business and nonbusiness income, subject to the constitutional constraints discussed above. Most states have adopted a definition of nonbusiness income that more or less conforms to the UDITPA definition of nonbusiness income, which is "all income other than business income." [UDITPA §1(e)] Thus, the key is the definition of business income.

According to UDITPA §1(a), *business income* is defined as:

> Income arising from transactions and activity in the regular course of the taxpayer's trade or business and includes income from tangible and intangible property if the acquisition, management, and disposition of the property constitute integral parts of the taxpayer's regular trade or business operations.

In determining whether an item of income is business or nonbusiness in nature, state courts have arrived at different conclusions as to whether the UDITPA definition of business income includes both a *transactional test* (i.e., "income arising from transactions and activity in the regular course of the taxpayer's trade or business") and a *functional test* (i.e., "income from tangible and intangible property if the acquisition, management, and disposition of the property constitute integral parts of the taxpayer's regular trade or business operations"), or just a transactional test.

The transactional test looks at the frequency and regularity of the income-producing transaction in relation to the taxpayer's regular trade or business. The critical issue is whether the transaction is frequent in nature, as opposed to a rare and extraordinary event.

In contrast, the *functional test* looks at the relationship between the underlying income-producing asset and the taxpayer's regular trade or business. The critical issue is whether the asset is integral, as opposed to incidental, to the taxpayer's business operations.

The view that the UDITPA definition of business income includes both a transactional test and a functional test, and that an item of income is properly classified as business in nature if either test is met, is supported by state supreme court decisions in California, Illinois, North Carolina, Oregon, and Pennsylvania.

On the other hand, state supreme court decisions in Alabama, Iowa, Kansas, Minnesota and Tennessee support the view that the UDITPA definition contains only a transactional test and that an item of income is nonbusiness income. In each instance, however, the state supreme court decision interpreting the statutory definition of business income to include only a transactional test was followed by a legislative change to broaden the applicable statute to include both a transactional and a functional test. In 2003, the Multistate Tax Commission (MTC) amended MTC Reg. IV.1(a) to provide that business income means income that meets either the transactional test or the functional test.

When an item of income is determined to be nonbusiness income, most states allocate the income to a specific state under guidelines similar to §4 through §8 of UDITPA and the related MTC regulations. The basic thrust of these rules is that nonbusiness income derived from real and tangible personal property is allocable to the state in which the property is physically located, whereas nonbusiness income derived from intangible property is allocable to the state of commercial domicile (except for royalties, which are allocable to the state where the intangible asset is used).

STUDY QUESTIONS

3. Which of the following is an advantage of state conformity to federal tax provisions?

    a. It simplifies tax compliance for multistate corporations.

    b. Federal tax law changes affect state tax revenues.

    c. Complete conformity with federal tax laws would effectively cede control over state tax policy to the federal government.

    d. None of the above.

4. Which of the following is **not** a true statement regarding UDITPA?

    a. UDITPA was promulgated to provide uniformity among the states with respect to the taxation of multistate corporations.

    b. Under the UDITPA approach, a taxpayer apportions a percentage of its business income to each state in which it has nexus.

    c. UDITPA makes no distinction between business and nonbusiness income.

    d. All of the above are true statements.

APPORTIONMENT FORMULAS

A taxpayer's right to apportion its income is neither automatic nor elective; rather, it is a privilege that must be warranted by the corporation's activities. The requirements for establishing the right to apportion income vary from state to state, but they generally include:

- Carrying on business in another state
- Maintaining a regular place of business in another state
- Being taxable in another state

Some states take the restrictive position that permits apportionment only if the corporation is actually filing returns and paying tax in another state.

    Once a corporation has established its right to apportion income, the next step is to compute the applicable state apportionment percentages using the formulas provided by each taxing state. These formulas are usually based on the relative amounts of property, payroll, and/or sales that the corporation has in each taxing state. They reflect the notion that a corporation's business activity in a state is properly measured by the amount of property, payroll, and sales in the state. These three components of an apportionment formula are referred to as "factors." For any given state, each factor equals the ratio of the corporation's property, payroll or sales in the state to its property, payroll or sales everywhere.

Factor weights vary from state to state. At present, approximately 10 states use a three-factor apportionment formula that equally weights sales, property, and payroll. Most states use a modified three-factor formula, under which the sales factor is assigned more weight than the property or payroll factors. About 20 states double-weight the sales factor (i.e., 50 percent sales, 25 percent property, and 25 percent payroll).

In the 2008 tax year, 10 states use an apportionment formula that includes only a sales factor. These states include Georgia, Illinois, Iowa, Maine, Michigan, Nebraska, New York, Oregon, Texas, and Wisconsin.

In addition, Indiana and Minnesota have enacted legislation to adopt a *sales-only formula*, effective in 2011 and 2014, respectively. Other states that super-weight the sales factor include Ohio (60 percent weight), and Pennsylvania (70 percent weight).

Assigning more weight to the sales factor than to the property or payroll factor tends to increase the percentage of an out-of-state corporation's income that is subject to tax, because the out-of-state corporation's principal activity in the state—the sale of its products—is weighted more heavily than its payroll and property activities. At the same time, assigning more weight to the sales factor tends to reduce the tax on in-state corporations that have significant amounts of property and payroll in the state (factors that are given relatively less weight in the apportionment formula), but who make sales nationwide.

The standard three-factor formula was designed to apportion the income of multistate manufacturing and mercantile businesses, but it may not fairly apportion the income of businesses in other industries. To address this issue, many states provide special rules for computing apportionment percentages for businesses in certain industries. Typically, these special rules involve the modification or exclusion of the conventional factors or the use of unique, industry-specific factors.

EXAMPLE

Industries for which states provide special apportionment factor rules include airlines, railroads, trucking companies, financial institutions, television and radio broadcasters, publishers, telecommunication services companies, mutual funds, pipelines, ship transportation companies, and professional sports franchises.

In theory, apportionment prevents double taxation of a corporation's income. However, because each state is free to choose its own apportionment formula and its own rules for computing the factors, apportionment does not provide a uniform division of a taxpayer's income among the taxing states. There are significant differences among the states in terms of factor weights, as well as variations in the computation of the factors themselves.

Potentially Adverse Consequences of Apportionment, and Relief

This diversity can result in more than 100 percent of a corporation's income being subject to state taxation. Another potentially adverse consequence of apportionment occurs when a taxpayer's operations in one state result in a loss, but the corporation's overall operations are profitable. In such cases, the apportionment process will assign a percentage of the corporation's overall profit to the state in which the loss was incurred, even though no profit was generated by the taxpayer's operations in that state.

To address these issues, UDITPA §18 and the tax laws of most states allow a corporate taxpayer to petition for relief when the application of the state's apportionment formula does not fairly represent the taxpayer's business activity in the state.

In such situations, UDITPA §18 lists several possible alternatives to the standard formula, including the use of separate accounting, the exclusion of one or more factors, the inclusion of one or more additional factors, or some other method that provides a more equitable apportionment of the taxpayer's income.

Case law indicates that there is a presumption that a state's apportionment method is equitable. As a consequence, to receive relief from distortions caused by the state's standard formula, a corporation must prove by clear and convincing evidence that the apportionment method in question grossly distorts the amount of income actually earned in the state.

Sales Factor

Under UDITPA §15, the sales factor is a fraction whose numerator is the total sales of the taxpayer in the state during the tax period and whose denominator is the total sales of the taxpayer everywhere during the tax period. Because the sales factor is used to apportion a corporation's business income, only sales that generate apportionable business income are includible in the fraction. Nonbusiness sales are excluded from the sales factor.

Under UDITPA §1(g), the term *sales* means all gross receipts of the taxpayer other than receipts related to nonbusiness income. Consistent with this expansive view of the sales factor, MTC Reg. IV.15(b) provides that the sales factor generally includes all gross receipts derived by the taxpayer from transactions and activities in the regular course of its trade or business.

> **EXAMPLE**
>
> Examples of gross receipts that are included in the sales factor are gross receipts from sales of inventory or services, as well as interest, dividends, rentals, and royalties derived from other business assets and activities.

> Receipts from transactions with a related corporation are also generally included in the sales factor, unless a consolidated or combined return is filed with the related corporation, in which case intercompany receipts are generally excluded from the sales factor.

Under UDITPA §16(a), sales of tangible personal property are assigned to the sales factor numerator of the state in which the goods are delivered or shipped. This *destination test* reflects the original purpose of including a sales factor in the apportionment formula, which is to provide tax revenue to the states in which customers are located.

UDITPA §16(b) contains two exceptions to the destination test.

The first exception applies to sales to the U.S. government, which are assigned to the state from which the goods are shipped rather than to the state in which the purchaser is located.

The second exception is commonly known as *throwback*, and it requires that if the seller is not taxable in the destination state (in which case there is no sales factor numerator to which to assign the sale under the destination test), the sale is thrown back into the sales factor numerator of the state from which the goods are shipped. The rationale for throwback is to make sure that all of a company's sales are assigned to the numerator of some state's sales factor.

Despite the logical basis for adopting a throwback rule, approximately half of the states do not require throwback, primarily because not requiring throwback makes the state a more desirable place to locate a manufacturing or distribution facility from which to ship goods. The lack of a throwback rule results in *nowhere sales*, which are sales that are included in the denominator but not included in the numerator of any sales factor.

Under UDITPA §17, any sales other than sales of tangible personal property are considered in-state sales if the income-producing activity is performed in the state. This income-producing activity rule applies to fees for services, rental income, and income from intangibles (interest, dividends, royalties, and capital gains).

Under MTC Reg. IV.17(2), the term *income-producing activity* "applies to each separate item of income and means the transactions and activity engaged in by the taxpayer in the regular course of its trade or business."

EXAMPLE

Examples of income-producing activities include:

1. The rendering of personal services by employees or the use of tangible or intangible property by the taxpayer in performing a service
2. The sale, rental, leasing, licensing or other use of real property
3. The rental, leasing, licensing or other use of tangible personal property
4. The sale, licensing or other use of intangible personal property

If the income-producing activity is performed in two or more states, the sale is assigned to the state where the greater proportion of the income-producing activity is performed, based on the costs of performance [UDITPA §17].

Under MTC Reg. IV.17(3), the term *costs of performance* "means direct costs determined in a manner consistent with generally accepted accounting principles and in accordance with accepted conditions or practices in the trade or business of the taxpayer."

Direct costs include material and labor costs that have a causal relationship with the sale in question.

Indirect costs, which include general and administrative expenses that are not associated with any specific sale, are not taken in account in determining the costs of performance.

Property Factor

Under UDITPA §10, the *property factor* is a fraction whose numerator is the average value of the taxpayer's real and tangible personal property owned or rented and used in the state during the tax year and whose denominator is the average value of all the taxpayer's real and tangible personal property owned or rented and used during the tax year.

Under MTC Reg. IV.10(a), the definition *of real and tangible personal property* includes land, buildings, machinery, stocks of goods, equipment, and other real and tangible personal property but does not include coin or currency. Intangible property, such as accounts receivable and marketable securities, generally is excluded from the property factor.

Property owned by the corporation is typically valued at its average original cost plus the cost of additions and improvements, but without any adjustments for depreciation. Some states, however, require property to be included at its net book value or federal adjusted tax basis. Rented property is included in the property factor at a value equal to eight times the annual rental less any subrentals. For this purpose, annual rentals may include payments, such as real estate taxes and insurance, made by the lessee in lieu of rent.

Only property that is used in producing apportionable business income is included in the property factor. Therefore, construction-in-progress, property that has been permanently withdrawn from service, and property that is used for producing nonbusiness income generally is excluded. Property that is temporarily idled, however, generally remains in the property factor.

> **NOTE**
>
> Although the average value of the property is usually determined by averaging the beginning and ending property values, many states allow the average value to be calculated on a monthly or quarterly basis if the use of the annual computations substantially distorts the actual value of the property.
>
> This may occur if a significant amount of property is acquired or disposed of near the beginning or the end of the year.

Payroll Factor

Under UDITPA §13, the *payroll factor* is a fraction whose numerator is the total amount paid in the state during the tax year by the taxpayer for compensation and whose denominator is the total compensation paid everywhere during the tax year. For this purpose, compensation generally includes wages, salaries, commissions, and any other form of remuneration paid or accrued to an employee that is taxable to the employee for federal income tax purposes.

Payments made to an independent contractor or to any other person who is not properly classifiable as an employee generally are *excluded* from the payroll factor. Compensation related to the production of nonbusiness income is also excluded from the payroll factor. In addition, in an attempt to make the state a more desirable place to locate a headquarters office, some states exclude the compensation of top executives from the payroll factor.

The rules for computing an employee's *compensation*, and for assigning that compensation to a particular state, parallel those used to compute the employer's federal and state unemployment taxes. Federal Form 940, *Employer's Annual Federal Unemployment Tax Return*, summarizes taxable compensation amounts on a state-by-state basis, and generally can be used to compute state payroll factors.

In computing the numerator of the payroll factor for a particular state, the employee's compensation is included in the numerator for that state if an employee performs services *exclusively* within that state.

If an employee performs services both inside of and outside of a state, the entire amount of the employee's compensation generally is still assigned to a single state, based on a hierarchy of factors, including (in the order in which they are applied):

- The employee's base of operations
- Where the employee is directed from
- The employee's state of residence [UDITPA §14]

STUDY QUESTIONS

---

5. Assigning more weight to the sales factor than to the property or payroll factor tends to *decrease* the percentage of an out-of-state corporation's income that is subject to tax. ***True or False?***

6. Under UDITPA, sales of tangible personal property are generally assigned to the sales factor numerator of the state:

   a. from which the goods are shipped

   b. in which the goods are delivered or shipped

   c. where the company is commercially domiciled

   d. None of the above

CONSOLIDATED RETURNS AND COMBINED UNITARY REPORTING

For financial reporting purposes, a parent corporation must issue consolidated financial statements that include all of its majority-owned subsidiaries.

For federal income tax purposes, an affiliated group of corporations can elect to file a consolidated return [Code Sec. 1501]. A consolidated return is *not* mandatory, however, and the members of the affiliated group have the option of filing federal returns on a separate-company basis.

An *affiliated group* is a parent-subsidiary structure in which all of the affiliates, other than the common parent, are at least 80 percent owned by other members of the group [Code Sec. 1504(a)].

Generally, corporations organized in a foreign country are not includible in a federal consolidated return. Filing a federal consolidated return is a popular election, primarily because it allows the group to offset the losses of one affiliate against the profits of other affiliates.

The states that impose corporate income taxes employ a wide variety of filing options for groups of commonly controlled corporations. This makes it difficult to generalize about state filing options.

Roughly speaking, the different filing options fall into one of the following categories:

- Mandatory separate-company returns
- Elective consolidated returns
- Mandatory combined unitary reporting
- Discretionary combined unitary reporting
- A hybrid system, which includes both elective consolidated returns and discretionary combined unitary reporting

The lack of uniformity in state filing options means that tax practitioners must carefully analyze the filing options available in any given nexus state.

Mandatory Separate-Company Returns

Four states (Delaware, Maryland, Pennsylvania, and Wisconsin) require each member of a commonly controlled group of corporations to compute its income and file a return as if it were a separate economic entity. Under this mandatory separate company return approach, consolidated returns and combined unitary reporting are not permitted or required under any circumstances.

The filing of separate-company returns provides taxpayers with the opportunity to create legal structures and intercompany transactions that shift income from affiliates based in high-tax states to affiliates based in low-tax states.

EXAMPLE

If a multistate corporation's only activities in a high-tax state are sales and distribution (which are often relatively low-margin activities), and if the high-tax state allows separate-company returns, then the corporation may be able to insulate its higher-margin assets and activities from taxation in the high-tax state by forming a sales subsidiary that is responsible for marketing products in that state.

Disadvantages of the separate-company return approach include the inability to offset the losses of one affiliate against the profits of other affiliates and the need to develop defensible arm's-length transfer prices for intercompany transactions.

Elective Consolidated Returns

Roughly 20 states (including Alabama, Florida, Georgia, Iowa, Massachusetts, and South Carolina) generally allow affiliated corporations to file separate-company returns but also permit such corporations to elect to file a state consolidated return if certain conditions are met. The qualification requirements for including an affiliated corporation in a state consolidated return vary from state to state.

In terms of stock ownership requirements, most states piggyback on the federal rule requiring 80 percent or more ownership. A number of states also require that an affiliated group file a federal consolidated return as a prerequisite to filing a state consolidated return.

Examples of additional restrictions that a state may impose for including a specific affiliate in a state consolidated return include:

- Having nexus in the state
- Deriving income from sources in the state
- Not being subject to a special apportionment formula

The *advantages* of filing a consolidated return include:

- The ability to offset the losses of one affiliate against the profits of other affiliates
- Elimination of intercorporate dividends
- Deferral of gains on intercompany transactions
- The use of credits that would otherwise be denied because of a lack of income

One major disadvantage of filing a consolidated return is that it can prevent a taxpayer from creating legal structures and intercompany transactions to shift income from affiliates based in high-tax states to affiliates based in low-tax states.

Combined Unitary Reporting

Approximately 20 states (including California, Colorado, Illinois, Michigan, Minnesota, and Texas) require members of a unitary business group to compute their taxable income on a combined basis. New York requires related corporations to file a combined report if there are "substantial intercorporate transactions" among the related corporations, regardless of the transfer price for the intercorporate transactions.

Despite its surface-level resemblance to a consolidated return, *combined unitary reporting* differs from a consolidated return in a number of important respects:

1. Apportionment methodology versus type of return. A consolidated return involves the filing of a single return for a group of affiliated corporations. In contrast, combined unitary reporting is not so much a return as the name given to the calculations (akin to a spreadsheet) by which a unitary business group apportions its income.

> **EXAMPLE**
>
> Under California's combined unitary reporting scheme, the first step is to compute the aggregate business income of all group members. The group's combined business income is then apportioned, first to California (based on the group's apportionment percentage) and then to each of the individual group members that have nexus in California (based on the ratio of each member's factors to the group's factors).
>
> The second level of apportionment is necessary, because each group member that has nexus in California is treated as a separate taxpayer. This is true even if taxpayers that are members of the same combined reporting group satisfy their reporting obligation by filing a single group return on which they report the sum of their individual tax liabilities.

2. Stock ownership requirement. Inclusion in a state consolidated return generally requires 80 percent or more ownership (which piggybacks on the ownership threshold for inclusion in a federal consolidated return), whereas inclusion in a combined unitary report generally requires more than 50 percent ownership.

3. Unitary business requirement. To be included in a combined report, an affiliate must be engaged in the same trade or business as the other group members, as exhibited by such factors as centralized management, functional integration, and economies of scale. This "unitary business" test is not a requirement for inclusion in an elective consolidated return.

4. Worldwide combination. Consistent with the federal approach to consolidation, affiliates organized in a foreign country generally are not included in a state consolidated return. On the other hand, states have the ability to require the inclusion of foreign country affiliates in a combined unitary report.

Despite these differences, the advantages and disadvantages of consolidated returns and combined reporting are similar. A primary disadvantage of both filing options is that they can prevent a taxpayer from creating legal structures and intercompany transactions that shift income from affiliates based in high-tax states to affiliates based in low-tax states. A major advantage of both filing options is the ability to offset the losses of one affiliate against the profits of other affiliates. In addition, the effect of apportioning income on a combined basis may be to shift income from a high-tax state to a low-tax state.

In addition to these mandatory combined reporting states, roughly 15 other states (including New Jersey, North Carolina, and Virginia) generally allow commonly controlled corporations to file separate-company returns, but also require or permit a combined unitary report if certain conditions are satisfied.

A common reason for requiring a combined report is the state tax authority's determination that a combined report is necessary to clearly reflect the group's income earned in the state or to prevent the evasion of taxes.

EXAMPLE

New Jersey does not permit an affiliated group to elect to file a consolidated return, nor does it require a unitary group to compute its income on a combined basis. Thus, every corporation with nexus in New Jersey is generally considered a separate entity and must file its own return.

The Director of the Division of Taxation may, however, require members of an affiliated group or a controlled group to file a consolidated return "if the taxpayer cannot demonstrate by clear and convincing evidence that a report by a taxpayer discloses the true earnings of the taxpayer on its business carried on in this State" [N.J. Rev. Stat. 54:10A-10.c.].

CONCEPT OF A UNITARY BUSINESS GROUP

Combined unitary reporting requires a determination of the unitary business group. History has shown that determining the boundaries of a unitary business can be a source of controversy.

Unfortunately, there is no simple, objective definition of what constitutes a unitary business. In fact, over the years the courts have developed a number of different tests for determining the existence of a unitary business. This has led one Supreme Court justice to make the observation that "the unitary business concept ... is not, so to speak, unitary." As a result of the many judicial interpretations of a unitary business, a taxpayer may be unable to determine which of the available tests will be applied. In addition, even if a taxpayer knows which test will be used, the subjective nature of the tests makes them difficult to apply with certainty.

Generally, a vertically integrated business, in which each of the separate affiliates or divisions performs an interdependent step that leads to a finished product only when the steps are combined, will be treated as unitary. A horizontally integrated business, in which there are parallel operations in different geographic locations (e.g., a chain of retail stores), generally will also be considered unitary if there is strong centralized management. A conglomerate may or may not be considered unitary, depending on whether there is strong centralized management, as exhibited by a centralized executive force and shared staff functions as well as economies of scale in the form of common employee benefit plans, insurance, and so on.

As mentioned above, the courts have developed a number of different tests for determining the existence of a unitary business, including the:

- Three-unities test
- Contribution or dependency test
- Flow-of-value test
- Factors-of-profitability test

The *three-unities test* [**Butler Bros. v. McColgan,** 315 US 501 (1942)] requires the presence of unity of ownership, unity of operation, and unity of use:

1. **Unity of ownership** generally is satisfied when 50 percent or more of the corporation's stock is owned directly or indirectly by another corporation in the group.
2. **Unity of operation** is evidenced by the performance of certain staff functions by one of the corporations on behalf of the entire group, such as centralized purchasing, advertising, accounting and legal services, and human resource functions.
3. **Unity of use** is associated with common executive forces and general systems of operations and is evidenced by major policy decisions that are made by centralized management, intercompany product flow, and services that are provided by one affiliate to other group members.

The *contribution or dependency test* [**Edison Cal. Stores, Inc. v. McColgan,** 176 P.2d 697 (Cal. 1947)] focuses on whether the enterprise's in-state business operations depend on, or contribute to, the enterprise's out-of-state business operations. Examples of business activities that may be considered contributing factors are substantial borrowing from out-of-state operations to finance in-state operations and transfers of top-level executives, manufacturing equipment or materials from out-of-state operations to in-state operations.

Under the *flow-of-value test*, "some sharing or exchange of value ... beyond the mere flow of funds arising out of a passive investment" is needed to establish the existence of a unitary business [***Container Corp. of Am. v. Franchise Tax Bd.***, 463 US 159 (1983)].

Finally, the *factors-of-profitability test* (***Allied-Signal***) looks to functional integration, centralization of management, and economies of scale to determine the existence of a unitary business. Functional integration includes product flow among affiliates and centralized functions such as advertising, accounting, purchasing, manufacturing, and financing. Indicators of centralized management include interlocking boards of directors, interchange of personnel at upper management levels, and required parent company approval on major policy decisions.

In addition to judicial interpretations, state-specific statutes and regulations are important sources of authority regarding what constitutes a unitary business group. Like their judicial counterparts, however, they generally leave much to be desired in terms of providing detailed and objective guidance.

To help states determine the existence of a unitary business, the MTC adopted a uniform regulation [MTC Reg. IV.1.(b)], which portrays the concept of a unitary business as follows:

> A unitary business is a single economic enterprise that is made up either of separate parts of a single business entity or of a commonly controlled group of business entities that are sufficiently interdependent, integrated and interrelated through their activities so as to provide a synergy and mutual benefit that produces a sharing or exchange of value among them and a significant flow of value to the separate parts.

More specifically, a unitary business is characterized by significant flows of value evidenced by the following factors:
- Functional integration—examples include common marketing programs, transfers or pooling of technical information or intellectual property, common distribution systems, common purchasing, and common or intercompany financing.
- Centralization of management—joint participation of corporate directors and officers in the management decisions that affect the different business units.
- Economies of scale—centralized purchasing, centralized administrative functions, etc.

The MTC regulation also identifies same type of business, steps in a vertical process, and strong centralized management as indicators of a unitary business. The MTC is an agency of state governments that was established in 1967 to promote fairness and uniformity in state tax laws.

STUDY QUESTIONS

> **7.** Which of the following states does **not** require each member of a commonly controlled group of corporations to file separate-company returns?
>
> **a.** Arizona
> **b.** Delaware
> **c.** Maryland
> **d.** Wisconsin
>
> **8.** Inclusion in a state consolidated return generally requires 50 percent or more common ownership. **True or False?**

BASIC MULTISTATE TAX-PLANNING STRATEGIES

The objectives of multistate income tax planning are to:
- Structure an organization's business activities
- Create the optimal mix of legal entities in order to minimize state income tax costs

Planning techniques generally involve an attempt either to reduce the total amount of the organization's taxable income subject to apportionment or to minimize the apportionment percentage in a given state. In determining which activities or entities to alter, the tax planner must carefully analyze the effects that each change has on the corporation's total state tax liability to ensure that the taxes saved in one state are not offset by tax increases in other states.

Therefore, effective state tax planning requires a review of a corporation's activities in all states and an understanding of the apportionment formulas and other tax laws of the states in which the corporation does business. Moreover, any tax-planning strategy must be reviewed in light of practical business considerations and the additional administrative or operational costs that might be incurred in implementing the strategy.

The remainder of this section briefly discusses the following selected tax-planning opportunities:
- Selecting the states in which to be taxed
- Establishing the right to apportion income
- Intangible property holding companies
- Other structure planning techniques
- Using the most beneficial group filing method

Selecting the States in Which to Be Taxed

When a corporation has only a limited connection with a state, it may be possible to discontinue that activity by using an alternative means of accomplishing the same result.

EXAMPLE

If maintaining a formal corporate office in a state creates an undesired nexus, the corporation might avoid nexus by providing the sales representatives with an office allowance rather than an actual office.

When nexus is created by sales representatives performing repair and maintenance services in the state, one strategy would be to separately incorporate the sales division that operates in the state. Assuming the state does not require combined reporting, this would prevent the state from taxing the profits attributable to the parent corporation's out-of-state assets and activities. Such a technique will be successful only if the incorporated division is a bona fide business operation and the state does not successfully assert that the corporation continues to have nexus under the concepts of affiliate or agency nexus. In addition, the pricing of any sales or services between the new subsidiary and the parent corporation must be at arm's length.

Although most planning techniques are designed to avoid nexus, there are situations in which a corporation can benefit from establishing nexus in a state.

Creating nexus in a particular state can be beneficial if the corporation:

- Does not currently have the right to apportion its income
- Wants to avoid the application of a sales throwback rule by creating nexus in a destination state
- Wants to have a loss affiliate create nexus in a state that allows only nexus affiliates to join in filing a state consolidated return

Establishing nexus is usually not difficult because of the relatively low threshold for creating constitutional nexus and the limited nature of the protection afforded by P.L. 86-272.

Establishing the Right to Apportion Income

A corporation that has nexus only in its state of domicile may not apportion its income and, therefore, is subject to tax on 100 percent of its income in that state. By establishing the right to apportion its income, the taxpayer may be able to reduce its state income tax costs substantially, particularly if the corporation is domiciled in a high-tax state. The income that is removed from the tax base of the state of domicile may escape state taxation altogether if the state in which the corporation establishes nexus does not impose a corporate income tax, or if the state imposes a corporate income tax but has more liberal nexus rules than the state of domicile.

Another major factor in determining the tax benefit of apportioning income is whether the state from which the taxpayer is shipping goods has a *sales throwback rule.* Many states do not require throwback, in which case sales in states where the taxpayer does not have nexus are not assigned to the numerator of any state's sales factor (so-called nowhere sales).

To acquire the right to apportion its income, the corporation generally must have nexus in at least one state other than its state of domicile. Whether a corporation's activities or contacts in another state are considered adequate to justify apportionment is generally determined by reference to the tax laws of the domicile state.

Typically, a corporation must carry on business in another state, maintain an office or other regular place of business in another state, or be taxable in another state in order to apportion its income. Some states take the restrictive position that apportionment is permitted *only* if the corporation is actually filing returns and paying tax in another state. A corporation should analyze its current activities in and contacts with other states to determine which, if any, activities or contacts could be redirected so that the corporation will be granted the right to apportion its income.

Intangible Property Holding Companies

Numerous states allow a group of commonly controlled corporations to file returns on a separate-company basis. This can provide a taxpayer with the opportunity to create legal structures and intercompany transactions that shift income from affiliates based in high-tax states to affiliates based in low- or no-tax states.

For example, a financial institution that holds a significant portfolio of marketable securities may be able to realize significant tax savings by transferring the securities to an intangible property holding company domiciled in a low- or no-tax state. Another example is a manufacturer or retailer that owns valuable trademarks, trade names, patents or other intellectual property. By transferring these assets to an intangible property holding company domiciled in a low- or no-tax state and then licensing the use of the intangibles back to the operating companies, a corporation can potentially avoid state taxation of the income attributable to the intangible assets.

Delaware is a popular location for an intangible property holding company, because Delaware does not tax the income of a corporation whose only activities in the state are the maintenance and management of intangible property or the collection and distribution of income from such property. Nevada is also a popular location for an intangible property holding company, because it does not levy a corporate income tax.

To realize the desired tax benefit, the holding company must avoid establishing nexus in other states. In addition, the holding company must have economic substance as a separate corporate entity, serve a bona fide business purpose other than tax avoidance, and charge an arm's-length royalty for the use of its intangibles.

> **COMMENT**
>
> The holding company should have its own office, books and records, and corporate officers, and should function as an independent operation.

For federal tax purposes, transfers of appreciated property to a newly formed domestic subsidiary corporation generally qualify as nontaxable transactions under Code Sec. 351, and the states generally conform to this treatment. In addition, because most states provide some type of dividends-received deduction, the earnings of an intangible property holding company can be distributed as a dividend to the parent at a minimal state tax cost.

The benefits of an intangible property holding company will not be realized in states that require the holding company to be included in a combined unitary report, because the income of the holding company, if it is business in nature, will be included in the total apportionable income of the unitary group.

The benefits of using a holding company are also curtailed in states that disallow deductions for royalty and interest payments made to related parties. By enacting a statute that requires an in-state operating company to add back deductions for royalty and interest payments made to related parties, states deny the tax benefit of establishing an out-of-state intangible property holding company. Moreover, a number of states take the position that the licensing of intangible property in the state is, by itself, sufficient to create nexus for an out-of-state intangible property holding company. Finally, the related-party transactions and structure must have economic substance and serve a business purpose other than tax avoidance.

> **EXAMPLE**
>
> In *Syms Corp. v. Commissioner* [No. SJC-08513 (Mass. Apr. 10, 2002)], the Massachusetts Supreme Judicial Court ruled that transactions consisting of the transfer of trademarks to a Delaware holding company and the subsequent licensing of those intangibles back to Syms lacked a business purpose and economic substance.

Other Structure Planning Techniques

The ability in some states to file separate-company returns provides taxpayers with the opportunity to create legal structures and intercompany transactions that shift income from affiliates based in high-tax states to affiliates based in low- or no-tax states.

> **EXAMPLE**
>
> If a multistate corporation's only activity in a high-tax state is sales and distribution—which are often relatively low-margin activities—and if the high-tax state allows separate-company returns, the corporation may be able to insulate its out-of-state assets and activities from taxation in the high-tax state by forming a sales subsidiary that is responsible for marketing its products in the state.

Structure planning can also be used to take advantage of net operating losses in states that do not allow any form of consolidated or combined reporting. One way to use such losses is to merge an unprofitable affiliate into a profitable affiliate.

Another potential strategy for better utilizing an affiliate's net operating losses is to convert the unprofitable affiliate into a single member limited liability company (SMLLC). An SMLLC is generally treated as a disregarded entity for both federal and state income tax purposes, and therefore the use of an SMLLC effectively produces the same result as a consolidated return. Care must be taken, however, when dealing with SMLLCs because some states impose entity-level taxes on such entities. Moreover, the federal and state tax consequences of converting a corporation into an LLC must be considered.

Another structure planning technique is the formation of a real estate subsidiary to take advantage of the differences in how owned and rented real property are accounted for in computing a state's property factor. Owned property is usually included in the property factor at its original cost, whereas rented property is included in the property factor at a value equal to eight times the net annual rent. Depending on the taxpayer's facts and circumstances, the difference between the valuation of owned and rented property can reduce a state's apportionment percentage.

Finally, it may be possible to realize tax savings by forming a separate corporation that employs only the minimum amount of capital in states that tax the value of capital or net worth employed in the state. The operations in the state would then be limited to those of the newly formed subsidiary, and the parent corporation's entire capital or net worth would be removed from the tax base.

Using the Most Beneficial Group Filing Method

In states that permit an affiliated group to file a consolidated return, such an election can be beneficial when one affiliate has losses that can be offset against the income generated by other affiliates. Other potential benefits of filing a consolidated return include the elimination of intercorporate dividends, deferral of gains on intercompany transactions, and the use of credits that would otherwise be limited by the lack of income.

In choosing whether to file a consolidated return, the corporation should determine whether the advantages of a consolidated return can be realized without adverse consequences.

> **EXAMPLE**
>
> A corporation that is eligible to file a consolidated return in a given state may choose not to do so if it has significant losses on intercompany transactions and would lose the deduction as a result of the election. On the other hand, a corporation that is a member of the same affiliated group may file a consolidated state return in another state to defer recognition of intercompany gains.

A major disadvantage of filing a consolidated return is that it can prevent a taxpayer from creating legal structures and intercompany transactions that shift income from affiliates based in high-tax states to affiliates based in low-tax states.

Finally, most states that permit affiliated corporations to file a consolidated return have adopted a reporting-consistency requirement similar to that imposed for federal consolidated return purposes. Thus, once an election to file a consolidated return is made, the affiliated group generally must continue to file on a consolidated basis, unless the group receives permission from state tax authorities to file separate-company returns.

STUDY QUESTIONS

9. Which of the following is *not* a way to avoid nexus in a state?
    a. Reimbursing a sales representative in that state for the use of his or her own personal equipment used in non-solicitation activity
    b. Strictly limiting the activities of a sales representative in that state to the solicitation of orders for tangible personal property
    c. Providing a sales representative in that state with an office allowance rather than an actual office
    d. None of the above.

10. Which of the following is *not* a popular location for an intangible property holding company?
    a. Wisconsin
    b. Delaware
    c. Nevada
    d. All of the above are popular states for intangible property holding companies

MODULE 1: STATE CORPORATE INCOME TAXES — CHAPTER 2

Combined Unitary Reporting

This chapter discusses state combined reporting methodologies, the concept of a unitary business, and the difference between combined unitary reporting and consolidated returns.

LEARNING OBJECTIVES

Upon completing this chapter, the student will:

- Understand the difference between combined unitary reporting and consolidated returns
- Understand worldwide versus water's-edge combined reporting
- Be familiar with judicial and statutory definitions of a unitary business
- Be familiar with various state laws regarding unitary businesses

OVERVIEW

The *unitary business principle* was developed in the late 1800s as states sought to impose property taxes on railroad companies that operated across state lines. The essential idea of the unitary business principle is that, to effectively tax a business enterprise whose operations span numerous states, all of the activities constituting a single trade or business must be viewed as a whole, rather than as separate activities conducted in a given taxing state.

In the corporate income tax arena, the U.S. Supreme Court stated in *Mobil Oil Corp. v. Commissioner of Taxes* [445 US 425 (1980)] that "the linchpin of apportionability in the field of state income taxation is the unitary business principle." For example, based on the unitary business principle, a state can require a corporation that has divisions located both inside and outside of the state to compute its income using *formulary apportionment*, rather than geographic separate accounting if the out-of-state divisions conduct a unitary business with the in-state divisions [*Butler Bros. v. McColgan*, 315 US 501 (1942); *Exxon Corp. v. Wisconsin Dept. of Rev.*, 447 US 207 (1980)].

Even if a business enterprise structures its in-state and out-of-state operations as separately incorporated affiliates rather than as separate divisions of the same corporate entity, a state can require the affiliates to apportion their income on a combined basis if the out-of-state affiliates conduct a unitary business with the in-state affiliates [*Edison Cal. Stores, Inc. v. McColgan*, 176 P.2d 697 (Cal. 1947); *Container Corp. of Am. v. Franchise Tax Bd.*, 463 US 159 (1983)].

COMBINED REPORTING VERSUS CONSOLIDATED RETURNS

The unitary business principle ignores the separate legal existence of separately incorporated affiliates and, instead, focuses on the practical business reality that different affiliates often function as a single, economic entity. The unitary business principle allows states to require a commonly controlled group of corporations engaged in a unitary business to compute their state taxable income on a combined basis.

Despite its surface-level resemblance to a consolidated return, combined unitary reporting *differs* from consolidated returns in a number of important respects including:

- Apportionment methodology versus type of return
- Stock ownership requirements
- Unitary business requirement
- Worldwide combinations

Apportionment Methodology Versus Type of Return

A consolidated return involves the filing of a single return for a group of affiliated corporations. In contrast, combined unitary reporting is not so much a type of return as the name given to the calculations (akin to a spreadsheet) by which a unitary business group apportions its income.

For example, under California's combined unitary reporting scheme, the first step is to compute the aggregate business income of all members of the unitary business group. The group's combined business income is then apportioned, first to California (based on the group's apportionment percentage), and then to each of the individual group members that have nexus in California (based on the ratio of each member's factors to the group's factors).

The second level of apportionment is necessary because each group member that has nexus in California is treated as a separate taxpayer. This is true even if taxpayers that are members of the same combined reporting group satisfy their reporting obligation by filing a single group return on which they report the sum of their individual tax liabilities.

> **EXAMPLE**
>
> The importance of this distinction was illustrated in *General Motors Corp. v. Franchise Tax Board* [No. S127086 (Cal. Sup. Ct., Aug. 18, 2006)], in which the California Supreme Court ruled that a research and development credit could *only* reduce the tax of the member who earned the credit—it may not be used to reduce the tax of any other group members.

NOTE

Not all states require each member of a unitary group to compute its own tax separately.

EXAMPLE

Illinois requires a unitary business group to file a single Illinois combined report. In that report, the business income of each group member is aggregated, and then the combined income is apportioned to Illinois using the aggregated apportionment factors of the unitary group.

Stock Ownership Requirements

Inclusion in a state *consolidated return* generally requires stock ownership of 80 percent or more (which piggybacks on the ownership threshold for inclusion in a federal consolidated return). Membership in a *combined unitary report* generally requires stock ownership of more than 50 percent.

Unitary Business Requirement

To be included in a combined unitary report, an affiliate must be engaged in the same trade or business as the other group members, as exhibited by such factors as functional integration and centralized management. This *unitary business test* generally is not a requirement for inclusion in an elective consolidated return.

Worldwide Combinations

Consistent with the federal approach to consolidation, affiliates organized in a foreign country generally are not included in a state consolidated return. On the other hand, states have the ability to require the inclusion of foreign country affiliates in a combined unitary report. Despite these differences, the advantages and disadvantages of consolidated returns and combined unitary reporting are similar.

- Major *advantages* of both group filing options include the:
- Ability to offset the losses of one affiliate against the profits of other affiliates
- Elimination of intercorporate dividends
- Deferral of gains on intercompany transactions

A primary *disadvantage* of both filing options is that they can prevent a taxpayer from creating legal structures and intercompany transactions that shift income from affiliates based in high-tax states to affiliates based in low-tax states.

Note that the comparison of consolidated returns and combined unitary reporting is complicated by the wide variety of filing options employed by the states, which makes it difficult to generalize.

STUDY QUESTIONS

---

1. All of the following are true of combined unitary reporting *except:*

  a. Combined unitary reporting is not so much a type of return as the name given to a methodology for apportioning income.

  b. Inclusion in a combined unitary report generally requires stock ownership of more than 50 percent.

  c. To be included in a combined unitary report, an affiliate must be engaged in the same trade or business as the other group members.

  d. Affiliates organized in a foreign country may *not* be included in a combined unitary report.

2. Which of the following is a *disadvantage* of both consolidated returns and combined unitary reporting?

  a. Ability to offset the losses of one affiliate against the profits of other affiliates

  b. Elimination of intercorporate dividends

  c. Limitation of the taxpayer's ability to shift income from affiliates in high-tax states to affiliates in low-tax states

  d. None of the above

MANDATORY VERSUS DISCRETIONARY COMBINED REPORTING

About 20 states require members of a unitary business group to compute their taxable income on a combined basis. These states include Alaska, Arizona, California, Colorado, Idaho, Illinois, Kansas, Maine, Massachusetts (effective in 2008), Michigan (effective in 2008), Minnesota, Montana, Nebraska, New Hampshire, New York (effective in 2007 for related corporations that have substantial intercorporate transactions), North Dakota, Oregon, Texas (effective in 2007), Utah, Vermont (effective in 2006), and West Virginia (effective in 2009).

In addition to these mandatory combined reporting states, roughly 15 other states (including New Jersey, North Carolina, and Virginia) generally allow commonly controlled corporations to file separate company returns, but also require or permit a combined unitary report if certain conditions are satisfied. A common reason for requiring a combined report is the state tax authority's determination that a combined report is necessary to clearly reflect the group's income earned in the state or to prevent the evasion of taxes.

> ### EXAMPLE
>
> The Indiana Department of Revenue may require commonly controlled corporations to file a combined return, but only if the Department is unable to fairly reflect the taxpayer's income through other statutory means [Ind. Code §6-3-2-2(p)].
>
> For instance, in Letter of Findings No. 05-0175 [Ind. Dept. of Rev., May 1, 2006], a manufacturing corporation that divided its operations among various subsidiaries was required to file a combined Indiana income tax return to fairly reflect its income from Indiana sources. On a separate company basis, the parent had a loss of $25 million during the four-year audit period, while the other companies in the group had a profit of $500 million. The parent and its subsidiaries engaged in numerous intercompany transactions and were part of a unitary business.

New Jersey does *not* permit an affiliated group to elect to file a consolidated return, nor does it require all unitary groups to compute their tax on a combined basis. Thus, every corporation with nexus in New Jersey generally is considered a separate entity and must file its own return. The Director of the Division of Taxation may, however, require members of an affiliated group or a controlled group to file a consolidated return "if the taxpayer cannot demonstrate by clear and convincing evidence that a report by a taxpayer discloses the true earnings of the taxpayer on its business carried on in this State" [N.J. Rev. Stat. 54:10A-10.c.].

Likewise, North Carolina does *not* permit an affiliated group to elect to file a consolidated return; however, the Secretary of Revenue may require two or more commonly controlled corporations to file a consolidated return if a separate-company return "does not disclose the true earnings of the corporation on its business carried on in this State" [N.C. Gen. Stat. §105-130.6].

WORLDWIDE VERSUS WATER'S-EDGE COMBINED REPORTING

When a *unitary group* is required to compute its tax on a combined basis, there are two general approaches to dealing with unitary group members that are incorporated in a foreign country and/or conduct most of their business abroad:

1. **Worldwide combination.** The combined report includes all members of the unitary business group, regardless of the country in which the member is incorporated or the country in which the member conducts business.
2. **Water's-edge combination.** The combined report includes all members of the unitary business group, *except* for certain unitary group members that are incorporated in a foreign country and/or conduct most of their business

abroad. A common approach is to exclude so-called 80/20 corporations. An 80/20 corporation is a corporation whose business activity outside the United States, as measured by some combination of apportionment factors, is 80 percent or more of the corporation's total business activity. Other approaches to defining a water's-edge combination include excluding only the 80/20 corporations organized abroad, or excluding all corporations organized abroad, regardless of their degree of foreign business activity.

EXAMPLE

For Illinois tax purposes, an 80/20 company is defined as any member whose business activity outside the United States is 80 percent or more of the member's total business activity, as measured by its property and payroll factors [Rev. Stat. §1501(a)(27)].

Worldwide Combination

Requiring the use of worldwide combined reporting is controversial for a number of reasons, including:

- The distortion of the property and payroll factors caused by lower wage rates and property values in developing countries
- The difficulty of converting books and records maintained under foreign accounting principles and in a foreign currency into a form that is acceptable to the states
- The inability of states to readily access or audit records located in foreign countries
- The uncertainties about which affiliates are properly included in the unitary group

Despite the practical difficulties of apportioning income on a worldwide basis, the constitutionality of requiring a corporation to compute its state taxable income on a worldwide combined unitary basis has been firmly established.

In *Container Corp. of America v. Franchise Tax Board* [463 US 159 (1983)], the Supreme Court held that California's worldwide combined reporting method was constitutional with respect to a U.S.-based parent corporation and its foreign country subsidiaries. In *Barclays Bank plc v. Franchise Tax Board* [512 US 298 (1994)], the Supreme Court held that California's worldwide combined reporting method was also constitutional with respect to a foreign-based parent corporation and its U.S. subsidiaries.

The U.S. business community generally takes a dim view of combined unitary reporting and, in particular, the practice of requiring a worldwide combination. The major trading partners of the United States, such as the United Kingdom (the country in which Barclays Bank was based), are also generally opposed to worldwide combined reporting. In this regard, it is worth noting that no major industrialized country, including the United States, requires a worldwide consolidated return for income tax purposes.

Water's-Edge Combination

California repealed mandatory worldwide combined reporting in 1988, and it permits a unitary group to make a *water's-edge* election. Once the water's-edge election is made, the unitary group must continue to file on a water's-edge basis for a seven-year period. For California tax purposes, a water's-edge group includes the following unitary members:

- Corporations whose average property, payroll, and sales factors in the United States is 20 percent or more
- Corporations organized in the United States that have more than 50 percent of their stock controlled by the same interests
- Foreign sales corporations and domestic international sales corporations
- Controlled foreign corporations, whose income and factors are included based on the ratio of the corporation's current year Subpart F income to its current year earnings and profits
- Any other corporations with U.S. located business income which are included to the extent of U.S. located income and factors [Cal. Rev. & Tax. Code §25110]

> **PLANNING POINTER**
>
> Whether it is beneficial for a taxpayer to make a water's-edge election depends on the facts and circumstances. A major advantage of making a water's-edge election is that it avoids the compliance burden of a worldwide combination, which can be substantial, particularly if the unitary business group includes a large number of foreign affiliates. On the other hand, a water's-edge election may increase the taxpayer's California tax if the taxpayer's U.S. operations are more profitable than its foreign operations.

Other mandatory combined unitary reporting states that have adopted the concept of a worldwide combination, including Alaska, Idaho, Montana, North Dakota, and Utah, also permit a unitary group to make a water's-edge election. Alaska, however, requires the use of worldwide combined reporting by oil companies. Other mandatory combined reporting states, such as Arizona, Illinois, Kansas, Maine, Minnesota, and New Hampshire, generally require some type of water's-edge combination.

Massachusetts allows taxpayers to elect worldwide combined reporting. The election is binding for 10 years. A taxpayer that does not elect worldwide combined reporting determines its taxable income on a water's-edge basis. West Virginia generally requires water's-edge combined reporting, unless the Tax Commissioner requires worldwide combined reporting or the taxpayer elects to report on a worldwide basis. The election is binding for 10 years.

STUDY QUESTIONS

> **3.** Approximately how many states require members of a unitary business group to compute their taxable income on a combined basis?
>
> **a.** 30
> **b.** 20
> **c.** 15
> **d.** 10
>
> **4.** It may be beneficial for a taxpayer to make a water's-edge election if:
>
> **a.** The unitary business group includes a large number of foreign affiliates.
> **b.** The unitary business group includes no foreign affiliates.
> **c.** The taxpayer's U.S. operations are more profitable than its foreign operations.
> **d.** None of the above is a situation in which a taxpayer may benefit from a water's-edge election.

CONCEPT OF A UNITARY BUSINESS

Combined unitary reporting requires a determination of the *unitary business group*, which can be a source of controversy. The problem is that there is no simple, objective definition of what constitutes a unitary business. In fact, over the years the courts have developed a number of different tests for determining the existence of a unitary business. As one Supreme Court Justice observed, "the unitary business concept ... is not, so to speak, unitary." Because of the many judicial interpretations of a unitary business, it is not always clear which of the available tests should be applied. In addition, even if a taxpayer knows which test will be used, the subjective nature of the tests makes them difficult to apply with any certainty.

Generally speaking, a *vertically integrated business*, in which each of the separate affiliates or divisions performs an interdependent step that leads to a finished product only when the steps are combined, will be treated as unitary.

A *horizontally integrated business*, in which there are parallel operations in different geographic locations (e.g., a chain of retail stores), will generally be considered unitary if there is centralized management.

A *conglomerate* may or may not be considered unitary, depending on whether there is strong centralized management, as exhibited by a centralized executive force and shared staff functions, as well as economies of scale in the form of common employee pension and benefit plans, common insurance policies, and so on.

Judicial Interpretations of Unitary Business

Over the years the courts have developed a number of different tests for determining the existence of a unitary business. They are the:

1. Three-unities test
2. Contribution or dependency test
3. Factors-of-profitability test
4. Flow-of-value test

Three-Unities Test

The Supreme Court articulated the three-unities test in **Butler Bros. v. McColgan** [315 US 501 (1942)]. Under this test, a unitary business exists if the following three factors are present:

1. **Unity of ownership.** Generally, to establish unity of ownership other than the common parent, more than 50 percent of each corporation's voting stock must be directly or indirectly owned by another corporation in the group. Note that the unitary theory does not recognize minority interests. Thus, if *control* is established through a 51 percent ownership interest, *all* of the income of that corporation and all of its property, payroll, and sales factors are included in the combined report, even though there is a substantial minority interest.
2. **Unity of operation.** Unity of operation is exhibited by centralized staff functions performed by one of the corporations on behalf of the entire group. Examples include centralized purchasing, advertising, accounting and legal services, and human resources functions, as well as common personnel policies, pension and employee benefit plans, and insurance.
3. **Unity of use.** Unity of use is similar to unity of operation, except that unity of use is associated with *line functions* (executive force and general systems of operation), whereas unity of operation relates to *staff functions*. Unity of use is exhibited by a centralized executive force (e.g., shared officers and directors) that makes major decisions regarding strategy and operations, as well as by intercompany transfers of products, know-how, and expertise.

Contribution or Dependency Test

A second judicial test for the existence of a unitary business is whether "the operation of the portion of the business done within the state is dependent upon or contributes to the operation of the business without the state" [***Edison Cal. Stores, Inc. v. McColgan,*** 176 P.2d 697 (Cal. 1947)].

Examples of factors that suggest contributions by or dependency among commonly controlled corporations include:

- Intercompany loans
- Intercompany sales of goods or services
- Exchanges of products or expertise
- A shared executive force and staff functions

Some courts have made a distinction between essential contributing activities and other contributing activities.

Examples of activities that may be considered essential are:

- Substantial borrowing from out-of-state operations to finance in-state operations
- Transfers of top-level executives from out-of-state operations
- Transfers of manufacturing equipment and raw materials from out-of-state operations

Factors-of-Profitability Test

The Supreme Court has referred to the factors-of-profitability test in several cases, including *Mobil Oil Corp. v. Commissioner of Taxes* [445 US 425 (1980)], *F.W. Woolworth Co. v. Taxation & Rev. Dept.* [458 US 354 (1982)], and *Allied-Signal, Inc. v. Division of Taxation* [504 US 768 (1992)].

The indicia of a *unitary business*, or so-called *factors of profitability*, include:

1. Functional integration
2. Centralization of management
3. Economies of scale

Functional integration is exhibited by intercompany flows of goods, services, personnel, and expertise.

Centralization of management is indicated by shared directors and officers, exchanges of upper-level management, and required parent corporation approval of major policy decisions.

Economies of scale are demonstrated by the collective negotiation and purchase of goods and services, shared staff functions, and common insurance policies and employee pension and benefit plans.

Flow-of-Value Test

In *Container Corp. of America v. Franchise Tax Board* [463 US 159 (1983)], the Supreme Court arguably established a fourth test for the existence of a unitary business. Under the flow-of-value test, a parent corporation and its subsidiary are unitary if "there [is] some sharing or exchange of value not capable of precise identification or measurement—beyond the mere flow of funds arising out of a passive investment or a distinct business operation." The Court also indicated that "the prerequisite to a constitutionally acceptable finding of unitary business is a flow of value, not a flow of goods."

Statutory Definitions of Unitary Business

Other important sources of authority regarding the meaning of the term *unitary business* are state statutes, regulations, and administrative rulings. Like their judicial counterparts, however, they generally leave much to be desired in terms of providing detailed and objective guidance.

MTC Regulations

Created in 1967, the Multistate Tax Commission (MTC) is an agency of state governments whose mission is to promote fairness and uniformity in state tax laws. To help states determine the existence of a unitary business, the MTC adopted a uniform regulation [MTC Reg. IV.1.(b), *Principles for Determining the Existence of a Unitary Business*], which describes the concept of a *unitary business* as follows:

> A unitary business is a single economic enterprise that is made up either of separate parts of a single business entity or of a commonly controlled group of business entities that are sufficiently interdependent, integrated and interrelated through their activities so as to provide a synergy and mutual benefit that produces a sharing or exchange of value among them and a significant flow of value to the separate parts.

More specifically, a *unitary business* is characterized by significant flows of value evidenced by the following factors:

- **Functional integration.** Common marketing programs, transfers or pooling of technical information or intellectual property, common distribution systems, common purchasing, and common or intercompany financing.
- **Centralization of management.** Joint participation of corporate directors and officers in the management decisions that affect the different business units
- **Economies of scale.** Centralized purchasing, centralized administrative functions, etc.

The MTC regulation also identifies same type of business, steps in a vertical process, and strong centralized management as indicators of a unitary business. Additionally, the MTC has approved a model combined reporting statute [Proposed Model Statute for Combined Reporting, August 17, 2006].

STUDY QUESTIONS

---

5. Which of the following tests for determining the existence of a unitary business explicitly considers *economies of scale* as a factor?

 a. The three-unities test
 b. The contribution or dependency test
 c. The flow-of-value test
 d. The factors-of-profitability test

6. A conglomerate is *always* considered to be unitary. ***True or False?***

7. Which of the following is an example of *centralized management*?

 a. Joint participation of corporate officers in management decisions that affect different business units
 b. Common distribution systems
 c. Centralized administrative functions
 d. Centralized purchasing

California

Although California has not adopted a statutory definition of a unitary business, California Code of Regulations Title 18, §25120 (Definition of Business and Nonbusiness Income), provides guidelines on what a unitary business is. Under California law, the determination of whether two or more commonly controlled corporations are unitary depends on the facts in each case, and there is a strong presumption that the taxpayer's operations are unitary if any of the following factors is present:

- Same type of business
- Steps in a vertical process
- Strong centralized management

Common control means that the voting power of each member, other than the common parent, is more than 50 percent owned (directly or constructively) by other members of the group [Cal. Rev. & Tax. Code §25105].

In determining the existence of a unitary business, the California courts have also applied both the *three-unities test* and the *contribution or dependency test*. In *A.M. Castle & Co. v. Franchise Tax Board*, the court indicated that a unitary business exists if *either* the three-unities test or the contribution or dependency test is satisfied [No. A064957 (Cal. Ct. App. 1995)]. In *Appeal of Leland Corp.*, the California State Board of Equalization found that *either* the three-unities test or the contribution or dependency test must be satisfied to determine that a unitary business exists, but it is not required that both tests be met [No. 94A-0916 (Cal. St. Bd. of Equal. 1997)].

The existence of multiple criteria (three-unities test, contribution or dependency test, and the California regulation) creates a degree of uncertainty regarding California's application of the unitary business principle. This unpredictability of result is illustrated by the *Woolworth* and *Yellow Freight* cases.

In *F. W. Woolworth Co. v. Franchise Tax Board* [No. A075506 (Cal. Ct. App. 1998)], a mass merchandise retailer (Woolworth), owned 100 percent of a shoe manufacturer and retailer (Kinney). Although the two companies were arguably in the same industry (i.e., retail), they had decentralized management and staff functions and virtually no intercompany transactions. The California Franchise Tax Board determined that Woolworth and Kinney were *not* unitary. This prevented Kinney from offsetting its profits against the losses suffered by Woolworth.

The Court of Appeals applied the three-unities test, the contribution or dependency test, and the state's regulatory definition. The court determined that Woolworth and Kinney were *not* in the same line of business, and that there was an absence of strong centralized management, unity of use, and unity of operation. Based on these findings, the court concluded that a unitary business did *not* exist.

In *Yellow Freight System, Inc. v. Franchise Tax Board* [No. A070143 (Cal. Ct. App. 1996)], Yellow Freight Systems (Yellow) was an interstate trucking company that owned 100 percent of Overland Energy Inc. (OEI), an oil and gas exploration subsidiary. The California Franchise Tax Board determined that Yellow and OEI were *not* unitary. This prevented Yellow from offsetting the losses suffered by OEI against its profits.

The California Court of Appeals applied both the three-unities test and the contribution or dependency test, and concluded that Yellow and OEI were unitary under either test. Although Yellow and OEI were in different industries, and Yellow never used OEI to acquire fuel for its trucking operations, the fact that they shared a common executive force and common staff functions, as well as economies of scale in the form of shared insurance and employee benefit plans, was sufficient to establish the existence of a unitary business.

Illinois

Under Illinois Revenue Statutes §1501(a)(27), a *unitary business group* is defined as "a group of persons related through common ownership whose business activities are integrated with, dependent upon and contribute to each other." *Common ownership* is defined as direct or indirect control or ownership of more than 50 percent of the outstanding voting stock. A unitary business group also does *not* include any member that is ordinarily required to apportion its business income using a specialized formula, such as a financial organization.

Illinois Revenue Statutes §1501(a)(27) defines unitary business activity as follows:

> Unitary business activity can ordinarily be illustrated where the activities of the members are:
>
> (1) in the same general line (such as manufacturing, wholesaling, retailing of tangible personal property, insurance, transportation or finance); or
>
> (2) steps in a vertically structured enterprise or process (such as the steps involved in the production of natural resources, which might include exploration, mining, refining, and marketing); and, in either instance, the members are functionally integrated through the exercise of strong centralized management (where, for example, authority over such matters as purchasing, financing, tax compliance, product line, personnel, marketing and capital investment is not left to each member).

Case law indicates that the Illinois courts have interpreted the definition of unitary business activity broadly.

EXAMPLE

In *A.B. Dick Co. v. McGraw* [No. 4-96-0057 (Ill. App. Ct. 1997)], an office equipment manufacturer (A.B. Dick) owned 100 percent of Videojet, a company which manufactured a specialized line of printing equipment that was originally developed by A.B. Dick. Despite a general lack of functional integration in the key areas of manufacturing, marketing, engineering, purchasing, advertising, and distribution, the court held that the two companies *did* constitute a unitary business group under the *applicable statutory* definition. The two companies:

1. Were in the same line of business
2. Had a centralized executive force
3. Shared staff functions
4. Shared insurance and employee benefit plans
5. Engaged in intercompany financing

The court also found it significant that A.B. Dick did not acquire Videojet, but developed it from within.

> In **Borden, Inc. v. Dept. of Revenue** [No. 1-96-2408 (Ill. App. Ct. 1998)], Borden, a manufacturer and distributor of food, consumer, and chemical products, owned 100 percent of the Pepsi-Subs, which were independent bottlers that operated under an exclusive agreement with PepsiCo. Despite the general lack of functional integration in key areas such as manufacturing and marketing, the court held that the two companies constituted a unitary business group because of the restrictive nature of the bottling agreements between the Pepsi-Subs and PepsiCo. There was strong centralized management, as evidenced by shared staff functions, such as accounting, internal audit, tax compliance, cash management, employee relations, legal, insurance, and employee benefit programs. In addition, Borden had control over the Pepsi-Subs' operating budgets, capital expenditures, appointment of officers, and determination of officer salaries.

In *Envirodyne Industries, Inc.* [No. 02-1632 (US Ct. of App., 7th Cir., Jan. 6, 2004)], which involved a bankruptcy matter, the U.S. Court of Appeals ruled that despite the existence of common management, several steel manufacturing subsidiaries were *not* unitary with several food packaging subsidiaries because there was no functional integration of the activities of the two subsets of subsidiaries. As a consequence, the losses of the steel subsidiaries could not offset the income of the food-packaging subsidiaries for Illinois tax purposes. In making this determination, the federal court relied on a *wheel and spoke* theory of unity, under which unity between the common parent and the steel subsidiaries was not sufficient to establish unity between the steel subsidiaries and the food packaging subsidiaries.

Colorado

The Colorado statutory definition of a *unitary business* is noteworthy because it attempts to provide a *bright-line test* for the existence of a unitary business. Specifically, Colorado Revised Statutes §39-22-303 provides that a unitary business exists if there is common ownership, defined as more than 50 percent ownership, and three of the following six factors are present for the current tax year and the two preceding tax years:

1. Intercompany sales or leases constitute 50 percent or more of the gross operating receipts of the affiliate making the sales or leases (or 50 percent or more of the cost of goods sold or leases of the affiliate making the purchases or leases).
2. Five or more of the following services are provided by one or more affiliates for the benefit of other affiliates:
    −   Advertising and public relations services
    −   Accounting and bookkeeping services
    −   Legal services

- Personnel services
- Sales services
- Purchasing services
- Research and development services
- Insurance procurement and servicing exclusive of employee benefit programs
- Employee benefit programs

3. Twenty percent or more of the *long-term debt* of one affiliate is owed to or guaranteed by another affiliate. *Long-term debt* is defined as debt due more than one year after it is incurred.

4. One affiliate substantially uses the patents, trademarks, service marks, logo-types, trade secrets, copyrights, or other proprietary materials owned by another affiliate.

5. Fifty percent or more of the members of the board of directors of one affiliate are members of the board of directors or are corporate officers of another affiliate.

6. Twenty-five percent or more of the 20 highest ranking officers of one affiliate are members of the board of directors or are corporate officers of another affiliate.

Massachusetts

For Massachusetts tax purposes, the term *unitary business* means the activities of a group of two or more corporations under common ownership that are "sufficiently interdependent, integrated or interrelated through their activities so as to provide mutual benefit and produce a significant sharing or exchange of value among them or a significant flow of value between the separate parts." The term is construed to the broadest extent permitted under the U.S. Constitution [Mass. Gen. Laws, Ch. 63, Code §32B(b)(1)].

Common ownership means that more than 50 percent of the voting control of each member of the group is directly or indirectly owned by a common owner or owners, either corporate or non-corporate, and whether or not the owner or owners are members of the combined group [Mass. Gen. Laws, Ch. 63, Code § 32B(b)(2)].

Minnesota

For Minnesota tax purposes, a unitary business is defined as business activities that result in a flow of value, as determined by all of the facts and circumstances. Business activities conducted by two or more commonly controlled corporations are presumed to be unitary when one of the following is true:

■ The business activities or operations are of mutual benefit, dependent on, or contributory to one another individually or as a group.

- There is unity of operation evidenced by staff functions, such as centralized advertising, accounting, financing, management, or centralized, group, or committee purchasing.
- There is unity of use evidenced by line functions, centralized executive force, and general system of operation.

Two or more commonly controlled corporations are also presumed to be unitary when contributions to income result from functional integration, centralized management, and economies of scale.

Based on the state's statutory definition of a unitary business for the tax years in question (1986 to 1990), in *Amoco Corp. v. Comm'r of Rev.* [658 N.W.2d 859 (Minn. Sup. Ct. April 3, 2003)], the Minnesota Supreme Court ruled that an oil company's exploration and production subsidiary was *not* unitary with its refining, marketing, and transportation subsidiary, because the two companies did not depend on or contribute to one another in order to earn a profit. The two subsidiaries were independently managed, and their operations were driven by market conditions rather than each other's needs. In addition, all sales of crude oil by the exploration and production business were at market prices, including sales to its sister company.

Michigan

Starting in 2008, a unitary business group must compute both the Michigan business income tax and the modified gross receipts tax on a combined basis [Mich. Comp. Laws §208.1511]. A *unitary business group* is defined in Mich. Comp. Laws § 208.1117(6) as:

> (i) a group of United States persons, other than a foreign operating entity, one of which owns or controls, directly or indirectly, more than 50 percent of the ownership interests with voting rights of the other United States persons, and (ii) that has business activities or operations which result in a flow of value between or among persons included in the unitary business group or has business activities or operations that are integrated with, are dependent upon, or contribute to each other. The flow of value is determined by reviewing the totality of the facts and circumstances.

For this purpose, a *United States person* has the same meaning as in Internal Revenue Code Sec. 7701(a)(30), and includes corporations or partnerships organized in the United States or under the law of the United States. A *foreign operating entity* is a United States person (e.g., a corporation organized in the United States) that would otherwise be a part of a unitary business group, but has substantial operations outside the United States and at least 80 percent of its income is active foreign business income [Mich. Comp. Laws §208.1109(5)].

Non-U.S. persons, such as foreign corporations and foreign partnerships, are *not* includible in the unitary business group. Financial institutions and insurance companies are also excluded from the combined return [Mich. Comp. Laws §208.1511].

New York

For tax years beginning on or after January 1, 2007, under N.Y. Tax Law §211, related corporations are required to file a New York combined report "if there are substantial intercorporate transactions among the related corporations, regardless of the transfer price for such intercorporate transactions." Related corporations that do not satisfy the substantial intercorporate transactions requirement may still be required or permitted to file a combined report if necessary to properly reflect the related corporations' tax because of intercorporate transactions or some agreement, understanding, arrangement, or transaction.

According to N.Y. Regs. §6-2.2, a *related corporation* includes:

(i) any corporation 80 percent or more of the voting stock of which is owned or controlled directly or indirectly by the taxpayer, (ii) any corporation which owns or controls directly or indirectly 80 percent or more of the voting stock of the taxpayer; and (iii) any corporation the voting stock of which is owned or controlled directly or indirectly by the same interests that own or control directly or indirectly 80 percent or more of the voting stock of the taxpayer.

In determining whether there are substantial intercorporate transactions, according to N.Y. Tax Law §211, all activities and transactions of the related corporations are considered, including (but not limited to) the following:

(i) manufacturing, acquiring goods or property, or performing services, for related corporations; (ii) selling goods acquired from related corporations; (iii) financing sales of related corporations; (iv) performing related customer services using common facilities and employees for related corporations; (v) incurring expenses that benefit, directly or indirectly, one or more related corporations; and (vi) transferring assets, including such assets as accounts receivable, patents or trademarks from one or more related corporations.

On March 3, 2008, the New York State Department of Taxation and Finance issued TSB-M-08(2)C, which provides the following tests for determining whether related corporations satisfy the substantial intercorporate transactions requirement:

- **Substantial intercorporate receipts.** The substantial intercorporate transactions requirement is satisfied if, during the tax year, 50 percent or more of a corporation's receipts, excluding dividends and nonrecurring items, are from related corporations. However, a multi-year test (described below) applies if intercorporate receipts are between 45 percent and 55 percent.

- **Substantial intercorporate expenditures.** The substantial intercorporate transactions requirement is satisfied if, during the tax year, 50 percent or more of a corporation's expenditures, including expenditures for inventory but excluding nonrecurring items, are from related corporations. However, a multi-year test applies if intercorporate expenditures are between 45 percent and 55 percent.
- **Multi-year tests.** When a corporation's intercorporate receipts (or expenditures) during the tax year are between 45 percent and 55 percent, the substantial intercorporate transactions requirement is satisfied if 50 percent or more of a corporation's receipts (or expenditures), excluding nonrecurring items, during the current and prior two tax years are from related corporations.
- **Substantial intercorporate asset transfers.** A transfer of assets to a related corporation (including through incorporation) satisfies the substantial intercorporate transactions requirement if 20 percent or more of the transferee's gross income, including any dividends received, is derived directly from the transferred assets and the corporations are engaged in a unitary business. However, only the assets that are transferred in exchange for stock or paid-in capital of the transferee are taken into account for purposes of this test. Transfers of cash in exchange for stock or paid-in capital are ignored.

TSB-M-08(2)C describes a complex, 10-step process for determining which corporations are included in the combined group by identifying the specific related corporations which are engaged in substantial intercorporate transactions with either a taxpayer corporation, or another member of the combined group which includes a taxpayer corporation.

Oregon

For tax years beginning after 2006, a business enterprise is deemed to be a unitary business if there exists between its members a sharing or exchange of value as demonstrated by *one* of the following conditions [S.B. 178, June 11, 2007]:

- Centralized management or a common executive force
- Centralized administrative services or functions resulting in economies of scale
- Flow of goods, capital resources or services demonstrating functional integration

Under prior law, each of the three conditions had to be satisfied in order for a unitary business to exist.

Texas

For purposes of computing the Texas margin tax, taxable entities that are part of an affiliated group engaged in a unitary business must file a combined report. An *affiliated group* means a group of one or more taxable entities in which a controlling interest is owned by a common owner or owners, either corporate or noncorporate, or by one or more of the member entities.

Under Texas Tax Code §171.0001, a *controlling interest* in a corporation means direct or indirect ownership of more than 50 percent of the total combined voting power of all classes of stock of the corporation, or a more than 50 percent direct or indirect beneficial ownership interest in the voting stock of the corporation.

A taxable entity that conducts business outside the United States is excluded from the combined report if 80 percent or more of its property and payroll are assigned to locations outside the United States. If a taxable entity that conducts business outside the United States has no property or payroll and 80 percent or more of its gross receipts are assigned to locations outside the United States, the entity is excluded from the combined report [Texas Tax Code §171.1014(a)].

Under Texas Tax Code §171.0001(17), a unitary business means "a single economic enterprise that is made up of separate parts of a single entity or of a commonly controlled group of entities that are sufficiently interdependent, integrated, and interrelated through their activities so as to provide a synergy and mutual benefit that produces a sharing or exchange of value among them and a significant flow of value to the separate parts."

All relevant factors are considered in determining whether a unitary business exists, including [Texas Tax Code §171.0001(17)] :

> (i) whether the activities of the group members are in the same general line, such as manufacturing, wholesaling, retailing of tangible personal property, insurance, transportation, or finance; (ii) whether the activities of the group members are steps in a vertically structured enterprise or process, such as the steps involved in the production of natural resources, including exploration, mining, refining, and marketing; and (iii) whether the members are functionally integrated through the exercise of strong centralized management, such as authority over purchasing, financing, product line, personnel, and marketing.

The comptroller may also consider guidelines in Supreme Court decisions that presume activities are unitary. All affiliated entities are presumed to be engaged in a unitary business [34 Tex. Admin. Code 3.590].

STUDY QUESTIONS

8. New York provides which of the following tests for determining whether related corporations satisfy the substantial intercorporate transactions requirement?

   a. Unity-of-operation

   b. Substantial intercorporate asset transfers

   c. Unity-of-use

   d. Functional integration

9. Which of the following states does *not* use the 80/20-type test to determine whether to exclude foreign country affiliates from the combined report?

   a. California

   b. Illinois

   c. Texas

   d. None of the above

10. California has adopted a statutory definition of a unitary business. *True or False?*

Pass-Through Entities

This chapter discusses how states tax the income of S corporations, partnerships, and limited liability companies (LLCs).

LEARNING OBJECTIVES

Upon completing this chapter, the student will:

- Understand the federal tax treatment of pass-through entities
- Understand how the federal tax treatment of pass-through entities relates to the state tax treatment of these entities
- Be familiar with different types of entity-level taxes imposed by states on pass-through entities
- Comprehend the federal and state tax treatment of S corporation shareholders, partners and limited liability company members
- Understand how partnership income is apportioned
- Be familiar with state composite returns and withholding requirements for nonresident owners of pass-through entities
- Know fiscal year restrictions on pass-through entities

S CORPORATIONS

Federal Tax Treatment

The federal government taxes earnings of a regular corporation twice, by imposing both a *corporate-level tax* when the income is earned and a *shareholder-level tax* when the corporation distributes its earnings as a dividend to individual shareholders.

In 1958, Congress enacted Internal Revenue Code ("the Code") Secs. 1361 to 1379, or Subchapter S, to permit closely held corporations to enjoy the nontax advantages of the corporate form, like limited liability and ownership interests that are readily transferable, without being subject to double taxation of corporate income. This is achieved by allowing the income of an S corporation to be taxed only at the shareholder level. The S corporation form also allows entity-level operating losses to pass through to shareholders, who can claim a deduction for those losses on their individual income tax returns.

To be eligible to make an S corporation election, a domestic corporation must have *both*:
- Only one class of stock
- No more than 100 shareholders

In addition, Code Sec. 1361 requires all the shareholders to be *either*:
- Individuals who are U.S. citizens
- Resident aliens, estates, or certain types of trusts

> **NOTE**
>
> The election is made by filing federal Form 2553.

Although an S corporation's year-to-year operating profits are taxed much like those of a partnership, Subchapter C provisions still generally apply to incorporation, reorganization and liquidation transactions. In addition, entity-level taxes may be imposed on an S corporation that was a C corporation in a prior tax year. These include taxes on excess passive investment income (Code Sec. 1375), built-in gains (Code Sec. 1374), and the LIFO recapture amount (Code Sec. 1363(d)).

A qualified Subchapter S subsidiary (QSSS) is a domestic corporation that qualifies as an S corporation, that is owned 100 percent by another S corporation, and whose parent S corporation elects to treat it as a QSSS (Code Sec. 1361). For reporting purposes, the assets, liabilities, income, deductions, and other tax attributes of the QSSS are combined with those of its S corporation parent and reported on the parent's tax return.

State Conformity to Federal Pass-Through Treatment

States generally conform to the federal pass-through treatment of S corporations, but only if the corporation has filed a valid S corporation election for federal tax purposes. Although most states provide that the filing of a federal S corporation election automatically qualifies the corporation as an S corporation for state tax purposes, a handful of states require taxpayers to comply with additional special procedures in order to make a valid S corporation election.

> **EXAMPLE**
>
> A federal S corporation that wishes to be recognized as an S corporation for New Jersey income tax purposes must make a separate New Jersey S corporation election using New Jersey form CBT-2553.

States That Impose Entity-Level Taxes on S Corporations

Although most states treat S corporations as pass-through entities, a number of states impose entity-level taxes on S corporations. In many cases, the entity-level tax is imposed in addition to a shareholder-level personal income tax. For example, California imposes an income tax on S corporations doing business in California, and also imposes a personal income tax on a shareholder's pro-rata share of an S corporation's income.

States that impose entity-level taxes on S corporations include the following:

California

An S corporation doing business in California must pay the greater of an $800 minimum tax or a 1.5 percent corporate franchise tax on the S corporation's income. The tax rate is 3.5 percent for S corporations that are financial corporations.

Connecticut

Connecticut imposes a $250 business entity tax on S corporations.

District of Columbia

The District of Columbia does not conform to the federal pass-through entity treatment of an S corporation. As a consequence, S corporations are subject to the District's 9.975 percent corporate income tax.

Illinois

Illinois imposes a 1.5 percent income tax (referred to as the *personal property replacement tax*) on S corporations.

Kansas

Kansas imposes a franchise tax on S corporations. The tax base is net worth (stockholders' equity). The tax rate is $0.09375 per $1,000 of net worth, with a maximum tax of $20,000. The tax is scheduled to be phased out by 2011.

Kentucky

For tax years beginning on or after January 1, 2007, S corporations are subject to a limited liability entity tax equal to the lesser of 0.095 percent of Kentucky gross receipts or 0.75 percent of Kentucky gross profits. The tax does *not* apply to S corporations with gross receipts or gross profits of $3 million or less, and is reduced for S corporations with gross receipts or gross profits over $3 million but less than $6 million. For tax years beginning in 2005 and 2006, S corporations were subject to the greater of a 7 percent income tax or an alternative minimum calculation based on gross receipts or gross profits.

Massachusetts

An S corporation that has total annual receipts of $6 million or more is subject to a 3 percent corporate income tax. The rate increases to 4.5 percent for S corporations with total annual receipts of $9 million or more. Massachusetts also subjects S corporations to a $456 minimum tax and a 0.26 percent franchise tax based on either tangible property located in Massachusetts or net worth.

The Massachusetts corporate income tax rate of 9.5 percent is scheduled to be reduced to 8.75 percent in 2010, 8.25 percent in 2011, and 8.0 percent in 2012. The tax rate for S corporations with total annual receipts of $9 million or more is modified to equal the excess of the corporate tax rate over the personal income tax rate imposed for the year. The tax rate for S corporations with total annual receipts of at least $6 million but less than $9 million is two-thirds of the rate above (H.B. 4904 July 3, 2008).

Michigan

Prior to 2008, Michigan subjected S corporations to its 1.9 percent single business tax, which is a type of value-added tax. In 2007, Michigan repealed the single business tax, effective December 31, 2007, and replaced it with a new 4.95 percent business income tax and 0.80 percent modified gross receipts tax that apply to business activity occurring on or after January 1, 2008. Both taxes apply to S corporations.

New Hampshire

New Hampshire subjects S corporations to an 8.5 percent business profits tax and a 0.75 percent business enterprise tax.

New Jersey

For tax years ending on or after July 1, 2001, but on or before June 30, 2006, New Jersey imposed a 1.33 percent income tax on S corporations. The rate dropped to 0.67 percent for tax years ending on or after July 1, 2006, but on or before June 30, 2007. The tax does *not* apply for tax years ending on or after July 1, 2007.

New York City

New York City does *not* recognize a federal or New York State S corporation election. Therefore, S corporations are subject to New York City's 8.85 percent corporate income tax.

Ohio

Ohio imposes a commercial activity tax (CAT) on the annual gross receipts of an S corporation. The CAT is being phased in over a five-year period from 2005 to 2009. The initial tax rate was 0.06 percent (July 1, 2005), and it eventually rises to 0.26 percent (Apr. 1, 2009). Examples of *taxable gross receipts* include sales of property delivered to locations within Ohio, fees for services where the purchaser receives the benefit in Ohio, and rents from property used in Ohio.

In addition, an S corporation with a *qualifying investor* (e.g., a non-resident individual for whom the S corporation does not file an Ohio composite nonresident shareholder return) is subject to a five percent pass-through entity tax. The tax is imposed on the qualifying investor's distributive share of the S corporation's taxable income apportioned to Ohio, and the qualifying investor can claim a credit for his or her share of the pass-through entity tax paid by the S corporation.

Pennsylvania

S corporations are *not* subject to the Pennsylvania corporate income tax. However, S corporations are subject to a capital stock tax imposed on the corporation's capital stock value, as determined by a statutory formula. The capital stock tax rate is 0.289 percent in 2008. The tax is scheduled to be phased out by 2011.

Tennessee

Tennessee taxes S corporations in the same manner as it taxes regular corporations. Thus, S corporations are subject to *both* the Tennessee corporate excise tax, which equals 6.5 percent of net earnings, and the Tennessee corporate franchise tax, which equals 0.25 percent of net worth.

If an out-of-state S corporation owns stock in a corporation that is treated as a QSSS for federal tax purposes and has nexus in Tennessee, the QSSS is subject to the Tennessee corporate excise and franchise taxes as a separate entity, and the out-of-state S corporation owner is *not* subject to Tennessee tax solely because of its ownership of the in-state QSSS (Letter Ruling No. 05-07, Tenn. Dept. of Revenue, Jan. 31, 2005).

Texas

Texas subjects S corporations to its margin tax. The tax base equals the *lesser* of the following three amounts:

1. Total revenue, minus cost of goods sold
2. Total revenue, minus compensation
3. 70 percent of total revenue

The tax rate is 0.5 percent for S corporations primarily engaged in retail or wholesale trade and one percent for all other S corporations.

Prior to 2007, S corporations were subject to the Texas corporate franchise tax, which equaled the greater of 0.25 percent of net taxable capital (a net worth tax) or 4.5 percent of net taxable earned surplus (an income tax).

Washington
Washington subjects S corporations to its business and occupation (B&O) tax, which is a type of gross receipts tax. The B&O tax rate varies with the type of business activity, but generally is between 0.471 percent and 1.5 percent.

West Virginia
West Virginia imposes a business franchise tax on S corporations. For tax years beginning in 2007 and 2008, the tax is the greater of $50 or 0.55 percent of the S corporation's capital. The tax is scheduled to be phased out by 2014.

State Taxation of Shareholders
Again, Code Sec. 1361 requires that shareholders of an S corporation be either individuals who are U.S. citizens or resident aliens, estates, or certain types of trusts. Therefore, to the extent a state conforms to the federal pass-through treatment of an S corporation, the operative state income tax is usually the individual income tax. However, not all states have an individual income tax. Alaska, Florida, Nevada, South Dakota, Texas, Washington, and Wyoming do *not* impose individual income taxes. In addition, New Hampshire and Tennessee tax only *selected* types of income, not including salaries or wages.

The state in which an S corporation shareholder resides generally taxes the *entire* amount of the resident shareholder's pro rata share of S corporation income, regardless of where the income is earned. In contrast, states in which the shareholder does not reside tax a nonresident shareholder's distributive share of S corporation income *only* if the S corporation has nexus in the state, and then only to the extent the nonresident shareholder's pro rata share of income is attributable to sources within the state.

If a portion of a shareholder's pro rata share of income is subject to tax in two states (one by virtue of the shareholder's residence and the other by virtue of the source of the S corporation's income), the state of residence usually allows the individual to claim a credit for income taxes paid to the other state as a means of avoiding double taxation.

Some states, such as California, also allow a shareholder to claim a credit for income taxes imposed directly on the S corporation. In *MacFarlane v. Utah Tax Comn.*, the Utah Supreme Court ruled that Utah residents who were shareholders in S corporations were entitled to claim credits against their Utah personal income taxes for their pro rata shares of corporate franchise taxes paid by the S corporations to California and Texas [Nos. 20040956, 20030949, and 20030887 (Utah S. Ct., Mar. 24, 2006)]. The applicable statute provided a credit for taxes paid to other states "on income." The court held that the statute did not exclude franchise taxes imposed on the privilege of doing business in the state, provided the franchise taxes were measured by or calculated according to income.

Composite Returns and Withholding Requirements

The requirement that nonresident shareholders file returns and pay taxes in every state in which an S corporation has nexus can create a significant compliance burden for shareholders of an S corporation that has nexus in numerous states. To foster compliance, states require S corporations to file an annual informational return (similar to federal Form 1120S) and issue K-1s for shareholders. Another method of enhancing compliance is to require or permit an S corporation to file a composite return on behalf of the nonresident shareholders. A composite return is a single filing in which the participating shareholders report their distributive shares of the S corporation's income and the S corporation pays the state tax on behalf of the nonresident shareholders.

> **EXAMPLE**
>
> A State X Subchapter S corporation has five shareholders, all of whom are individuals who reside in State X. The S corporation also has nexus in State Z, and State Z allows an S corporation to file a composite return on behalf of shareholders who are nonresidents. The five shareholders do *not* have to file separate State Z tax returns. Instead, the S corporation can file a single composite State Z return on their behalf.

Another technique for promoting compliance on the part of nonresident shareholders is to require the S corporation to withhold and remit any taxes due on the shareholders' distributive shares of S corporation income.

The Multistate Tax Commission has adopted a model statute governing reporting options for nonresident owners of pass-through entities, including composite returns and withholding requirements (Proposed Statutory

Language on Reporting Options for Non-resident Members of Pass-through Entities with Withholding Requirement, Dec. 18, 2003).

STUDY QUESTIONS

1. To be eligible to make an S corporation election at the federal level, a domestic corporation must:
   - **a.** Have two classes of stock
   - **b.** Have more than 100 shareholders
   - **c.** File federal Form 2553
   - **d.** Have shareholders that are corporations

2. Which of the following statements is true?
   - **a.** States generally conform to the federal pass-through treatment of S corporations.
   - **b.** *All* states provide that the filing of a federal S corporation election automatically qualifies the corporation as an S corporation for state tax purposes.
   - **c.** *Most* states require taxpayers to comply with special procedures in addition to federal procedures in order to make a valid S corporation election.
   - **d.** None of the above

3. Most states treat S corporations as pass-through entities. ***True or False?***

4. Which of the following states no longer imposes an entity-level income tax on S corporations for tax years ending on or after July 1, 2007?
   - **a.** Kansas
   - **b.** Michigan
   - **c.** New Jersey
   - **d.** Tennessee

5. Which of the following is **not** a way states promote tax compliance by nonresident shareholders?
   - **a.** Requiring the S corporation to withhold taxes due on the shareholders' distributive shares of S corporation income
   - **b.** Requiring the S corporation to file an annual informational return and issue K-1s for shareholders
   - **c.** Permitting an S corporation to file a composite return on behalf of nonresident shareholders
   - **d.** None of the above

PARTNERSHIPS

Federal Tax Treatment

A partnership is an unincorporated trade or business owned and managed by two or more persons. For federal income tax purposes, a partnership is *not* a taxpaying entity. Instead, it is treated as a pass-through entity, whereby its gross income, deductions, and credits flow through to the partners, who report the items on their own tax returns. For federal tax purposes, each year a partnership must file a tax return (Form 1065) to report its results from operations, and it must send each partner a statement (Schedule K-1 of Form 1065) that details the partner's distributive share of the partnership's gross income, deductions, and credits. In the case of corporate partners, each partner then reports these items on Form 1120. In the case of a partner who is an individual, each partner then reports these items on Form 1040.

A partnership generally takes one of two legal forms—that of either a general partnership or a limited partnership. In a *general partnership*, each partner has unlimited liability for the partnership's debts and has the right to participate in the management of the partnership.

In a *limited partnership*, there must be at least one general partner and one limited partner. A *general partner* has unlimited liability and is responsible for managing the partnership. In contrast, a *limited partner* cannot lose more than its investment in the partnership and generally may not participate in the management of the partnership.

A third partnership form is the *limited liability partnership*, which allows partners of certain types of professional service firms (e.g., public accounting firms) to reduce their exposure to lawsuits relative to operating as a general partnership.

The principal state income tax issues with respect to partnerships include:

- Conformity to the federal pass-through treatment of partnerships
- State entity-level taxes on partnerships
- Nexus considerations for corporate general and limited partners
- Apportionment of a corporate partner's distributive share of partnership income
- State taxation of partners who are individuals
- Composite returns and withholding requirements

State Conformity to Federal Pass-Through Treatment

The federal income tax classification of an entity as a partnership is determined by an elective system for entity classification (Treas. Reg. §301.7701-3). The regime is known as *check-the-box* because an entity's owners can merely check a box on federal Form 8832 to determine an eligible entity's classification. If Form 8832 is not filed, default classification rules determine an eligible entity's classification for federal income tax purposes. Under these regulations, the owners of a partnership organized in the United States have the option of electing to have the entity classified as a regular corporation. If no election is made, the entity is classified as a partnership under the default rules.

The check-the-box regime also applies to a partnership organized under the laws of a foreign country, although the default classification rules are different. Under the default rules, a foreign partnership that does not affirmatively make an election is classified as a corporation if *all* the partners have limited liability, and as a partnership if *at least one* of the partners does *not* have limited liability. Like the owners of a domestic partnership, however, the owners of a foreign partnership have the option of electing a different classification than that provided by the default rules, as long as the entity is not on the Treasury Department's list of *per se* corporations (Treas. Reg. §301.7701-3).

The states generally conform to the federal classification rules for partnerships. Thus, in most cases, an entity that is treated as a partnership for federal tax purposes is also treated as a partnership for state income tax purposes. State conformity to the federal pass-through treatment of a partnership generally extends to a limited liability company classified as a partnership for federal tax purposes. Under the federal check-the-box regulations, the default classification for a domestic limited liability company that has two or more members is a partnership.

States That Impose Entity-Level Taxes on Partnerships

Although most states treat partnerships as pass-through entities, a number of states impose entity-level taxes on partnerships. Examples include, but are not limited to, the following:

Alabama
Alabama imposes a business privilege tax on limited partnerships and limited liability partnerships. The tax is based on Alabama net worth. The tax is a minimum of $100 and a maximum of $15,000.

California
California imposes an annual tax of $800 on limited partnerships and limited liability partnerships doing business in California.

District of Columbia
The District of Columbia imposes a 9.975 percent income tax on unincorporated businesses, including partnerships. The tax does *not* apply to a professional firm in which more than 80 percent of the gross income is derived from personal services and capital is not a material income-producing factor.

Illinois
Illinois imposes a 1.5 percent income tax (referred to as the *personal property replacement tax*) on partnerships. An exemption is provided for investment partnerships.

Kansas

Kansas imposes a franchise tax on limited partnerships and limited liability partnerships that have net capital accounts located or used in Kansas, but only if the entity reports income of $1 million or more on a federal partnership return. The tax rate is $0.09375 per $1,000 of net worth, with a maximum tax of $20,000. The tax is scheduled to be phased out by 2011.

Kentucky

For tax years beginning on or after January 1, 2007, limited partnerships, limited liability partnerships, and limited liability companies are subject to a limited liability entity tax equal to the lesser of 0.095 percent of Kentucky gross receipts or 0.75 percent of Kentucky gross profits. The tax does *not* apply to entities with gross receipts or gross profits of $3 million or less, and is reduced for entities with gross receipts or gross profits over $3 million but less than $6 million. For tax years beginning in 2005 and 2006, these entities were subject to the greater of a 7 percent income tax or an alternative minimum calculation based on gross receipts or gross profits.

Michigan

Prior to 2008, Michigan subjected partnerships to its 1.9 percent single business tax, which is a type of value-added tax. In 2007, Michigan repealed the single business tax, effective December 31, 2007, and replaced it with a new 4.95 percent business income tax and 0.80 percent modified gross receipts tax that apply to business activity occurring on or after January 1, 2008. Both taxes apply to partnerships.

New Hampshire

New Hampshire subjects partnerships to an 8.5 percent business profits tax and a 0.75 percent business enterprise tax.

New Jersey

A limited partnership or limited liability company with a nonresident partner or member must pay *both* a:
1. 6.37 percent tax on a nonresident noncorporate partner's share of partnership income apportioned to New Jersey
2. 9 percent tax on a nonresident corporate partner's share of partnership income apportioned to New Jersey. If the nonresident partner or member files a New Jersey return, it may claim a credit for its share of the tax paid by the pass-through entity.

New York City
New York City imposes a 4 percent income tax on partnerships.

Ohio
Ohio imposes a commercial activity tax (CAT) on the annual gross receipts of a partnership. The CAT is being phased in over a five-year period from 2005 to 2009. The initial tax rate is 0.06 percent (July 1, 2005), and eventually rises to 0.26 percent (April 1, 2009). Examples of taxable gross receipts include sales of property delivered to locations within Ohio, fees for services where the purchaser receives the benefit in Ohio, and rents from property used in Ohio.

In addition, a partnership with a qualifying corporate investor (i.e., an out-of-state corporation that does not have nexus in Ohio) is subject to a 1.7 percent (2008) pass-through entity tax. Likewise, a partnership with a qualifying individual investor (i.e., a nonresident individual for whom the partnership does not file an Ohio composite nonresident return) is subject to a 5 percent pass-through entity tax. The tax is imposed on the qualifying investor's distributive share of the partnership's taxable income apportioned to Ohio, and the investor can claim a credit for its share of the tax paid by the partnership. The pass-through entity tax rate on an out-of-state corporate partner is being phased out at a rate of 20 percent per year from 2005 to 2009. The rate prior to 2005 rate was 8.5 percent.

Tennessee
Tennessee imposes a 6.5 percent income tax and a 0.25 percent net worth tax on limited liability companies, limited partnerships and limited liability partnerships.

Texas
Texas subjects partnerships to its margin tax. However, general partnerships directly owned entirely by natural persons and passive investment partnerships are not subject to the margin tax. The tax base equals the lesser of the following three amounts:

1. Total revenue minus cost of goods sold
2. Total revenue minus compensation
3. 70 percent of total revenue

The tax rate is 0.5 percent for partnerships primarily engaged in retail or wholesale trade and one percent for all other partnerships.

Washington

Washington subjects partnerships to its business and occupation (B&O) tax, which is a type of gross receipts tax. The B&O tax rate varies with the type of business activity, but generally is between 0.471 percent and 1.5 percent.

West Virginia

West Virginia imposes a business franchise tax on partnerships. For tax years beginning in 2007 and 2008, the tax is the greater of $50 or 0.55 percent of the partners' capital accounts. The tax is scheduled to be phased out by 2014.

In addition, a number of states (e.g., Delaware, Florida, Illinois, New Jersey, and New York) impose per partner annual filing fees on limited liability partnerships.

STUDY QUESTIONS

6. In a _____ partnership, one or more partners do **not** have the right to participate in the management of the partnership.
   a. General partnership
   b. Limited partnership
   c. Limited liability partnership
   d. All of the above

7. Which of the following statements is **not** true?
   a. If Form 8832 is not filed, default classification rules determine an eligible entity's classification for federal income tax purposes.
   b. The default classification for a domestic limited liability company that has two or more members is a partnership.
   c. Although most states treat partnerships as pass-through entities, a number of states impose entity-level taxes on partnerships.
   d. None of the above

8. An entity that is treated as a partnership for federal tax purposes is usually **not** treated as a partnership for state income tax purposes. **True or False?**

Nexus Issue

A state has jurisdiction to tax a corporation organized in another state *only* if the nondomiciliary corporation's contacts with the taxing state are sufficient to create nexus. The types of contacts that create nexus are determined by U.S. constitutional law, Public Law 86-272, and the applicable state statutes.

The principal issue with respect to corporate partners is whether a state has jurisdiction to tax the income of a nondomiciliary corporation that has no contacts with the state other than its ownership interest in a partnership doing business in the state. In asserting nexus, the states rely primarily on the aggregate theory of partnership. The *aggregate theory* holds that a partnership (unlike a corporation) is the aggregation of its owners rather than an entity that is separate and distinct from its owners. Under this theory, the partners are viewed as direct owners of fractional interests in the partnership's assets. Based on the aggregate theory, most states take the position that the mere ownership of a partnership interest is sufficient to create constitutional nexus for a nondomiciliary corporation, regardless of whether the corporation is a general or limited partner.

Some states (e.g., New Jersey and New York) have adopted statutes or regulations that provide different nexus standards for corporate limited partners, reflecting the view that a limited partnership interest is a passive investment akin to a share of corporate stock. Other states (e.g., California and Illinois) provide special exemptions for corporate partners of investment partnerships and/or partnerships engaged in trading securities.

The issue of whether a state has jurisdiction to tax a nondomiciliary corporation whose only contact with the state is through a limited partnership interest has been litigated in a number of cases, with the taxpayer prevailing in some cases [e.g., *Appeals of Amman & Schmid Finanz AG*, No. 96-SBE-008 (Cal. St. Bd. of Equalization Apr. 11, 1996)], and state tax authorities prevailing in other cases [e.g., *In re Borden Chem. & Plastics, LP*, No. 96-L-51039 (Ill. Cir. Ct. Oct. 7, 1998); *In re CRIV Invs., Inc.*, No. 4046 (Or. T.C. Apr. 23, 1997); *In re Perkins Restaurants, Inc.*, N.C. Admin. Decision 351 (Jan. 28, 1999)].

In *SAHI USA Inc. v. Commissioner of Revenue*, the taxpayer (SAHI) was a Delaware corporation and a limited partner in a New York partnership that invested in a Massachusetts joint venture, which owned and operated a hotel in Boston [No. C262668 (Mass. App. Tax Bd., Oct. 27, 2006)]. The higher-tier New York partnership sold its interest in the lower-tier Massachusetts partnership, and the income from the sale was distributed to partners, including SAHI. The Massachusetts Appellate Tax Board ruled that because both the higher-tier and lower-tier partnerships were doing business in Massachusetts, their income-producing activities were imputed to SAHI through the tiered-partnership arrangement. Because SAHI had income tax nexus with Massachusetts through a tiered-partnership arrangement, the income that SAHI realized from the sale of the lower-tier partnership interest *was* taxable by Massachusetts.

Apportionment of Partnership Income

There are two approaches to apportioning a corporate partner's distributive share of partnership income:

1.   Partner-level apportionment
2.   Partnership-level apportionment

Partner-Level Apportionment

Partner-level apportionment is analogous to the federal pass-through entity theory, under which the partnership's items of income and deduction pass through and are reported on the tax returns of the partners. Under this approach, the partnership's activities are treated as part of the same trade or business as the corporate partner's other activities. Accordingly, when a state adopts this approach, the corporate partner's entire distributive share of partnership income is combined with the partner's other income to determine the total apportionable income of the single trade or business.

Likewise, the partner computes its state apportionment percentage by combining its share of the partnership's property, payroll, and sales with its other apportionment factors. In other words, the corporate partner is allowed factor relief with respect to the inclusion of the entire distributive share of partnership income in the partner's apportionable income tax base [e.g., *Homart Dev. Co. v. Norberg*, 529 A.2d 115 (R.I. 1987)].

The *numerator* of the apportionment formula equals the corporate partner's property, payroll, and sales within the state, plus its share of the partnership's property, payroll, and sales within the state. The *denominator* equals the corporate partner's property, payroll, and sales everywhere, plus its share of the partnership's property, payroll, and sales everywhere. The corporate partner's state tax base is determined by multiplying the partner's apportionable income (which includes its distributive share of partnership income) by the partner's apportionment percentage (which reflects the partner's share of the partnership's factors).

Partnership-Level Apportionment

The second approach, partnership-level apportionment, treats the corporate investment in the partnership as a separate trade or business. Under this approach, the corporate partner's distributive share of partnership income is apportioned to the nexus state based solely on the property, payroll, and sales of the partnership. In effect, the partnership's activities are treated as a trade or business that is *separate and distinct* from the trade or business of the corporate partner.

As a consequence, the corporate partner's distributive share of partnership income is *not* combined with the partner's other apportionable income, nor is the partner's share of the partnership's property, payroll, and sales combined with the partner's other apportionment factors. Instead, the corporate partner's distributive share of partnership income is independently apportioned to the state by multiplying the distributive share of partnership income by the partnership's apportionment percentage. The corporate partner's state tax base is then determined by combining the apportioned partnership income with any other income that the corporate partner allocates or apportions to the state by virtue of its other (non-partnership) activities.

Determining the Applicable Methodology

The applicable methodology, partner-level or partnership-level apportionment, depends on both state law and the facts and circumstances. A number of states require *partner*-level apportionment if the activities of the corporate partner and the partnership constitute a unitary business, but require partner*ship*-level apportionment if the corporate partner and partnership are not unitary.

In determining whether a corporate partner is unitary with a partnership, the conventional tests for the existence of a unitary business generally apply [e.g., ***Luhr Bros., Inc. v. Director of Revenue,*** 780 S.W.2d 55 (Mo. 1989)], with the exception of ownership requirements [e.g., ***Appeal of Willamette Indus., Inc.,*** No. 87-SBE-053 (Cal. St. Bd. of Equalization, June 17, 1987)]. A general partner is typically unitary with the partnership, whereas a limited partner may or may not be unitary, depending on the facts of the case [e.g., ***Appeals of GasCo Gasoline, Inc.,*** 88-SBE-017 (Cal. St. Bd. of Equalization, June 1, 1988)].

For example, California Code of Regulations Title 18, §25137-1 (Apportionment and Allocation of Partnership Income), states:

> If the partnership's activities and the taxpayer's activities constitute a unitary business under established standards, disregarding ownership requirements, the taxpayer's share of the partnership's trade or business shall be combined with the taxpayer's trade or business as constituting a single trade or business. ... When the activities of the partnership and the taxpayer do not constitute a unitary business under established standards, disregarding ownership requirements, the taxpayer's share of the partnership's trade or business shall be treated as a separate trade or business of the taxpayer.

New Jersey Administrative Code Title 18, §7-7.6 (Corporate Partners), adopts essentially the same principle, as follows:

> For purposes of apportionment (allocation) of corporate income, where the subject corporation and the partnership are not part of a single unitary business, including a business carried on directly by the foreign corporate partner, separate accounting apportionment should be used to arrive at corporate income. If the New Jersey business of the partnership is part of a single unitary business including a business carried on directly by the foreign corporate partner, flow

through accounting apportionment should be used with respect to the income of the two entities.

Other states that require partner-level apportionment, regardless of whether there is a unitary relationship between the partner and the partnership, include Georgia (Ga. Comp. R. & Regs. r. 560-7-7.03) and Pennsylvania (Pa. Admin. Code §153.29).

In *Sasol North America v. Commissioner of Revenue* [No. C273084 (Mass. App. Tax Bd., Sept. 5, 2007)], the Massachusetts Appellate Tax Board ruled that an out-of-state corporation's distributive share of the income of a limited partnership was subject to apportionment, rather than being 100 percent allocable to the state, because the business activities of the limited partnership were closely related to that of the corporation and served an operational rather than a passive investment function. Treating the income as entirely allocable to Massachusetts would also be improper because other states in which the corporate partner conducted business operations were entitled to tax an apportioned share of the limited partnership interest.

Partners Who Are Individuals

The operative state income tax for partners who are individuals is the state individual income tax; however, not all states have an individual income tax. Alaska, Florida, Nevada, South Dakota, Texas, Washington, and Wyoming do not impose individual income taxes. In addition, New Hampshire and Tennessee tax only selected types of income, not including salaries and wages.

The state in which a partner resides generally taxes the entire amount of a resident partner's distributive share of partnership income, regardless of where the income is earned. In contrast, states in which the partner does not reside tax a nonresident partner's distributive share of partnership income only if the partnership has nexus in the state, and then only to the extent the nonresident partner's distributive share of income is attributable to sources within the state.

If a portion of a partner's distributive share of income is subject to tax in two states (one by virtue of the partner's residence and the other by virtue of the source of the partnership's income), the state of residence usually allows the partner to claim a credit for income taxes paid to the other state as a means of mitigating double taxation. Some states also allow an individual partner to claim a credit for income taxes imposed directly on the partnership.

Composite Returns and Withholding Requirements

The requirement that out-of-state partners file returns and pay taxes in every state in which a partnership has nexus can create a significant compliance burden for partners in a partnership that has nexus in numerous states. One method of enhancing compliance is to require or permit a partnership to file a composite return on behalf of the out-of-state partners. A composite return is a single filing in which the participating partners report their distributive shares of the partnership's income, and the partnership pays the state tax on behalf of the partners.

> **EXAMPLE**
>
> A State X partnership has five partners, all of whom are individuals who reside in State X. The partnership also has nexus in State Z, and State Z allows a partnership to file a composite return on behalf of partners who are nonresidents. The five partners do *not* have to file separate State Z tax returns. Instead, the partnership can file a single composite State Z return on their behalf.

Most states permit partners who are individuals and meet certain other requirements (e.g., the distributive share of partnership income is the only income that the partner derives from sources within the state) to file a composite return.

Another popular technique for promoting compliance on the part of out-of-state partners is to require the partnership to withhold and remit any taxes due on the partners' distributive shares of partnership income. Most states require some form of withholding with respect to nonresident partners.

STUDY QUESTIONS

9. In asserting that an out-of-state corporation has nexus solely by virtue of its ownership interest in a partnership doing business in the state, states rely *primarily* on:
   a. Applicable state statutes
   b. The aggregate theory
   c. Public Law 86-272
   d. The U.S. Constitution

10. Which one of the following is *not* true of partnership-level apportionment?
    a. The partner computes its state apportionment percentage by combining its share of the partnership's property, payroll, and sales with its other apportionment factors.
    b. The partnership's activities are treated as a trade or business that is separate and distinct from the trade or business of the corporate partner.
    c. The corporate partner's state tax base is determined by combining the apportioned partnership income with any other income that the corporate partner allocates or apportions to the state.
    d. Corporate investment in the partnership is treated as a separate trade or business.

11. Which one of following states requires partner-level apportionment, regardless of whether there is a unitary relationship between the partner and the partnership?

   a. California
   b. New Jersey
   c. Pennsylvania
   d. None of the above.

LIMITED LIABILITY COMPANIES

Federal Tax Treatment

As is the case with partnerships, the federal income tax treatment of a limited liability company (LLC) is determined by an elective system of entity classification known as *check-the-box*, because an entity's owners can merely check a box on federal Form 8832 to determine an entity's classification. If Form 8832 is not filed, default classification rules determine the entity's classification.

For example, for an LLC that is organized in the United States and has two or more members, the default classification is partnership. The default classification for a single-member limited liability company (SMLLC) is a branch if the single member is a corporation, and a sole proprietorship if the single member is an individual. In other words, the separate legal existence of an SMLLC is disregarded for federal income tax purposes. In the case of both multi-member LLCs and SMLLCs, the members have the option of electing to have the LLC classified as a regular corporation for federal tax purposes.

Different default classification rules apply to an LLC organized in a foreign country. If the foreign LLC has two or more owners and at least one owner does not have limited liability, the foreign LLC is classified as a partnership. If the foreign LLC has only one owner and that member does not have limited liability, the entity is treated as a disregarded entity. If all the members have limited liability, the foreign LLC is classified as a corporation. Like the owners of a domestic LLC, however, the owners of a foreign LLC have the option of electing a different classification than that prescribed by the default rule, as long as the foreign entity is not on the Treasury Department's list of *per se* corporations (Treas. Reg. §301.7701-3).

State Conformity to Federal Pass-Through Treatment

Virtually all of the states conform to the federal approach of allowing an LLC to be treated as a partnership or a disregarded entity.

> ### PLANNING POINTER
> When structuring new operations, a major advantage of using the LLC form is that an SMLLC that is treated as a disregarded entity can provide results similar to those provided by a consolidated return in states in which the taxpayer is filing on a separate-company basis. In other words, the disregarded entity's start-up losses can be used to offset the profits of the corporate parent. If the new operations are structured as a subsidiary corporation, the losses may *not* be used by the corporate parent in separate-company return states, but instead have to be carried forward and offset against the future profits, if any, of the subsidiary.

States That Impose Entity-Level Taxes on LLCs

Although virtually all states conform to the federal classification of an LLC as a pass-through entity, a number of states impose entity-level taxes on LLCs. Examples include, but are not limited to, the following:

Alabama

Alabama imposes a business privilege tax on LLCs. The tax is based on Alabama net worth. The tax is a minimum of $100 and a maximum of $15,000.

California

California imposes an annual tax of $800 on any LLC doing business in California. An LLC must also pay a fee based on its total gross receipts. The maximum fee is $11,790, and applies if the LLC's total gross receipts are $5 million or more. The fee applies even if the LLC is classified as a disregarded entity or partnership for federal income tax purposes.

For tax years beginning on or after January 1, 2007, the LLC fee is determined on the basis of the LLC's gross receipts attributable to California (A.B. 198, Oct. 10, 2007). Under prior law, the LLC fee was based on an LLC's gross receipts without apportionment. In both *Northwest Energetic Services, LLC v. Franchise Tax Board* [No. A114805 (Cal. Ct. of App., Jan. 31, 2008)], and *Ventas Finance I, LLC v. Franchise Tax Board* [No. A116277 (Cal. Ct. of App., Aug. 11, 2008)], state appellate courts ruled that basing the fee on an LLC's total gross receipts without apportionment is contrary to the Commerce Clause's fair apportionment requirement, and therefore the fee was an unconstitutional tax. California Franchise Tax Board Notice 2008-2 (April 14, 2008) provides guidance regarding the processing of refund claims.

District of Columbia

The District of Columbia imposes a 9.975 percent income tax on unincorporated businesses, including LLCs. The tax does *not* apply to a professional firm in which more than 80 percent of the gross income is derived from personal services and capital is not a material income-producing factor.

Illinois

Illinois imposes a 1.5 percent income tax (referred to as the *personal property replacement tax*) on LLCs classified as partnerships.

Kansas

Kansas imposes a franchise tax on an LLC that has net capital accounts located or used in Kansas, but only if the LLC reports income of $1 million or more on a federal partnership return. The tax rate is $0.09375 per $1,000 of net worth, with a maximum tax of $20,000. The tax is scheduled to be phased out by 2011.

Kentucky

For tax years beginning on or after January 1, 2007, LLCs are subject to a limited liability entity tax equal to the lesser of 0.095 percent of Kentucky gross receipts or 0.75 percent of Kentucky gross profits. The tax does *not* apply to LLCs with gross receipts or gross profits of $3 million or less, and it is reduced for LLCs with gross receipts or gross profits over $3 million but less than $6 million. For tax years beginning in 2005 and 2006, LLCs were subject to the greater of a 7 percent income tax or an alternative minimum calculation based on gross receipts or gross profits.

Michigan

Prior to 2008, Michigan subjected LLCs to its 1.9 percent single business tax, which is a type of value-added tax. In 2007, Michigan repealed the single business tax, effective December 31, 2007, and replaced it with a new 4.95 percent business income tax and 0.80 percent modified gross receipts tax that apply to business activity occurring on or after January 1, 2008. Both taxes apply to LLCs.

New Hampshire

New Hampshire subjects LLCs classified as partnerships to an 8.5 percent business profits tax and a 0.75 percent business enterprise tax.

New Jersey

An LLC with a nonresident member must pay a 6.37 percent tax on a nonresident noncorporate member's share of LLC income apportioned to New Jersey, and a 9 percent tax on a nonresident corporate member's share of LLC income apportioned to New Jersey. If the nonresident member files a New Jersey return, it may claim a credit for its share of the tax paid by the LLC.

Ohio

Ohio imposes a commercial activity tax (CAT) on the annual gross receipts of an LLC. The CAT is being phased in over a five-year period from 2005 to 2009. The initial tax rate is 0.06 percent (July 1, 2005), and eventually rises to 0.26 percent (April 1, 2009). Examples of taxable gross receipts include sales of property delivered to locations within Ohio, fees for services where the purchaser receives the benefit in Ohio, and rents from property used in Ohio.

In addition, an LLC with a qualifying corporate investor (i.e., an out-of-state corporation that does not have nexus in Ohio) is subject to a 1.7 percent (2008) pass-through entity tax. Likewise, an LLC with a qualifying individual investor (i.e., a nonresident for whom the LLC does not file an Ohio composite nonresident return) is subject to a 5 percent pass-through entity tax. The tax is imposed on the qualifying investor's distributive share of the LLC's taxable income apportioned to Ohio, and the investor can claim a credit for its share of the tax paid by the LLC. The pass-through entity tax rate on an out-of-state corporate member is being phased out at rate of 20 percent per year from 2005 to 2009. The rate prior to 2005 was 8.5 percent.

Pennsylvania

An LLC is subject to a capital stock tax based on the LLC's capital stock value, as determined by a statutory formula. The capital stock tax rate is 0.289 percent in 2008. The tax is scheduled to be phased out by 2011.

Tennessee

Tennessee imposes a 6.5 percent income tax and a 0.25 percent net worth tax on LLCs.

Texas

Texas subjects LLCs to its margin tax. The tax base equals the lesser of three amounts:

1. Total revenue minus cost of goods sold
2. Total revenue minus compensation
3. 70 percent of total revenue

The tax rate is 0.5 percent for LLCs primarily engaged in retail or wholesale trade, and one percent for all other LLCs.

Prior to 2007, LLCs were subject to the Texas corporate franchise tax, which equaled the greater of 0.25 percent of net taxable capital (a net worth tax) or 4.5 percent of net taxable earned surplus (an income tax).

Washington

Washington subjects LLCs to its business and occupation (B&O) tax, which is a type of gross receipts tax. The B&O tax rate varies with the type of business activity, but generally is between 0.471 percent and 1.5 percent.

West Virginia

West Virginia imposes a business franchise tax on LLCs classified as partnerships. For tax years beginning in 2007 and 2008, the tax is the greater of $50 or 0.55 percent of the partners' capital accounts. The tax is scheduled to be phased out by 2014.

In addition, a number of states (e.g., New Jersey and New York) impose per member annual filing fees on LLCs.

State Taxes Other Than Income Taxes

Treating an LLC as a disregarded entity for income tax purposes does not necessarily relieve the LLC from liability as a separate legal entity for other tax purposes, such as registration fees, sales and use taxes, employment taxes, and property taxes. Such taxes generally are imposed on each separate legal entity, and an LLC is a legal entity separate from its members, even if the LLC's existence is disregarded for income tax purposes.

> **EXAMPLE**
>
> A state may require an SMLLC and its corporate owner to file separate sales and use tax reports, even though for income tax purposes the SMLLC is viewed as a branch of the corporate parent. Similarly, although intercompany transactions between a disregarded entity and its owner are ignored for income tax purposes, such transactions could create a sales and use tax or real estate transfer tax liability. The payroll tax consequences of operating a disregarded entity must also be analyzed on a state-by-state basis.

Nexus Issue

A state has jurisdiction to tax a corporation organized in another state *only* if the nondomiciliary corporation's contacts with the taxing state are sufficient to create nexus. The types of contacts that create nexus are determined by U.S. constitutional law, Public Law 86-272, and the applicable state statutes. As discussed in the previous section, states generally take the position that an ownership interest in a partnership doing business in the state is sufficient to create constitutional nexus for a nondomiciliary corporation. In asserting nexus, the states rely on nexus theories developed primarily for general partnerships.

For example, under the aggregate theory of partnership, the partners are viewed as direct owners of fractional interests in the partnership's assets. Therefore, the physical presence of any partnership assets within a state is imputed to the partners. Based on these nexus theories, most states take the position that they have jurisdiction to tax a corporate partner's distributive share of income from a general partnership that is doing business in the state, even if the partner has no other contacts with the state.

The extent to which these nexus principles apply to nonresident corporate members of an LLC has yet to be addressed in a comprehensive fashion by the states. It is reasonable to assume, however, that most states would take the position that a state *does* have jurisdiction to tax a nonresident corporate member of an LLC that is classified as a partnership and doing business in the state, even if the member has no other contacts with the state.

> **EXAMPLE**
>
> In Directive No. CD-02-1 (May 31, 2002), the North Carolina Department of Revenue indicated that a corporate member of an LLC doing business in North Carolina must file a state income tax return if the LLC is treated as a partnership for federal tax purposes.

Unlike a general partner's risk, a limited partner's risk is restricted to its initial investment in the partnership, and a limited partner generally does not participate in the management of the partnership. Therefore, a limited partnership interest is more akin to owning shares of a corporation. As a result, some states treat corporate limited partners differently than corporate general partners.

Based on the analogy of the general versus limited partner distinction, a corporate member that is actively engaged in the management of an LLC within the state arguably is doing business in the state, whereas it is arguable that a member that does not participate in the management of the LLC is not doing business in the state.

Members Who Are Individuals

If an LLC is classified as a pass-through entity, the operative state income tax for members who are individuals is the state individual income tax; however, not all states have an individual income tax. Alaska, Florida, Nevada, South Dakota, Texas, Washington, and Wyoming do not impose an individual income tax. In addition, New Hampshire and Tennessee tax only selected types of income, not including salaries and wages. The state in which a member resides generally taxes the entire amount of a resident member's distributive share of LLC income, regardless of where the income was earned.

In contrast, states in which the member does not reside tax a nonresident member's distributive share of LLC income only if the LLC has nexus in the state, and then only to the extent the nonresident member's distributive share of income is attributable to sources within the state. If a portion of a member's distributive share of income is subject to tax in two states (one by virtue of the member's residence and the other by virtue of the source of the LLC's income), the state of residence usually allows the member to claim a credit for income taxes paid to the other state as a means of mitigating double taxation. Some states also allow a credit for income taxes imposed directly on the LLC.

Composite Returns and Withholding Requirements

The requirement that nonresident members file returns and pay taxes in every state in which an LLC that is treated as a partnership has nexus can create a significant compliance burden for members of an LLC that has nexus in numerous states. One method of enhancing compliance is to require or permit an LLC to file a composite return on behalf of the nonresident members. A *composite return* is a single filing in which the participating nonresident members report their distributive shares of the LLC's income and the LLC pays the state tax on behalf of the members.

> **EXAMPLE**
>
> A State X LLC is classified as a partnership and has five members, all of whom are individuals who reside in State X. The LLC also has nexus in State Z, and State Z allows an LLC to file a composite return on behalf of members who are nonresidents. The five members do *not* have to file separate individual income tax returns in State Z. Instead, the LLC can file a single composite State Z return on their behalf.

Most states allow members who are individuals to file a composite return.

Another popular technique for promoting compliance on the part of nonresident members of an LLC that is treated as a partnership is to require the LLC to withhold and remit any taxes due on a nonresident member's distributive share of the LLC's income.

STUDY QUESTIONS

---

12. What is the default classification for an LLC that is organized in the United States and has two or more members?

   a. Corporation
   b. Branch
   c. Sole proprietorship
   d. Partnership

13. Which of the following states subjects LLCs to its margin tax?

   a. Illinois
   b. Michigan
   c. Texas
   d. Washington

14. In the case of an LLC with two or more members, states in which an individual LLC member does *not* reside generally tax the entire amount of the nonresident member's distributive share of LLC income if the LLC has nexus in the state. *True or False?*

FISCAL-YEAR ELECTIONS: PARTNERSHIPS, S CORPORATIONS, AND PERSONAL SERVICE CORPORATIONS

Federal Tax Treatment
Personal Service Corporations

A regular corporation's taxable income is subject to tax at graduated rates; that is, the first $50,000 of income is taxed at 15 percent, the next $25,000 of income is taxed at 25 percent, etc. A personal service corporation (PSC) is denied the benefit of these low tax brackets. Instead, a 35 percent flat tax is imposed on all of the PSC's taxable income. Code Sec. 448 defines a PSC as a corporation that meets the following two tests:

1. Substantially all of its activities involve performing services in accounting, actuarial science, architecture, consulting, engineering, health, law, or the performing arts.
2. Substantially all of its stock (by value) is held directly or indirectly by employees performing the services, retired employees who performed the services in the past, their estates, or persons who hold stock by reason of the death of an employee or retired employee within the past two years.

PLANNING POINTER

The 35 percent flat tax on all of a PSC's income encourages shareholder-employees to withdraw all of the earnings of a PSC as deductible salary payments.

Fiscal-Year Restrictions on Pass-Through Entities

A partnership generally must adopt the same tax year as one or more partners that own more than 50 percent of the partnership (Code Sec. 706).

EXAMPLE

If all of the partners of a partnership are calendar-year individuals, the partnership also must file its tax returns on a calendar-year basis.

A similar rule applies to S corporations and PSCs (Code Sec. 1378). The purpose of these restrictions is to prevent owners of a pass-through entity from deferring income by choosing a different tax year for the partnership, S corporation, or PSC. For example, calendar-year shareholders of an S corporation might choose a January 31 tax year for the S corporation, thereby deferring the taxation of the S corporation's income because that income is deemed to pass through to the shareholders on the last day of the S corporation's tax year. Similarly, a PSC owned by calendar-year individuals might choose a January 31 year-end, and then wait each fiscal year until January to distribute a significant portion of the income earned from February to December of the prior year, thereby achieving a deferral of income at the shareholder level.

An exception applies if a partnership, S corporation, or PSC can establish to the satisfaction of the IRS that there is a substantial business purpose for adopting a different tax year [Treas. Reg. §1.441-1(c)(2)]. The primary method for establishing a substantial business purpose is to satisfy a mechanical natural business year test. A *natural business year* is one in which at least 25 percent of the taxpayer's gross receipts are received in the last two months of the 12-month period (Rev. Proc 2002-38).

Code Sec. 444 Elections

Many pass-through entities are unable to meet the IRS's strict business purpose test. This led Congress to create the Code Sec. 444 election, which allows partnerships, S corporations, and PSCs to elect a tax year that results in a tax deferral of three months or less. The deferral period signifies the number of months from the beginning of the entity's fiscal year to December

31. Therefore, an S corporation or PSC with calendar-year shareholders may elect a September 30, October 31, or November 30 year-end. A Code Sec. 444 election is made on federal Form 8716.

A partnership or S corporation making a Code Sec. 444 election must reimburse the IRS for the benefit of the tax deferral obtained when a fiscal year is used. Under Code Sec. 7519, the required payment is the product of the maximum tax rate for individuals, plus one percent times the previous year's taxable income times a deferral ratio. The deferral ratio equals the number of months in the deferral period divided by the number of months in the tax year.

PSCs that elect a fiscal year are *not* required to reimburse the IRS for the benefit of the tax deferral. Instead, they must make minimum distributions to shareholders during the deferral period (Code Sec. 280H). These minimum distributions are designed to prevent a distribution pattern that achieves a deferral of income at the shareholder level. Roughly speaking, these rules require that deductible payments made to shareholder-employees during the deferral period be made at a rate that is no lower than the rate at which they were made during the previous fiscal year.

STUDY QUESTION

> **15.** A *natural business year* is one in which at least 25 percent of the tax-payer's gross receipts are received in the last ___ month(s) of the 12-month period
>
> **a.** One
> **b.** Two
> **c.** Three
> **d.** Four

> **CPE NOTE:** When you have completed your study and review of chapters 1-3, which comprise Module 1, you may wish to take the Quizzer for this Module.
>
> For your convenience, you can also take this Quizzer online at **www.cchtestingcenter.com.**

MODULE 2: SALES AND USE TAXES — CHAPTER 4

Nexus

This chapter discusses which activities performed by a taxpayer in a particular state will cause the taxpayer to have income tax and/or sales and use tax nexus with that state.

LEARNING OBJECTIVES

Upon completing this chapter, the student will:

- Comprehend the concept of economic nexus
- Understand which activities of a multistate corporation may create nexus
- Understand the impact of affiliates and independent agents on nexus
- Identify which activities of a multistate corporation are protected by P.L. 86-272
- Know how electronic commerce affects state and local taxes

OVERVIEW

Whether a corporation is required to collect sales or use tax or pay income tax hinges on whether it has economic nexus with the state.

Nexus is defined as some definite link, some minimum connection, between the state and the corporation it seeks to tax. Nexus embodies the spirit that a state cannot impose a tax on persons doing business or activities that occur outside the state's borders.

Different taxes may have differing threshold standards for establishing nexus. Those standards are usually the outgrowth of judicial decisions that are accepted or modified as a result of legislative activity.

Sales and Use Tax Nexus

The nexus standards for establishing a sales or use tax collection responsibility have traditionally been very broad. However, they have been curtailed to a certain extent by the U.S. Supreme Court in the *Quill* decision.

Quill Corporation was a mail-order vendor of office supplies. Sales were solicited through catalogs mailed to potential customers in North Dakota, with deliveries made through common carriers. Quill was a Delaware corporation with offices and warehouses in California, Georgia, and Illinois. Quill did not have an office, warehouse, retail outlet, or other facility located in North Dakota, nor were any Quill employees or sales representatives physically present in North Dakota. Thus, with respect to North Dakota, Quill was strictly an out-of-state mail-order vendor. Nevertheless, during the tax years in question, Quill made sales to roughly 3,000 North Dakota customers, and was the sixth largest office supply vendor in the state.

North Dakota attempted to impose on Quill an obligation to collect North Dakota use tax on sales to North Dakota customers. The North Dakota Supreme Court ruled that Quill *did* have constitutional nexus in North Dakota, reasoning that Quill's *economic presence* in North Dakota depended on services and benefits provided by the state and, therefore, generated "a constitutionally sufficient nexus to justify imposition of the purely administrative duty of collecting and remitting the use tax."

The U.S. Supreme Court reversed the lower court's ruling, and held that, although an economic presence was sufficient to satisfy the Due Process Clause requirement of a minimal connection, it was *not* sufficient to satisfy the Commerce Clause requirement of substantial nexus. Consistent with its ruling 25 years earlier in *National Bellas Hess,* the Court further ruled that substantial nexus exists only if a corporation has a nontrivial physical presence in a state. Therefore, a *physical presence* is an essential prerequisite to establishing constitutional nexus, at least for sales and use tax purposes.

It is important to highlight the fact that *Quill* is a use tax case, and that the Supreme Court did not address the issue of whether the physical presence test also applied to income taxes. This has resulted in a significant amount of controversy and litigation (see discussion under the heading of Economic Nexus).

To support a position not to collect use tax, some taxpayers point to the decision made in *Quill Corp. v. North Dakota* [504 US 298 (1992)]. Although *Quill* was decided in favor of the taxpayer, application of the decision may be limited in scope. This raises the following questions:

- What activities in a state will create sufficient contact with the state to impose a use tax collection responsibility?
- Will *de minimis* activities create a sufficient connection?
- Should a taxpayer voluntarily register to collect use tax?

Income Tax Nexus

Another issue for any corporation operating in more than one state is determining in which states it must file returns and pay income tax. A corporation is generally subject to income tax in the state in which it is incorporated. It may also be subject to income tax in any other states in which its property, employees, or other agents are physically present on a regular and systematic basis.

Large corporations with customers nationwide clearly have nexus in each state in which the company has offices and other facilities, accompanied by resident employees. A more difficult issue is determining in which, if any, market states the company has nexus.

Such corporations generally want to minimize the number of states in which they must file returns and pay income tax. Fortunately, the U.S. Constitution and Public Law (P.L.) 86-272 provide important protections against state income taxation. These federal protections also provide a degree of uniformity in state tax laws because they govern income tax nexus determinations in all 50 states.

PLANNING POINTER

When looking at expansion plans, taxpayers should consider the impact on nexus that their new plans may have. Many times, offices or employees can be assigned to new locations without consideration of the tax impact of such changes. Acceptable alternatives that do not require additional compliance or tax expense can be developed.

CONSTITUTIONAL NEXUS

Due Process and Commerce Clause Restrictions

Historically, states have asserted that virtually any type of in-state business activity creates nexus for an out-of-state corporation. Such behavior reflects the reality that it is politically more appealing to tax out-of-state corporations than to raise taxes on in-state business interests. The desire of state lawmakers and tax officials to, in effect, export the local tax burden has been counterbalanced by the Due Process Clause and Commerce Clause of the U.S. Constitution.

The *Due Process Clause* states that no state shall "deprive any person of life, liberty or property, without due process of law." The U.S. Supreme Court has interpreted this clause as prohibiting a state from taxing an out-of-state corporation unless there is a *minimal connection* between the company's interstate activities and the taxing state [e.g., ***Mobil Oil Corp. v. Commissioner of Taxes***, 445 US 425 (1980)].

The *Commerce Clause* expressly authorizes Congress to "regulate Commerce with foreign Nations, and among the several States." The Supreme Court has interpreted the Commerce Clause as prohibiting states from enacting laws that might unduly burden or otherwise inhibit the free flow of trade among the states. With respect to the nexus issue, in ***Complete Auto Transit, Inc. v. Brady***, [430 US 274 (1977)] the Supreme Court has interpreted the Commerce Clause as prohibiting a state from taxing an out-of-state corporation unless that company has a *substantial nexus* with the state.

In ***Complete Auto***, the U.S. Supreme Court determined that Commerce Clause analysis is governed by a four-pronged test, which provides that a state tax is valid if all of the following are true:

1. It is applied to an activity having *substantial nexus* with the taxing state.
2. It is fairly apportioned.

3. It does not discriminate against interstate commerce.
4. It is fairly related to services provided by the state.

In summary, a state cannot impose a tax obligation on an out-of-state corporation unless the Due Process Clause minimal connection and Commerce Clause substantial nexus requirements are satisfied. Therefore, a critical question in the nexus arena is: what do minimal connection and substantial nexus mean? The landmark case for sales and use tax in this regard is *Quill.*

PHYSICAL PRESENCE REQUIREMENT

In *Quill,* the U.S. Supreme Court upheld the *bright-line physical presence test* established in *National Bellas Hess, Inc. v. Illinois* [386 US 753 (1967)], an earlier mail-order/use tax collection Supreme Court case.

National Bellas Hess involved an attempt by Illinois to require a mail-order business to collect and pay use taxes on goods purchased within the state. National Bellas Hess was incorporated in Delaware and had its principal place of business in Missouri. It had neither outlets nor employees in Illinois. Twice a year, the company mailed catalogues to the company's customers in Illinois. Orders for merchandise were mailed by customers to National Bellas Hess' Missouri plant, and the ordered items were mailed to the customers either by mail or common carrier. The company challenged the Illinois use tax levied against it on the basis that it created an unconstitutional burden on interstate commerce. The Supreme Court held that Illinois had *no* power to impose the use tax on National Bellas Hess. The Court based its decision in part on the undue burden placed on interstate commerce by compliance with a host of administrative regulations governing the collection of sales and use taxes.

In 1992, the Supreme Court reaffirmed in *Quill* its *Bellas Hess* holding to the extent that *Bellas Hess* held that a showing of the taxpayer's physical presence in the taxing state was necessary to sustain a sales and use tax against a challenge under the Commerce Clause.

Many commentators have argued that there is no reason to believe that the Commerce Clause would impose a different standard for income taxes than for sales and use taxes. Therefore, the same physical presence test should apply. Nevertheless, until the Supreme Court rules on the issue, it will be uncertain.

In summary, the Supreme Court has ruled that a corporation does *not* have constitutional nexus in a state unless that company has a nontrivial physical presence within the state's borders. Thus, a physical presence, established through the presence of either company-owned property or company employees or other agents, is generally regarded as an essential prerequisite for establishing constitutional nexus in a state for sales and use tax purposes.

CAUTION

Taxpayers and their advisors should continuously challenge assumptions regarding nexus and physical presence of employees. Changes are often made in business operations without considering the tax effects of the changes or consulting with a tax advisor regarding the implications of the change. Because of an unlimited statute of limitations for non-filers, taxpayers need to be particularly cautious in dealing with nexus issues.

P.L. 86-272: Income Tax Safe Harbor

In *Northwestern States Portland Cement Co. v. Minnesota* [358 US 450 (1959)], the Supreme Court held, for the first time, that the Commerce Clause did *not* prohibit a state from imposing a fairly apportioned, direct corporate income tax on an out-of-state corporation carrying on an exclusively interstate business within the taxing state. This ruling created a furor among the business community, which lobbied Congress to exercise its Commerce Clause powers to limit the ability of the states to tax out-of-state corporations.

Congress responded in 1959 by enacting P.L. 86-272, which provides multistate corporations with a limited safe harbor from the imposition of state taxes imposed on *net income*. Specifically, P.L. 86-272 prohibits a state from taxing the income of a nondomiciliary corporation (i.e., a corporation that is not incorporated in the taxing state) if the company's only in-state activity is solicitation of orders by company representatives for sales of tangible personal property, and any orders are sent outside the state for approval or rejection and, if approved, are filled by shipment or delivery from a point outside the state.

NOTE

Taxpayers frequently misinterpret P.L. 86-272 provisions as providing some shield from the obligation to collect use tax. However, P.L. 86-272 does *not* apply to taxes that are measured by gross receipts or sales. Therefore, physical presence, beyond some *de minimis* level, triggers an obligation to collect sales and use tax.

> **EXAMPLE**
>
> If employees regularly visit an out-of-state location and solicit sales of tangible personal property that are then forwarded to the out-of-state headquarters for approval and subsequent shipment from stocks located at that out-of-state location, the seller *would* be required to collect use tax on the sale. This is because the level of physical presence exceeds some *de minimis* amount.
>
> Absent from any other considerations, however, the taxpayer would *not* be liable for income tax in the destination state because the requirements of P.L. 86-272 have been met.

P.L. 86-272: Limitations

Although P.L. 86-272 can provide significant protections for a multistate business, it has several important limitations. These limitations include the following:

1. It applies *only* to taxes imposed on net income. Therefore, it does not provide protection against the imposition of a sales and use tax collection obligation, property taxes, the Michigan single business tax (a type of value-added tax) and its recently enacted replacement (the Michigan Business Tax), or the Washington business and occupations tax (a gross receipts tax).
2. It does not provide protection against franchises taxes imposed on a corporation's capital or net worth, such as those employed by Pennsylvania or Tennessee. Likewise, in ***Home Impressions, Inc. v. Division of Taxation*** [No. 000099-2003 (N.J. Tax Ct., June 7, 2004)], the New Jersey Tax Court ruled that P.L. 86-272 does not protect a taxpayer from the imposition of a flat dollar minimum tax that is part of the state's corporate business tax regime.
3. The protection of P.L. 86-272 is available *only* to businesses that sell tangible personal property. It provides no protection to businesses that lease tangible personal property, sell services, sell or lease real estate, or sell or license intangibles.
4. For businesses that do sell tangible personal property, their employees or representatives must limit their in-state activities to the solicitation of orders that are sent outside the state for approval, and if approved, are filled by shipment or delivery from a point outside the state.

> **EXAMPLE**
>
> P.L. 86-272 does *not* provide protection if salespersons are given the authority to approve merchandise orders. Likewise, P.L. 86-272 does not protect the presence of salespersons who perform nonsolicitation activities, such as repairs, customer training, or technical assistance, within a state.

In *Schering-Plough Healthcare Products Sales Corp. v. Commonwealth* [161 MAP 2002 (Pa. Sup. Ct., Oct. 20, 2004), *aff'g* 805 A.2d 1284 (Pa. Commw. Ct. 2002)], the Pennsylvania Supreme Court ruled that P.L. 86-272 did protect an out-of-state corporation that was a manufacturer's representative that limited its in-state activities to the solicitation of orders on behalf of its parent company, even though the taxpayer did not own the products it sold.

The court reasoned that the "plain language of the statute is devoid of any suggestion that ownership of the goods is significant," and that it "cannot seriously be argued that a company which limits its activity in a State to solicitation of orders for goods to which it will never take title has a greater nexus to that State than a company taking similar orders for goods it owns someplace else."

MEANING OF SOLICITATION [*WRIGLEY* (1992)]

To qualify for the safe harbor provided by P.L. 86-272, a corporation must limit its employees' in-state activities to the *solicitation of orders*. Despite its importance as a qualification requirement, P.L. 86-272 does not define the phrase *solicitation of orders*.

However, the proper interpretation of the phrase was addressed by the Supreme Court in *Wisconsin Department of Revenue v. William Wrigley, Jr., Co.* [505 US 214 (1992)] Wrigley was a chewing gum manufacturer headquartered in Illinois. Wrigley marketed its goods in Wisconsin through employee sales representatives who were residents of Wisconsin. All Wisconsin orders were sent to Chicago for acceptance and were filled by shipment through common carrier from outside the state. Wrigley did not own or lease any offices or other facilities in Wisconsin.

> **PLANNING POINTER**
>
> Because certain solicitation activities are protected, a taxpayer may be required to collect sales and use tax but not be liable for income tax. This can be a frequent point of audit contention. The taxpayer in such circumstances should be prepared to defend its position by demonstrating that, although there is a physical presence, the employees operate within the limits of P.L. 86-272 in terms of their duties in the state.

In determining whether Wrigley's activities in Wisconsin exceeded the protection of P.L. 86-272, the Supreme Court was faced with two fundamental questions:

1. What is the scope of the phrase *solicitation of orders*?
2. Does a *de minimis* exception exist for activities other than solicitation of orders?

With respect to the scope of the phrase, Wisconsin argued that *solicitation of orders* should be narrowly construed to mean "any activity other than requesting the customer to purchase the product." Wrigley, on the other hand, argued for a much broader definition—specifically, "any activities that are ordinary and necessary business activities accompanying the solicitation process or are routinely associated with deploying a sales force to conduct the solicitation, so long as there is no office, plant, warehouse or inventory in the State."

The Supreme Court rejected both definitions as too extreme, and instead crafted its own interpretation, defining *solicitation of orders* as encompassing "requests for purchases" and "those activities that are entirely ancillary to requests for purchases—those that serve no independent business function apart from their connection to the soliciting of orders."

The Court then applied this definition to the activities of Wrigley employees within Wisconsin. It found that providing the following were entirely ancillary to solicitation because they served no purpose apart from their role in facilitating requests for purchases:

- A company-owned car or stock of free samples to salespeople
- In-state recruitment, training, and evaluation of sales representatives
- The use of hotels and homes for sales-related meetings

In contrast, the Court found that the following activities within the state were *not* ancillary to Wrigley's solicitation activities:

- Replacing stale gum
- Supplying gum through agency stock checks
- Storing gum within the state

With respect to the issue of *de minimis* nonsolicitation activities, the Supreme Court held that a *de minimis* level of nonsolicitation activities does not cause a company to lose the protections afforded by P.L. 86-272. It also determined that whether nonsolicitation activities are sufficiently *de minimis* to avoid the loss of tax immunity depends on whether that activity establishes a "nontrivial additional connection with the taxing state."

The Court then held that, in the aggregate, Wrigley's unprotected activities (i.e., the replacement of stale gum, the supplying of gum through agency stock checks, and the storage of gum) did *not* meet its *de minimis* standard, even though the relative magnitude of those activities was not large in comparison to Wrigley's total Wisconsin activities.

In summary, although taxpayers and the states can be expected to interpret the phrases *entirely ancillary* and *nontrivial additional connection* differently, the Supreme Court's ruling in **Wrigley** nevertheless provides a uniform standard applicable to all 50 states. Moreover, the **Wrigley** decision clearly establishes that there is a *de minimis* exception to the activities that are not protected by P.L. 86-272.

STUDY QUESTIONS

1. Which of the following cases dealt with whether or not the taxpayer should pay state income taxes?
   a. National Bellas Hess
   b. Quill Corp.
   c. William Wrigley, Jr.
   d. None of the above

2. Which of the following **prohibits** a state from taxing an out-of-state corporation, unless that company has *substantial nexus* with the state?
   a. Commerce Clause
   b. Due Process Clause
   c. Public Law 86-272
   d. None of the above

3. According to the U.S. Supreme Court **Wrigley** decision, which of the following activities is **not** ancillary to solicitation of sales?
   a. Providing a company-owned car to salespeople in the state
   b. Providing a stock of free samples to salespeople in the state
   c. Storage of inventory within the state
   d. Use of hotels and homes in the state for sales-related meetings

De Minimis Exception

The U.S. Supreme Court noted in **Quill** that the slightest presence in the state does *not* meet the substantial nexus requirements of the Commerce Clause, but it did not define how much physical presence is necessary to establish substantial nexus.

A company may, therefore, have a physical presence in the state and not create sales tax nexus—as long as the activities in the state are *de minimis* in nature. Previous court decisions indicate that the relative value of the company's in-state property, the number of in-state employees, or the relative amount of sales made in the state may *not* be determinative if the company is otherwise found to have activities in the state that are more than *de minimis*.

The Florida Supreme Court upheld a district court's *insufficient nexus* decision in **Share International, Inc.** [676 So.2d 1362 (Fla. 1996), *cert. denied*, No. 96-647 (US Jan. 6, 1997)]. Share International is in the business of manufacturing and distributing chiropractic supplies, which are sold primarily via mail order from its office in Texas. Between 1986 and 1989, Share International participated in annual seminars in Florida, each lasting three days. The company collected sales tax on items sold at each seminar, but did not collect tax on the mail-order sales.

The Florida Department of Revenue's contention that the taxpayer's presence at each seminar was enough to satisfy nexus requirements was *rejected* by the trial court and the district court. Relying principally on **National Geographic Society v. State Board of Equalization** [97 S. Ct. 1386 (1977)], the district court held that, under the Commerce Clause, the slight presence of an out-of-state mail-order company within the state was not sufficient to permit the state to enforce a use tax against the company.

Instead, the district court held that the state may only enforce such a tax against an out-of-state company whose activities create a *substantial* nexus to the state. The Florida Supreme Court found that "[w]hile this law may require courts to fill in the gaps and give meaning to the terms 'slightest presence' and 'substantial nexus' it is apparent that those are the standards established by the U.S. Supreme Court." Accordingly, the Florida Supreme Court found no error in the district court's interpretation and application of those terms.

The Florida Supreme Court also agreed with the district court that the bright-line test adopted in **National Bellas Hess** clearly insulates from state taxation only out-of-state vendors whose sole activities in the taxing state are mail-order sales. If such a company has additional connections to the taxing state, those connections must be analyzed under the substantial nexus test.

In **Dell Catalog Sales v. Commissioner, Department of Revenue Services** (No. CV 00 05031465 July 10, 2003), the Connecticut Superior Court held that the national retailer of computer equipment did not have a sufficient physical presence in Connecticut to constitute nexus for sales and use tax purposes. Although Dell had a third party perform service work on its behalf, that level of contact was deemed to be *de minimis* because the actual number of onsite calls was minimal.

It does appear that some states will narrowly interpret the *Wrigley* definition of solicitation of orders. For example, in *Kennametal Inc. v. Massachusetts Commissioner of Revenue* [No. SJC-07448 (Mass. 1997)] the Massachusetts Supreme Judicial Court ruled that Kennametal's frequent in-plant presentations, inventory analyses for tool standardization programs, and sample testing using Kennametal's products exceeded *solicitation*. According to the court, those activities not only invited orders, but they also ingratiated customers to the company and assisted customers with making buying decisions.

Likewise, in *Amgen, Inc. v. Commissioner of Revenue* [No. SJC-07563 (Mass. 1998)], the Massachusetts Supreme Judicial Court held that the in-state activities of Amgen employees exceeded the mere solicitation of Amgen's pharmaceutical products. In particular, the employees monitored the research and clinical studies performed in Massachusetts, provided educational seminars, maintained ownership and control of the supplies used in such studies, and retained employees to review specific patient charts and answer patient-specific questions. The court ruled that these activities were not entirely ancillary to the solicitation of orders, but that they served an independent business purpose.

In *Alcoa Building Products, Inc. v. Commissioner of Revenue* [No. SJC-08939 (Mass. Sup. Jud. Ct., Oct. 21, 2003)], the Massachusetts Supreme Judicial Court held that various warranty claims activities performed by in-state sales personnel, such as initiating warranty claims, analyzing the merits of claims, and assisting customers in filing claims, exceeded mere solicitation and created income tax nexus for an out-of-state manufacturer.

Although taxpayers generally prefer to avoid nexus, a narrow interpretation of the meaning of *solicitation* can be helpful in avoiding the application of a state's sales factor throwback rule, as was illustrated in *Colgate-Palmolive Company v. Commissioner of Revenue* [No. C255116 (Mass. App. Tax Bd. April 3, 2003)].

On the other hand, the Texas Comptroller of Public Accounts rejected a taxpayer's argument that throwback did not apply to the company's sales to Alabama customers because, while visiting family in Alabama, an employee checked the company's voice mail system and responded to work-related telephone calls. [Tex. Comp. of Pub. Accts., Hearing No. 42,586, Jan. 6, 2004]

In *Tyson Foods, Inc. v. Illinois Department of Revenue* [No. 1-98-1476 (Ill. App. Ct. Feb. 8, 2000)], an out-of-state company that sold products only through independent brokers also rented an unstaffed office in Illinois solely for the purpose of registering a fleet of trucks in Illinois under interstate transportation laws. The state appellate court ruled that the registration of the trucks served an independent business function apart from the solicitation of orders, and therefore was *not* protected by P.L. 86-272.

Multistate Tax Commission (MTC) Statement of Practices: Protected Versus Unprotected Activities

Created in 1967, the MTC is an agency of state governments whose mission is to promote fairness and uniformity in state tax laws. The MTC adopted a policy statement in 1986 regarding the proper application of P.L. 86-272, modified the statement in 1993 and 1994 (in light of the *Wrigley* decision), and modified it again in 2001 to remove deliveries in company-owned vehicles from the list of unprotected activities.

In the MTC's Statement of Information Concerning Practices of Multistate Tax Commission and Signatory States Under P.L. 86-272, the states indicate that "it is the policy of the state signatories hereto to impose their net income tax, subject to State and Federal legislative limitations, to the fullest extent constitutionally permissible." The statement goes on to list *protected activities* (considered to be entirely ancillary to the solicitation of orders) and *unprotected activities* (considered to serve an independent business function).

UNPROTECTED ACTIVITIES

The following in-state activities (if they are not of a *de minimis* level) are *not* considered either the solicitation of orders or ancillary to the solicitation of orders or otherwise protected under P.L. 86-272, and they will cause otherwise protected sales to lose their protection under P.L. 86-272:

- Making repairs or providing maintenance or service to the property sold or to be sold
- Collecting current or delinquent accounts, whether directly or by third parties, through assignment or otherwise
- Investigating creditworthiness
- Installation or supervision of installation at or after shipment or delivery
- Conducting training courses, seminars, or lectures for personnel other than personnel involved only in solicitation
- Providing any kind of technical assistance or service (including, but not limited to, engineering assistance or design service) when one of the purposes thereof is other than the facilitation of the solicitation of orders
- Investigating, handling, or otherwise assisting in resolving customer complaints, other than mediating direct customer complaints when the sole purpose of the mediation for sales personnel is to ingratiate themselves with customers
- Approving or accepting orders
- Repossessing property
- Securing deposits on sales
- Picking up or replacing damaged or returned property
- Hiring, training, or supervising personnel--other than personnel involved only in solicitation

- Using agency stock checks or any other instrument or process by which sales are made within the state by sales personnel
- Maintaining a sample or display room in excess of two weeks (14 days) at any one location within the state during the tax year
- Carrying samples for sale, exchange, or distribution in any manner for consideration or other value
- Consigning stock of goods or other tangible personal property to any person, including an independent contractor, for sale
- Conducting maintenance, by any employee or other representative, on an office or place of business of any kind (other than an in-home office located within the residence of the employee or representative) that is both:
    1. Not publicly attributed to the company or to the employee or representative of the company in an employee or representative capacity
    2. Used only for soliciting and receiving orders from customers, for transmitting such orders outside the state for acceptance or rejection by the company, or for other such activities protected under P.L. 86-272
- Entering into franchising or licensing agreements, selling or otherwise disposing of franchises and licenses, or selling or otherwise transferring tangible personal property pursuant to such franchise or license by the franchisor or licensor to its franchisee or licensee within the state
- Conducting any activity not listed as a protected activity (see the list of 'protected activities' below) that is not entirely ancillary to requests for orders, even if the activity helps to increase purchases
- Owning, leasing, using, or maintaining any of the following facilities or property in the state:
    - Repair shop
    - Parts department
    - Any kind of office, other than an in-home office
    - Warehouse
    - Meeting place for directors, officers, or employees
    - Stock of goods other than samples for sales personnel or samples whose use is entirely ancillary to solicitation
    - Telephone answering service that is publicly attributed to the company or to employees or agents of the company in their representative status
    - Mobile stores (i.e., vehicles with drivers who are sales personnel making sales from the vehicles)
    - Real property or fixtures to real property of any kind

PROTECTED ACTIVITIES

The following in-state activities will *not* cause the loss of protection for otherwise protected sales:

- Soliciting orders by any type of advertising
- Soliciting orders by an in-state resident employee or representative of the company, as long as such person does not maintain or use any office or other place of business in the state other than an in-home office
- Carrying samples and promotional materials only for display or distribution without charge or other consideration
- Furnishing and setting up display racks and advising customers on the display of the company's products without charge or other consideration
- Providing automobiles to sales personnel for their use in conducting protected activities
- Passing orders, inquiries, and complaints on to the home office
- Missionary sales activities (i.e., the solicitation of indirect customers for the company's goods, which would include, for example, a manufacturer's solicitation of retailers to buy the manufacturer's goods from the manufacturer's wholesale customers if such solicitation activities were otherwise immune)
- Coordinating shipment or delivery without payment or other consideration, and providing information relating thereto either prior or subsequent to the placement of an order
- Checking customers' inventories without charge (for reorder but not for other purposes such as quality control)
- Maintaining a sample or display room for two weeks (14 days) or less at any one location within the state during the tax year
- Recruiting, training, or evaluating sales personnel, including occasionally using homes, hotels, or similar places for meetings with sales personnel
- Mediating direct customer complaints when the purpose of the mediation is solely for sales personnel to ingratiate themselves with customers and to facilitate requests for orders
- Owning, leasing, or maintaining personal property for use in the employee's or representative's in-home office or automobile that is solely limited to conducting protected activities

It follows from the last item that use of personal property such as a cellular telephone, facsimile machine, duplicating equipment, personal computer, and computer software that is limited to carrying on protected solicitation and activity entirely ancillary to protected solicitation or permitted by the MTC's statement will not, by itself, remove the protection under the MTC's statement.

STUDY QUESTIONS

4. Which of the following activities in a state is considered "unprotected" under a policy statement adopted by the MTC?

  a. Solicitation of orders by a salesperson
  b. Order approval by a salesperson
  c. Replacing damaged or returned property
  d. None of the above

5. Which of the following activities in a state is considered "protected" under a policy statement adopted by the MTC?

  a. Solicitation of orders by a salesperson
  b. Order approval by a salesperson
  c. Repossession of property
  d. None of the above

6. A company may have a physical presence in a state and **not** create sales tax nexus, as long as the activities in the state are *de minimis* in nature. **True or False?**

MTC Nexus Bulletin 95-1

Nonancillary services, such as installation and repair services, performed by an employee-salesperson are *not* protected by P.L. 86-272 and will create income tax nexus for the employer if the unprotected activities are not *de minimis.* A number of states take the position that such in-state services create nexus, even if they are performed by unrelated third-party repairpersons (i.e., independent agents). Unlike the use of independent agents to perform continuous local solicitation, the use of independent agents to perform services that are not ancillary to the solicitation has yet to be addressed by the Supreme Court. Thus, this remains an unsettled area of the law.

In Nexus Bulletin 95-1 (1995), the MTC and roughly two dozen signatory states took the position that, with respect to mail-order computer vendors, the industry practice of providing in-state warranty repair services through third-party repair service providers creates constitutional nexus. As a consequence, the out-of-state mail-order vendors have nexus for sales and use tax purposes. This position is based on the Supreme Court's decision in *Scripto* and *Tyler Pipe,* both of which dealt with the use of independent sales representatives, as opposed to independent service providers.

The computer mail-order industry and many practitioners believe that there is not sufficient support in these two Supreme Court decisions for the position asserted by the MTC in Nexus Bulletin 95-1. Nevertheless, since its issuance, a number of states have taken a position similar to that espoused in Nexus Bulletin 95-1.

In TSB-A-00(42)S [Oct. 13, 2000], the New York Department of Taxation and Finance ruled that an out-of-state mail order computer vendor's use of independent contractors to perform warranty services in the state was sufficient to create sales/use tax nexus. On the other hand, a handful of states (most notably, California) have taken a position contrary to that in Nexus Bulletin 95-1 [See, e.g., *In re Gateway 2000 Inc.,* Declaratory Ruling No. 96-30-6-0033 (Iowa Dept. of Revenue and Finance, March 19, 1966)].

In *Dell Catalog Sales v. Commissioner of Revenue Services* [No. CV 00 0503146S (Conn. Super. Ct. July 10, 2003)], a Texas-based Internet and mail-order computer vendor (Dell) had no property or employees in Connecticut. Nevertheless, Dell offered on-site computer repair services to customers that elected to purchase a service contract when purchasing a computer. The services were performed by a third-party repair company (BancTec). The Connecticut Superior Court ruled that Dell did *not* have sales tax nexus because no evidence was produced to indicate that the in-state service calls were frequent or substantial in nature.

In another case involving Dell and BancTec [*Louisiana v. Dell International, Inc.,* No. 2006-C-0996 (La. Ct. of App., Feb. 15, 2006)], the Louisiana Court of Appeal concluded that BancTec's on-site repair services were crucial to Dell's ability to establish and maintain a market for its goods in Louisiana, and that Dell retained control over many aspects of the services provided by BancTec, such as requiring customers to contact Dell directly to determine whether a BancTec technician was dispatched, setting the price for the on-site services, compensating BancTec based on the number of service calls made, and training the BancTec technicians on how to perform the services.

As a result, the appellate court ruled that there was a genuine issue of fact as to whether Dell, through its contractual agreements with BancTec, had established constitutional nexus in Louisiana, and that the trial court had erred in granting summary judgment for Dell. Therefore, the case was remanded to the trial court for further proceedings.

AFFILIATE NEXUS

A number of states have taken the position that the existence of common ownership between a corporation that has a physical presence in a taxing state (e.g., an in-state brick-and-mortar retailer) and an out-of-state corporation that has no physical presence in the state but makes substantial sales into the state (e.g., an out-of-state mail-order vendor) is sufficient to create constitutional nexus for the out-of-state mail-order affiliate.

As with agency nexus, many of these cases concern the existence of nexus for sales and use tax purposes. For example, in *SFA Folio Collections, Inc. v. Tracy* [73 Ohio St. 3d 119, 652 N.E.2d 693 (1995)], SFA Folio

(Folio), a New York corporation, sold clothing and other merchandise by direct mail to customers in Ohio. Thus, Folio mailed catalogs to potential Ohio customers, the customers placed orders with Folio by telephone, and Folio shipped the merchandise via common carrier. Folio had no property or employees in Ohio. Folio's parent corporation, Saks & Company, also owned another subsidiary, Saks Fifth Avenue of Ohio, which operated a retail store in Ohio.

Ohio tax authorities argued that Folio did have *substantial nexus* in Ohio because it was a member of an affiliated group that included Saks-Ohio, a corporation that operated a store in Ohio and, therefore, was required to collect Ohio sales tax on its mail-order sales to Ohio customers. The state's position was based on a nexus-by-affiliate statute that the Ohio legislature had enacted (since repealed), as well as the argument that Saks-Ohio was an *agent* of Folio. The agency argument was based on the fact that Saks-Ohio accepted some returns of Folio sales and distributed some Folio catalogs.

The Ohio Supreme Court rejected the affiliate nexus argument, noting that Saks-Ohio was a separate legal entity, and to impute nexus to Folio merely because a sister corporation had a physical presence in Ohio ran counter to federal constitutional law and Ohio corporation law. The court also rejected the agency nexus argument, reasoning that, although the acceptance of Folio's returns and distribution of Folio's catalogs by Saks-Ohio might provide a minimal connection under the Due Process Clause, these contacts did not create substantial nexus under the Commerce Clause because Saks-Ohio accepted Folio's returns according to its own policy (not Folio's) and charged the returns to its inventory (not Folio's). Moreover, the returns were a minimal part of the returns Saks-Ohio received.

Consistent with the Ohio Supreme Court ruling in *SFA Folio*, other states have generally been unsuccessful in their attempts to argue that common ownership, by itself, creates nexus for an out-of-state affiliate [See, e.g., ***Current, Inc. v. State Bd. of Equalization,*** 24 Cal. App. 4th 382, 29 Cal. Rptr. 2d 407 (Ct. App. 1994); ***SFA Folio Collections, Inc. v. Bannon,*** 217 Conn. 220, 585 A.2d 666 (1991); ***Bloomingdale's By Mail, Ltd. v. Commonwealth,*** 130 Pa. Commw. 190, 567 A.2d 773 (Pa. 1989)].

On the other hand, based on the Supreme Court's decisions in ***Scripto*** and ***Tyler Pipe,*** if the in-state affiliate truly acts as an agent for the out-of-state affiliate, there is a stronger argument that continuous local solicitation on the part of the in-state affiliate may create nexus for an out-of-state affiliate.

In ***Borders Online, Inc.*** [No. A105488 (Cal. Ct. of App., May 31, 2005)], the California Court of Appeals ruled that an out-of-state online retailer had a substantial nexus in California for sales tax purposes because an affiliated corporation, which sold similar products in brick-and-mortar stores in California, performed return and exchange activities for the online retailer. The brick-and-mortar affiliate was considered to be an authorized representative of the online retailer because the online retailer posted a notice on its website that returns could be made to the brick-and-mortar retailer, and the brick-and-mortar retailer's acceptance of returns was an integral part of the online retailer's sales operations. Therefore, under the relevant state statute, the online retailer *was* considered to be engaged in business in California and subject to the obligation to collect sales tax on sales to California residents.

Likewise, in *Barnes & Noble.com* [SC OHB 97-732835 89872 (Sept. 12, 2002)], the California State Board of Equalization ruled that an out-of-state Internet vendor did have sales tax nexus in California because an in-state brick-and-mortar affiliate was acting as an authorized representative of the Internet vendor by distributing coupons that could be used to make online purchases at a discount, thereby assisting the Internet vendor in selling its goods within the state.

In *Reader's Digest Ass'n v. Franchise Tax Board* [No. C036307 (Cal. Ct. App. Dec. 31, 2001), *cert. denied*, Cal. Mar. 13, 2002], the California Court of Appeals held that an out-of-state parent corporation (*Reader's Digest*) had nexus for California corporate income tax purposes as a result of solicitation activities performed by its wholly owned in-state subsidiary (*Reader's Digest Sales & Services, Inc.*). P.L. 86-272 did not protect the in-state affiliate's California activities because the subsidiary had offices in the state and did *not* qualify as an *independent contractor*, with respect to its out-of-state parent.

In *Dillard National Bank, N.A. v. Johnson* [No. 96-545-III (Tenn. Ch. Ct., June 22, 2004)], the Tennessee Chancery Court ruled that an out-of-state subsidiary corporation that issued proprietary credit cards for use in a chain of in-state department stores that were operated by the parent corporation had income tax nexus in Tennessee because of the activities conducted on its behalf by the department stores and the store employees. These activities included placing advertisements in the stores, soliciting and taking credit card applications from store customers, answering questions for store customers regarding their credit card accounts, and accepting credit card payments in the stores.

The Tennessee Chancery Court's ruling in *Dillard National Bank* is consistent with the nexus principles articulated by the Tennessee Court of Appeals in *America Online, Inc. v. Johnson* [No. M2001-00927-COA-R3-CV (Tenn. Ct. App. July 30, 2002)], in which the court stated that "substantial nexus may be established by activities carried on within the state by affiliates and independent contractors." In addition, the facts in *Dillard National Bank* are distinguishable from those in *J.C. Penney National Bank v. Johnson* [No. M1998-00497-COA-R3-CV (Tenn. Ct. App. Dec. 17, 1999)], in which the Tennessee Court of Appeals rejected the affiliate nexus argument because the in-state retail stores conducted no activities that assisted the affiliated out-of-state bank in maintaining its credit card business in Tennessee.

On the other hand, in *St. Tammany Parish Tax Collector v. Barne-*

sandnoble.com [No. 05-5695, (E.D. La., Mar. 22, 2007)], the U.S. District Court ruled that an online retailer of books, movies, and music with no physical presence in Louisiana did *not* have sales and use tax nexus merely because of its close business relationship with an affiliated bricks-and-mortar retailer. The court stated that the "existence of a close corporate relationship between companies and a common corporate name does not mean that the physical presence of one is imputed to the other," and that "attributional nexus does not apply merely by virtue of the affiliation between the companies."

Instead of litigation, other states have simply passed legislation providing that companies are taxable in the state through affiliation.

EXAMPLES

Under Alabama legislation, the presence of an in-state retailer is imputed to a related out-of-state vendor if the out-of-state vendor and in-state retailer:

1. Use shared names, trade names, trademarks or goodwill to develop, promote or maintain sales
2. Pay for each other's services based upon the amount of sales
3. Share a common business plan or coordinate their business plans
4. The in-state retailer provides services to the out-of-state vendor related to developing, promoting or maintaining an in-state market [Ala. Stat. § 40-23-190]

Effective January 1, 2002, a remote seller affiliated with an Arkansas retailer has nexus with the state for the purposes of sales and use tax. The out-of-state or remote seller must collect and remit Arkansas use tax on sales into the state, if the seller is affiliated with an Arkansas retailer and "the vendor sells the same or substantially similar line of products ... under the same or substantially similar business name, or the facilities or employees of the Arkansas retailer are used to advertise or promote sales by the vendor to Arkansas purchasers" [Ark. Code Ann. §26-53-124(a)(3)(B)].

Like Arkansas, Minnesota has amended its statutes to require that an affiliated remote seller of an in-state retailer's products must collect the state's use tax. An out-of-state retailer or remote seller is an affiliate of an in-state entity if "the entity uses its facilities or employees in this state to advertise, promote, or facilitate the establishment or maintenance of a market for sales of items by the retailer to purchasers in this state ... or for the provision of services to the retailer's purchasers in this state, such as accepting returns of purchases for the retailer, providing assistance in resolving customer complaints of the retailer, or providing other services" [Minn. Stat. §297A.66(4)].

In TSB-A-03(25)S (June 11, 2003), the New York Department of Taxation and Finance indicated that the opening of a Bass Pro Outdoor World retail store in New York State would not create nexus for an out-of-state mail-order catalog company merely due to common ownership. For the catalog company to avoid nexus, the retailer should avoid performing the following functions:

1. Assist customers with catalog company sales, service, or returns
2. Refer customers
3. Compile mailing lists
4. Distribute advertising or merchandising materials (such as coupons)
5. Maintain common inventory, accounting/legal staff, and other advertising activity

The MTC's Executive Committee has approved a model affiliate nexus statute for sales tax nexus [Proposed Model Affiliate Sales Tax Nexus Provision, approved Apr. 28, 2005]. According to this model statute, an out-of-state vendor has sales tax nexus with a state if "(i) the out-of-state vendor and an in-state business maintaining one or more locations within this State are related parties; and (ii) the out-of-state vendor and the in-state business use an identical or substantially similar name, trade name, trademark or goodwill to develop, promote, or maintain sales, or the in-state business provides services to, or that inure to the benefit of, the out-of-state business related to developing, promoting, or maintaining the in-state market."

STUDY QUESTIONS

---

7. Which of the following statements is true regarding MTC Nexus Bulletin 95-1?

   a. In Nexus Bulletin 95-1, the MTC takes the position that providing in-state warranty repair services through third-parties does not create nexus.

   b. Most states have taken a position *contrary* to that in Nexus Bulletin 95-1.

   c. The position taken in the bulletin is based on the Supreme Court decision in **Quill.**

   d. The position taken in the bulletin is based on the Supreme Court's decisions in **Scripto** and **Tyler Pipe.**

8. In which of the following cases was the taxpayer not deemed to have nexus because of the activities of an in-state affiliate?

   a. Borders Online Inc.

   b. Reader's Digest Association

   c. Dillard National Bank

   d. J.C. Penney National Bank

AGENCY AND AFFILIATE NEXUS

Agency Nexus Principle

Under the *Quill* decision, a corporation generally has constitutional nexus in any state in which the corporation's property or employees are physically present on a regular and systematic basis.

What if, rather than conducting business in a state through employees (dependent agents), a corporation conducts business through independent contractors (independent agents)? Does the use of independent agents, rather than employees, allow the corporation to avoid constitutional nexus?

In *Scripto, Inc. v. Carson* [362 US 207 (1960)], the Supreme Court addressed whether the Florida marketing activities of 10 independent sales representatives created sales and use tax nexus for an out-of-state manufacturer of writing instruments. The Court held that for nexus purposes, the distinction between employees and independent contractors was "without constitutional significance" and that "to permit such formal 'contractual shifts' to make a constitutional difference would open the gates to a stampede of tax avoidance." In the Court's opinion, the critical fact was that the agents' activity in Florida helped create and maintain a commercial market for Scripto's goods. Thus, the presence of independent agents engaged in continuous local solicitation *did* create Florida sales and use tax nexus for Scripto.

The Supreme Court reaffirmed these principles 25 years later in *Tyler Pipe Industries, Inc. v. Washington Department of Revenue* [483 US 232 (1987)], holding that the activities of a single independent contractor residing in Washington was sufficient to create constitutional nexus for the out-of-state principal (Tyler Pipe). As in *Scripto,* the Court held that the critical test was "whether the activities performed in this state on behalf of the taxpayer are significantly associated with the taxpayer's ability to establish and maintain a market in this state for the sales."

More recently, in *Appeal of Family of Eagles, Ltd.* [No. 88,118 (Kan. Sup. Ct. Apr. 18, 2003)], the Kansas Supreme Court ruled that a Texas corporation whose only physical presence in Kansas was through its in-dependent sales representatives did have nexus for sales tax purposes. The court did not find any constitutionally significant differences between the taxpayer's independent sales representatives and the independent contractors in *Scripto.*

In *Jafra Cosmetics, Inc. v. Massachusetts* [No. SJC-08265 (Mass. Jan. 25, 2001)], the Massachusetts Supreme Judicial Court ruled that independent contractors (called *consultants*) who sold the products of an out-of-state cosmetics company (Jafra) in Massachusetts created sales tax nexus for Jafra. Although the consultants were not agents of Jafra, the nature of the relationship between the consultants and Jafra was such that the consultants did constitute representatives of Jafra, and, as such, created sales tax nexus for

Jafra. Under the applicable statute for the tax years in question, a vendor was considered to be "engaged in business" in Massachusetts if it regularly solicited orders for the sale of tangible personal property by "salesmen, solicitors or representatives" in the state.

P.L. 86-272 AND INDEPENDENT AGENTS

In addition to protecting solicitation activities of employee-salespersons, P.L. 86-272 protects certain in-state activities conducted by an independent contractor.

Specifically, P.L. 86-272 provides that independent contractors may engage in the following in-state activities on behalf of an out-of-state corporation without creating income tax nexus for the out-of-state principal:

1. Soliciting sales
2. Making sales
3. Maintaining an office

Thus, unlike employees, independent agents can maintain in-state offices without creating nexus for the principal [See, e.g., *Universal Instruments Corp. v. Massachusetts Comm'r of Revenue,* No. 196059 (Mass. App. Tax Bd. (1998)].

> **NOTE**
>
> Because P.L. 86-272 provides no protection for sales or use taxes, any of these activities would create sales and use tax nexus.

For this purpose, the term *independent contractors* means a commission agent, broker, or other independent contractor who is engaged in selling, or soliciting orders for the sale of, tangible personal property for more than one principal and who holds him or herself out as such in the regular course of business activities.

In *Dart Industries, Inc.* [No. 04-03, N.M. Dept. of Rev., Feb. 26, 2004], the New Mexico Department of Revenue ruled that P.L. 86-272 did *not* protect an out-of-state manufacturer from income tax nexus. The taxpayer sold its goods in New Mexico through an in-state distributor that maintained an office in the state, but did not qualify as an independent contractor because the distributor was contractually bound to represent only the taxpayer. The distributor also handled customer complaints, which was another activity that is not protected by P.L. 86-272.

Likewise, in *Reader's Digest Association v. Franchise Tax Board* [No. C036307 (Cal. Ct. App. Dec. 31, 2001), *cert. denied,* Cal. Mar. 13, 2002], the California Court of Appeals held that P.L. 86-272 did not protect an out-of-state parent corporation from nexus in California because its California sales subsidiary had offices in the state, but did not qualify as an independent contractor because it represented only its parent company.

Under the MTC's Statement of Information Concerning Practices of Multistate Tax Commission and Signatory States Under P.L. 86-272, the maintenance of a stock of goods within a state by the independent contractor under consignment or any other type of arrangement with the out-of-state principal, except for purposes of display and solicitation, is not protected by P.L. 86-272.

OTHER APPLICATIONS OF AGENCY NEXUS PRINCIPLE

State tax authorities have become increasingly creative in their application of the agency nexus principle. Two examples are the decisions in *Furnitureland South, Inc. v. Comptroller* [No. C-97-37872 OC (Md. Cir. Ct. Aug. 13, 1999)], and *Kmart Properties, Inc.* [No. 00-04 (N.M. Taxation and Revenue Dep't Feb. 1, 2000)]. In *Furnitureland South,* the Maryland court ruled that a trucking company (Royal Transport) created use tax nexus for an unrelated out-of-state furniture retailer (Furnitureland South) because the trucking company acted as the retailer's *agent* in Maryland.

Before 1991, Furnitureland had its own fleet of trucks and drivers to make deliveries. Royal Transport was established in 1991 as a for-hire motor carrier. Royal was not a subsidiary of Furnitureland. No employee, officer, director, or shareholder of Royal was at any time an employee, officer, director, or shareholder of Furnitureland. However, Furnitureland provided Royal with start-up capital, sold Royal its used trailers, assigned Royal its leased equipment, remained on the assigned equipment leases as guarantor, trained Royal drivers on the delivery and assembly of furniture, and provided Royal with rent-free office space in Furnitureland's distribution center.

The Maryland court concluded that Royal created a use tax withholding obligation for Furnitureland because it acted as its *agent* for the purpose of delivering, setting up, and servicing furniture in Maryland. Royal's drivers provided important services to Maryland customers on behalf of Furnitureland. The drivers carried tools that they used to repair damaged furniture, regularly set up new furniture in customers' homes, collected C.O.D. payments for Furnitureland, carried additional items (e.g., bed slats and mirror supports) that they sold to Furnitureland's customers, and routinely picked up damaged furniture. Royal's trucks also prominently displayed the Furnitureland logo. In addition, Furnitureland prepared and scheduled each trip to be taken by a Royal driver. As it emphasized in its marketing, this personalized delivery service helped Furnitureland, "your neighborhood furniture store," become the largest furniture retailer in the world.

In **Quill,** the Supreme Court observed that **National Bellas Hess** created a safe harbor for out-of-state vendors "whose only connection with customers in the taxing State is by common carrier or the U.S. mail." The Maryland court concluded, however, that the "personalized delivery service" provided by Royal to Furnitureland customers did *not* fall within the common carrier safe harbor.

When merchandise is shipped via common carrier (e.g., UPS), set-up and repair are not services expected by the typical consumer. Furthermore, when a package is shipped via common carrier, the shipper has little or no control over the time, manner, and means of delivery. In contrast, when Royal made deliveries for Furnitureland, Royal's drivers entered the customer's home, set up the furniture, made any necessary minor repairs, and even made sales of items not ordered. In addition, Furnitureland retained significant control over the time, manner, and means of delivery.

In **Kmart Properties, Inc.,** the taxpayer (Kmart Properties, Inc., or KPI) was a Michigan corporation that had no employees or tangible or real property located in New Mexico. KPI did, however, own highly valuable intangible property (trademarks, trade names) that it licensed for use by Kmart stores, which operated 22 retail stores in New Mexico.

As the owner of the intangible property, KPI controlled the terms of the licenses it granted, including where that property could be used by Kmart. The licensing agreement had been negotiated and executed in Michigan, and KPI's management of its intellectual property occurred in Michigan.

Despite the lack of tangible property or employees in New Mexico, the New Mexico Taxation and Revenue Department ruled that KPI *was* physically present in New Mexico by virtue of Kmart's (the parent company's) contractual obligations under the licensing agreements to establish, maintain, and enhance the market for KPI's trademarks in New Mexico in order to generate a revenue stream for KPI.

The license agreement provided that Kmart would:

- Maintain the quality of products and services bearing the trademarks and trade names
- Comply with quality standards set by KPI for such products and services
- Advise KPI of new or changed products and services
- Instruct Kmart not to use products or services failing to meet KPI's quality standards

In other words, Kmart was in effect an agent of KPI. Thus, the Department concluded, Kmart was in the same position as the salespersons in **Scripto** (1960) and **Tyler Pipe** (1987), both cases in which the Supreme Court had ruled that the actions of independent agents *were* sufficient to establish nexus for Commerce Clause purposes.

STUDY QUESTIONS

---

9. In which of the following cases did the U.S. Supreme Court hold that, for nexus purposes, the distinction between employees and independent contractors was "without constitutional significance?"

  a. Scripto Inc.
  b. Reader's Digest Association
  c. Kmart Properties Inc.
  d. Share International Inc.

Deliveries in Company-Owned Trucks

A corporation generally has constitutional nexus in any state in which it has property or employees located on a continuous basis. Thus, a number of state courts have held that the regular and systematic presence of company-owned delivery trucks driven by company employees is sufficient to create sales and use tax nexus [E.g., *Brown's Furniture, Inc. v. Wagner,* No. 78195 (Ill. Apr. 18, 1996); *Town Crier, Inc. v. Zehnder,* No. 1-98-4251 (Ill. App. Ct. June 30, 2000); *John Swenson Granite Co. v. State Tax Assessor,* 685 A.2d 425 (Me. Super. Ct. 1996). But see *Miller Bros. Co. v. Maryland,* 347 US 340 (1954) (ruling that "occasional delivery" of goods with no solicitation other than the "incidental effects of general advertising" was not sufficient to create nexus under the Due Process Clause)].

For income tax purposes, P.L. 86-272 shields an out-of-state corporation from taxation:

- If its only in-state activity is solicitation of orders by company representatives for sales of tangible personal property
- If those orders are sent outside the state for approval or rejection
- If approved, the orders are filled by shipment or delivery from a point outside the state

Over the years, taxpayers have taken the position that the phrase *shipment or delivery* implies that a seller is protected by P.L. 86-272 regardless of whether it ships the goods into the state using a common carrier or its own delivery trucks. Some states, however, have taken the position that the in-state delivery of goods in the seller's own delivery trucks exceeds solicitation and therefore is an activity that is *not* protected by P.L. 86-272.

State Supreme Courts in Massachusetts and Virginia have ruled that the activity of making deliveries in company-owned trucks is protected under P.L. 86-272 [*National Private Truck Council v. Virginia Dept of Taxation,* 253 Va. 74, 480 S.E.2d 500 (1997); and *National Private Truck Council v. Commissioner of Revenue,* 688 N.E.2d 936 (Mass. 1997), *cert. denied*].

In addition, reversing a 1997 decision, the Texas Comptroller of Public Accounts has held that a taxpayer could claim immunity from the earned surplus portion of the Texas franchise tax under P.L. 86-272, even though the taxpayer delivered tangible personal property into Texas using company-owned trucks [Hearing No. 36,590 (Comptroller of Public Accounts Jan. 20, 2000)]. Thus, there is a strong argument that the use of company-owned trucks to deliver products should not, by itself, cause a taxpayer to forfeit the protections granted by P.L. 86-272.

In 2001, the MTC revised its Statement of Information Concerning Practices of Multistate Tax Commission and Signatory States Under P.L. 86-272 by removing from the list of unprotected activities the following item: "Shipping or delivering goods into this state by means of private vehicle, rail, water, air or other carrier, irrespective of whether shipment or delivery fee or other charge is imposed, directly or indirectly, upon the purchaser." Several state revenue departments have also indicated that the activity of making deliveries using company-owned trucks *is* protected by P.L. 86-272 [Rev. Rul. 24-01-01, Neb. Dept. of Rev. (Feb. 22, 2001); Decision No. 2005-05-10-22, Okla. Tax Comm'n. (May 10, 2005); and Ala. Reg. 810-27-1-4-.19 (Feb. 28, 2006)].

Although deliveries may be a protected activity, other activities of a delivery truck driver (such as collecting payments or accepting returns (back-hauling)) are most likely *not* protected by P.L. 86-272.

For example, in Revenue Ruling No. 97-15, the Tennessee Department of Revenue ruled that a corporation's back-hauling and collection activities create nexus for Tennessee excise (income) taxes because such activities exceed solicitation.

Similarly, in TSB-A-97(8)C, the New York Department of Taxation and Finance held that, although the delivery of products to New York customers using company-owned vehicles would not subject the company to franchise (income) tax, post-delivery back-hauling activities in New York would subject the company to franchise (income) tax, unless those activities were *de minimis*. The Department held that the back-hauling activities of the company at issue unrelated to the delivery of products produced four percent of the company's total revenues earned in New York and therefore were not *de minimis*, thus subjecting the company to New York franchise (income) tax.

In *Asher Inc. v. Division of Taxation* [No. 004061-2003 (N.J. Tax Ct., Jan. 5, 2006)], the New Jersey Tax Court ruled that P.L. 86-272 did *not* protect the New Jersey activities of a Pennsylvania company's delivery drivers, which included picking up damaged or returned goods and the collection of delinquent accounts. These activities were not ancillary to the solicitation of sales and were not sufficiently *de minimis* to avoid the loss of immunity under the standard established by the Supreme Court in *Wrigley*.

ECONOMIC NEXUS

In *Quill,* the Supreme Court ruled that a corporation satisfies the Commerce Clause's *substantial nexus* requirement *only* if the taxpayer has a physical presence in the state. Yet, in *Geoffrey, Inc. v. South Carolina Tax Commissioner* [437 S.E.2d 13 (S.C.), *cert. denied,* 114 SCt 550 (1993)], the South Carolina Supreme Court held that a trademark holding company that licensed its intangibles for use in South Carolina had nexus for income tax purposes, despite the lack of any tangible property or employees in South Carolina.

Geoffrey was the trademark holding company of the toy retailer, Toys "R" Us. Geoffrey was incorporated and domiciled in Delaware and had a license agreement with South Carolina retailers allowing them to use its trademarks and trade names, including the Toys "R" Us trademark, in exchange for a percentage of net sales. The court rejected Geoffrey's claim that it had not purposefully directed its activities toward South Carolina and held that, by licensing intangibles for use in the state and receiving income in exchange for their use, Geoffrey had the minimum connection and substantial nexus with South Carolina required by the Due Process Clause and the Commerce Clause. The *Geoffrey* court did *not* follow the precedent established by *Quill* because it believed that ruling applied only to the issue of nexus for sales and use tax purposes.

Since 1993, many states have adopted *Geoffrey* rules or regulations, and there has been a significant amount of litigation related to the *Geoffrey* court's interpretation of the Commerce Clause's substantial nexus requirement.

For example, in *Cerro Copper Products Inc. v. Department of Revenue* [No. 94-444 (Ala. Admin. L. Div. 1995)] and *Dial Bank v. Department of Revenue* [No. 95-289 (Ala. Admin. L. Div. 1998)], an administrative law judge could find no reason why the *Quill* physical presence test should not also apply to nexus for corporate income taxes.

Likewise, in *Bandag Licensing Corp. v. Rylander* [No. 03-99-00427-CV (Tex. App. May 11, 2000)], the Texas appeals court saw no principled distinction between sales taxes and income taxes when the underlying issue was whether the Commerce Clause permits a state to impose a tax obligation on an out-of-state corporation. The court concluded that, consistent with the ruling in *Quill*, a state may *not* constitutionally impose its corporate franchise tax on an out-of-state corporation that lacks a physical presence in the state.

In *A&F Trademark, Inc. v. Tolson* [No. COA03-1203 (N.C. Ct. of App., Dec. 7, 2004); *appeal denied,* No. 23P05, N.C. Sup. Ct., Mar. 3, 2005; *cert. denied,* US No. 04-1625, Oct. 3, 2005], the North Carolina Court of Appeals held that, despite the fact that the holding company did not have a physical presence in North Carolina, licensing intangibles for use in North Carolina *was* sufficient to establish income tax nexus for an out-of-state trademark holding company.

In *Geoffrey, Inc. v. Tax Commission* [No. 99,938 (Okla. Ct. of Civ. App., Dec. 23, 2005)], the Oklahoma Court of Civil Appeals ruled that licensing intangibles for use in Oklahoma was sufficient to establish income tax nexus for a Delaware trademark holding company, even though the holding company had no physical presence in Oklahoma. The court concluded that the *Quill* physical presence test did not apply to taxes other than sales and use taxes.

In *Kmart Properties, Inc. v. Taxation and Revenue Department* [No. 21,140 (N.M. Ct. App. Nov. 27, 2001)], the taxpayer (Kmart Properties, Inc., or KPI) was a Michigan corporation that had no employees or property in New Mexico but did license trademarks to its parent corporation, which operated Kmart stores in New Mexico. The New Mexico Court of Appeals ruled that the use of the trademarks in New Mexico was sufficient to create income tax nexus for KPI, despite the lack of any direct physical presence in New Mexico.

The court also concluded that the *Quill* physical presence requirement did not apply to income taxes, and that the presence in New Mexico of a licensee that was working on KPI's behalf to maintain and enhance the market for its intangibles created nexus for KPI under the agency nexus principles of *Scripto, Inc. v. Carson* [362 US 207 (1960)].

The New Mexico Supreme Court granted *certiorari* with respect to numerous issues in this case, including a constitutional challenge regarding income tax nexus. However, the state Supreme Court did not address this issue in its opinion. Instead, it quashed the certiorari it had granted on the issue of income tax nexus and ordered that the appellate court's decision be filed concurrent with the filing of its opinion [*Kmart Corp. v. Taxation and Revenue Department*, No. 27,269 (N.M. Sup. Ct., Dec. 29, 2005)].

In *ACME Royalty Co. and Brick Investment Co.* (Mo. SCt, No. SC84225 and SC84226, Nov. 26, 2002), the Missouri Supreme Court ruled that two trademark holding companies were not subject to the Missouri corporate income tax, because they did not have any activity in Missouri in the form of payroll, property, or sales.

In *SYL, Inc.* and *Crown Cork & Seal Co. (Del.), Inc.* (Nos. 76 and 80, Md. Ct. of App. June 9, 2003), the Maryland Court of Appeals held that the trademark holding companies in question had nexus in Maryland because they were unitary with their parent companies which were doing business in Maryland, and had no economic substance as separate entities from their parent corporations.

In *Department of Revenue v. Gap (Apparel) Inc.* [No. 2004 CW 0263 (La. Ct. App., June 25, 2004)], the Louisiana Court of Appeal held that a California trademark holding company had income tax nexus in Louisiana, despite the lack of any type of physical presence in the state. The trademark holding company licensed its intangibles for use by affiliates which operated 2,600 retail stores nationwide, including about 40 stores in Louisiana. The court concluded that the trademark holding company's intangibles had "acquired a business situs in Louisiana," because the intangibles were an integral part of a business carried on within the state.

In *Bridges v. Autozone Properties, Inc.* [No. 2004-C-814 (La. Sup. Ct., Mar. 24, 2005)], the Louisiana Supreme Court ruled that, based on the *minimum contacts* nexus standard of the Due Process Clause, the State of Louisiana could tax an out-of-state corporation on the dividends that it received as a shareholder of a real estate investment trust (REIT). The REIT owned rental producing retail stores in Louisiana that were operated by another subsidiary of the taxpayer. Therefore, the state provided the "benefits, opportunities and protections that come from doing business in Louisiana."

In *Geoffrey, Inc. v. Commissioner of Revenue* [No. C271816 (Mass. App. Tax Bd., July 24, 2007], the Massachusetts Appellate Tax Board concluded that the Commerce Clause does not require that an out-of-state corporation have a physical presence in a state in order to support the imposition of that state's income-based corporate excise tax. Furthermore, a Delaware trademark holding company's receipt of royalty income from licensing intangibles used for retail business activities in Massachusetts constituted *substantial nexus* in the state under the Commerce Clause.

In *Lanco, Inc. v. Division of Taxation* [No. A-89-05 (N.J. Sup. Ct., Oct. 12, 2006); *cert. denied*, U.S. Sup. Ct., 06-1236, June 18, 2007], the New Jersey Supreme Court ruled that the Delaware trademark holding corporation of the clothing retailer Lane Bryant (Lanco) had income tax nexus with New Jersey, even though the corporation had no physical presence in the state. The court stated that, "We do not believe that the Supreme Court intended to create a universal physical-presence requirement for state taxation under the Commerce Clause," and concluded that, "The better interpretation of Quill is the one adopted by those states that limit the Supreme Court's holding to sales and use taxes."

In *Tax Commissioner v. MBNA America Bank, N.A.* [No. 33049 (W.V. Sup. Ct. of App., Nov. 21, 2006); *cert. denied*, U.S. Sup. Ct., 06-1228, June 18, 2007], the West Virginia Supreme Court of Appeals ruled that a Delaware bank that provided credit card services to customers in West Virginia had income tax nexus in West Virginia, even though it had no physical presence in the state. During the tax years in question, the bank regularly issued credit cards and extended unsecured credit to West Virginia customers, and it derived significant gross receipts from these activities. The court concluded that the *Quill* physical presence test "applies only to state sales and use taxes and not to state business franchise and corporation net income taxes," and that MBNA had "a significant economic presence sufficient to meet the substantial nexus" test under the Commerce Clause.

Likewise, in *Capital One Bank and Capital One F.S.B. v. Commissioner of Revenue* [Nos. C262391, C262598 (Mass. App. Tax Bd., June 22, 2007)], the Massachusetts Appellate Tax Board held that "the physical-presence requirement in *Quill* is not applicable to an income-based" tax. Consequently, two out-of-state credit card banks that "derived substantial economic gain from the Massachusetts market through a sophisticated marketing campaign that targeted Massachusetts customers" had substantial nexus for purposes of the Massachusetts financial institution excise (income) tax.

However, in *The Sherwin-Williams Co. v. Commissioner of Revenue* [No. SJC-08516, , 438 Mass. 71, , 778 N.E. 2d 504, 2002 Mass October 31, 2002; reversing Massachusetts Appellate Tax Board, No. F233560, July 19, 2000, ¶400-635], the Massachusetts Supreme Judicial Court found that the transfer and licensing back of trademarks was not a sham transaction but had economic substance. It determined there was no evidence that the transfer of the marks was specifically devised as a tax-avoidance scheme. The revenue earned by the subsidiaries was invested as part of ongoing business operations. The payments were reasonable and reflected the fair value of the services received.

In addition, in *America Online, Inc. v. Johnson* [No. 97-3786-III (Tenn. Ch. Ct. Mar. 3, 2000)], the court ruled that Tennessee did not have the right to tax the company's Internet services because the company did not have a physical presence in the state.

In *Praxair Technology, Inc. v. Division* [N.J. Tax Ct. (6/18/07)], The New Jersey Tax Court held that, based upon *Lanco, Inc. v. Director* [N.J. (10/12/06)] an intangible holding company that licensed patent/trade secret intangibles to an affiliate that used the technologies to manufacture industrial gases at facilities in New Jersey had state corporate income tax nexus, even though it lacked an in-state physical presence.

During the 110th session of Congress, a bill was introduced in the Senate to create a physical presence standard for income tax nexus. The Business Activity Tax Simplification Act of 2007 [S. 1726, introduced June 28, 2007] would prohibit a state from imposing a business activity tax unless the taxpayer has a physical presence in the state for 15 days or more during the year. Presence in a state "to conduct limited or transient business activity" would *not* establish physical presence. Similar legislation was introduced in the 109th session of Congress [e.g., H.B. 1956, introduced April 28, 2005, and S.B. 2721, introduced May 4, 2006], but was not enacted into law.

STUDY QUESTIONS

---

10. Which of the following activities is protected under P.L. 86-272 according to state Supreme Courts in Massachusetts and Virginia?

   a. Delivery drivers in company-owned trucks accepting returns
   b. Delivery drivers in company-owned trucks collecting payments
   c. Delivery drivers delivering products in company-owned trucks
   d. None of the above

11. In which of the following cases was the taxpayer determined *not* to have nexus and thereby not subject to income taxes in the state?

   a. Geoffrey Inc. v. South Carolina Tax Commissioner
   b. A&F Trademark Inc. v. Tolson
   c. Geoffrey Inc. v. Tax Commission
   d. ACME Royalty Co. and Brick Investment Co.

OTHER NEXUS ISSUES

State-Specific Statutory and Administrative Exemptions

States generally attempt to impose their income taxes to the fullest extent permissible under the U.S. Constitution and P.L. 86-272. In the name of supporting in-state business interests, however, many states provide targeted exemptions for selected activities that would otherwise create nexus.

EXAMPLE

Although the ownership of property in a state typically creates nexus, a number of states provide statutory or administrative exemptions for:

- The ownership of raw materials or finished goods at an unrelated in-state printer
- The ownership of equipment or tooling in the state for use by an unrelated in-state manufacturer
- Employees attending in-state trade shows or conventions

EXAMPLE

An out-of-state corporation does not have nexus in California if its only contact with the state is employees who *both*:

1. Enter the state to attend conventions and trade shows for a total of no more than 15 days in a given year
2. Earn no more than $100,000 from those activities [Cal. Rev. & Tax. Code § 6203(e)]

Ownership of Partnership Interest

States generally take the position that an ownership interest in a partnership doing business in the state is sufficient to create constitutional nexus for a nondomiciliary corporation. In asserting nexus, the states rely primarily on the *aggregate theory* of partnership, which holds that a partnership is the aggregation of its owners rather than an entity that is separate from its owners (unlike a corporation).

Under this theory, the partners are viewed as direct owners of the partnership's assets. Based on the *aggregate theory*, most states take the position that the mere ownership of a partnership interest is sufficient to create constitutional nexus for a nondomiciliary corporation, regardless of whether the corporation is a general or limited partner.

NOTE

Some states apply a different rule for limited partners. The basis for this distinction is that a limited partnership interest is a passive investment akin to shares of corporate stock.

Ownership of Leased Property

In general, the ownership of business property in a state is sufficient to create nexus. In the case of leased property, the lessee is subject to the state's jurisdiction because the property is being used in the state and sufficient nexus may also be established for the lessor because of the in-state presence of owned business property. In addition to the presence of property, factors that help to support nexus include the negotiation or execution of the lease agreement in the state or the receipt of the rental payments in the state.

In the case of leased property that is immobile, the creation of nexus generally is easier to identify because, in negotiating the agreement or in addressing the shipment or delivery of the property to the lessee, the lessor is informed of the state in which the property is expected to be located during the rental period. In contrast, when mobile property (e.g., airplanes and other transportation vehicles) is at issue, the lessor typically has no control over where the property will be used. Moreover, unless otherwise specified in the lease agreement, the lessee may be under no contractual obligation to provide the lessor with any information about where the property has been used at any time during the lease.

In the case of immobile property (e.g., machinery and equipment located within a manufacturing facility), the lessor typically is considered to have established nexus with each state where the leased property is located. For leased mobile property, many states provide that an isolated landing or trip through the state will not create nexus. The presence of leased property in the state on a regular or systematic basis, however, is typically sufficient nexus with the state to subject the lessor to the state's corporate income tax. Therefore, in negotiating lease agreements, the lessor should annually require the lessee to supply the appropriate information about the states in which the property is used during the tax period. Without that information, the lessor cannot determine the states with which nexus has been established or compute its apportionment factors in the various states.

In *TTX Co. v. Idaho State Tax Commission* [128 Idaho 483 (1996)], the Idaho Supreme Court held that an out-of-state corporation that leased railcars to railroads operating within Idaho did *not* have nexus in Idaho. Likewise, in *Airoldi Bros., Inc. v. Illinois Department of Revenue* [Admin. Hearing Decision No. 98-IT-0330 (Ill. Dep't of Revenue Sept. 29, 2000)], the Illinois Department of Revenue ruled that a Wisconsin truck leasing company whose customers used its trucks in Illinois did not have income tax nexus in Illinois. In both *Comdisco, Inc. v. Indiana Department of Revenue* [No. 49T10-9903-TA-19, Ind. Tax Ct. Dec. 8, 2002)] and *Enterprise Leasing Company of Chicago v. Indiana Department of Revenue* [No. 49T10-9807-TA-74, Ind. Tax Ct. Dec. 8, 2002)], the Indiana Tax Court ruled that two out-of-state leasing companies were not subject to Indiana tax on income from equipment and autos leased to Indiana customers, because their ownership of the leased property was the companies' only contact with the state. The out-of-state leasing companies did not exercise control over the leased equipment, and were not active participants in the leasing activities within the state.

On the other hand, in *Truck Renting & Leasing Ass'n, Inc. v. Commissioner of Revenue* [No. SJC-08308 (Mass. Apr. 17, 2001)], the Massachusetts Supreme Judicial Court ruled that the imposition of the Massachusetts corporate income tax on an out-of-state corporation whose leased trucks operated in Massachusetts violated neither the Due Process Clause nor the Commerce Clause of the U.S. Constitution, even though the lessor had no physical presence in Massachusetts beyond the presence of the leased trucks. By providing registration and licensing services that allowed the lessees to operate the trucks in Massachusetts, the out-of-state lessee was purposefully availing itself of the privilege of doing business in the state, as required by the Due Process Clause. In addition, the physical presence of the taxpayer's trucks within the state on a regular and systematic basis created a substantial nexus, as required by the Commerce Clause.

In *Alabama Dept. of Revenue vs. Union Tank Car Co.* [No. 2050652 (Ala. Ct. of Civ. App., April 13, 2007)], the taxpayer (Union Tank) was a Delaware corporation that was headquartered in Illinois. Union Tank manufactured specialty railroad cars in Illinois and Texas and leased them to customers nationwide. Some of Union Tank's leased railcars were used to transport materials through Alabama and to destinations within Alabama. None of the railcars were used strictly within Alabama.

The Department contended that Union Tank was subject to Alabama income tax, because the operative statute imposes an income tax on "[e]very corporation doing business in Alabama or deriving income from sources within Alabama, including income from property located in Alabama." The Alabama Court of Civil Appeals concluded, however, that Union Tank "derived income from the lease transactions in Illinois, not from sources in Alabama." Union Tank executed its lease contracts in Illinois, the railcars were picked up in Illinois or Texas, and the lessees made lease payments to Union Tank in Illinois. The amount of the lease payments were fixed, and Union Tank had no control over where the railcars were used after they had been leased.

Qualification to Do Business

A number of states have statutes or regulations that require a corporation to file an income or franchise tax return and pay tax if the corporation has the authority to do business in the state. For example, under Texas Tax Code Annotated §171.001(a)(1), the state's corporate franchise tax applies to "each corporation that does business in this state or that is chartered or authorized to do business in this state" [See also, e.g., Cal. Code Regs. tit. 18, §23038(a); Mass. Regs. Code tit. 830, §63.39.1].

The constitutionality of the Texas statute was tested in *Bandag Licensing Corp. v. Rylander.* [No. 03-99-00427-CV (Tex. App. May 11, 2000)] Bandag was incorporated in Iowa. It did not own or use any property in Texas, nor did it have any employees or other agents present in Texas. Nevertheless, the Texas Comptroller of Public Accounts imposed the Texas corporate franchise tax on Bandag solely on the basis that Bandag had obtained a certificate of authority to do business in Texas.

The Comptroller argued that the economic benefits conferred by the state on a company having the authority to do business in Texas were sufficient to create nexus. The Comptroller also argued that the *Quill* physical presence test applied only to sales taxes, and was not controlling for corporate franchise tax purposes. The Texas appeals court saw no principled distinction between sales and income taxes when the underlying issue was whether the Commerce Clause permits a state to impose a tax obligation on an out-of-state corporation. The court went on to conclude that, consistent with the ruling in *Quill,* a state cannot constitutionally impose its corporate franchise tax on an out-of-state corporation that lacks a physical presence in the state.

In response to the *Bandag* decision, the Comptroller issued a letter ruling indicating that an out-of-state corporation's possession of a certificate of authority to do business in Texas is *not,* by itself, sufficient to create nexus [Comptroller's Letter No. 200106294L (Tex. Comptroller of Public Accounts June 15, 2001)].

A related issue is whether the authority to do business in a state constitutes a separate business activity that is not protected by P.L. 86-272. This issue arises when a corporation's employees are soliciting sales in a state (in which case the corporation has constitutional nexus), but P.L. 86-272 protects the corporation from income tax nexus.

For example, in *Commissioner of Revenue v. Kelly-Springfield Tire Co.* [419 Mass. 262 (1994)], the taxpayer had employees who were physically present in Massachusetts on a continuous basis. The parties agreed, however, that the activities of the in-state employees were protected by P.L. 86-272. At issue was whether the taxpayer's authority to do business in Massachusetts constituted a separate business activity that was sufficient to establish income tax nexus. The Massachusetts Commissioner of Revenue argued that the authority to do business created a close relationship to the state by providing the taxpayer with the right to maintain litigation, convey land, limit individual liability under principles of corporate law, protect the corporate name, and appoint a resident agent for service of process. Based on the plain language of P.L. 86-272, which does not specifically exclude from immunity a corporation that has the authority to do business in a state, the Massachusetts Supreme Judicial Court ruled that the authority to do business in a state is not a separate business activity that creates nexus.

In another case involving the same company, the Connecticut Supreme Court also ruled that the authority to do business does not deny a corporation the protections afforded by P.L. 86-272. [*Kelly-Springfield Tire Co. v. Bajorski,* 228 Conn. 137 (1993)]

In *LSDHC Corp. v. Tracy* [No. 98-J-896 (Ohio Bd. of Tax App. Nov. 19, 2001)], the Ohio Board of Tax Appeals ruled that registration to do business was *not,* by itself, sufficient to create nexus for purposes of Ohio's corporate franchise tax on net income.

STUDY QUESTIONS

---

12. States generally attempt to impose their income taxes to the fullest extent permissible. ***True or False?***

13. In which of the following situations would a lessor be ***least*** likely to have nexus with a state where the leased property is used?
  a. Negotiation of the lease agreement in the state
  b. Receipt of the rental payments in the state
  c. Lease of mobile property that made a trip through the state
  d. Lease of immobile property to be used in the state

14. In which of the following cases was Texas' decision to tax a company that had authority to do business but no physical presence in the state ruled unconstitutional?
  a. Bandag Licensing Corp.
  b. Kelly-Springfield Tire Co. (1993)
  c. Kelly-Springfield Tire Co. (1994)
  d. LSDHC Corp.

State Versus Federal Nexus Standards for Foreign (non-U.S.) Corporations

State income tax nexus generally requires that an out-of-state corporation (including corporations organized in other countries):
- Purposefully direct its activities at the state
- Have some type of nontrivial physical presence within the state
- Have a type of physical presence that is *not* protected by P.L. 86-272

A different nexus standard applies with respect to federal taxation of a foreign (non-U.S.) corporation. The United States has bilateral income tax treaties with over 60 countries, and tax treaties routinely contain a *permanent establishment* provision, under which the business profits of a foreign corporation that is a resident of a treaty country are exempt from federal income tax, unless the foreign corporation conducts business through a permanent establishment situated in the United States (e.g., Articles 5 and 7, U.S. Model Income Tax Treaty of 2006). Treaty permanent establishment provisions are not binding for state nexus purposes, however, because income tax treaties generally do not apply to state taxes (e.g., Article 2 of the U.S. Model Treaty of 2006). As a consequence, it is possible for a foreign corporation to have nexus for state tax purposes but not federal income tax purposes.

A permanent establishment generally includes a fixed place of business (e.g., a sales office), or the presence of employees who habitually exercise an authority to conclude contracts that are binding on the foreign corporation within the United States.

Certain activities are specifically *excluded* from the definition of a *permanent establishment.* Excluded activities include the following:

1. Using facilities solely for the purpose of storing, displaying or delivering inventory belonging to the taxpayer
2. Maintaining inventory belonging to the taxpayer solely for the purpose of storage, display or delivery, or processing by another enterprise
3. Maintaining a fixed place of business solely for the purpose of purchasing goods or collecting information for the taxpayer, or any other activity of a preparatory or auxiliary character (e.g., Article 5, U.S. Model Income Tax Treaty of 2006)

Therefore, as an example, if a foreign corporation stores inventory in a state in which it has some U.S. customers, the physical presence of company-owned inventory would generally create state tax nexus but not federal income tax nexus, because the mere storage of inventory does not constitute a permanent establishment. Some states provide guidance regarding the foreign corporation's filing requirements in these situations.

EXAMPLE

A foreign corporation that has nexus in Florida but is exempted by a treaty from filing a federal income tax return does not need to file a Florida income tax return.

However, a foreign corporation that does not have any income effectively connected with a U.S. trade or business, but which is still subject to U.S. tax (e.g., withholding taxes on U.S. source dividend, interest, rental or royalty income) is required to file a Florida corporate income tax return (Fla. Reg. §12C-1.022 and TAA 03C1-003, Fla. Dept. of Rev., Sept. 3, 2003).

Electronic Commerce

Since the 1990s, the Internet has transformed how many companies transact business. Although electronic commerce provides significant benefits to the overall economy, it also threatens the viability of state income and sales and use tax systems. For example, as goods that have historically been sold by *brick-and-mortar* retailers (e.g., books, compact discs, clothing) are increasingly sold over the Internet, states have experienced an erosion of their sales and use tax base.

The states' predicament is largely due to the physical presence test for nexus, as mandated by the Supreme Court in *Quill.* Because electronic commerce allows companies to exploit a commercial market without establishing a physical presence in a state, the physical presence test significantly inhibits a state's ability to impose a tax obligation on an out-of-state, Internet vendor.

On the other hand, the business community has legitimate concerns about the future direction of the state taxation of electronic commerce and, in particular, the significant compliance burden of collecting sales tax on a nationwide basis.

There are currently thousands of sales tax jurisdictions (state, county, and city), which have different tax rates, different definitions of the tax base, and different administrative procedures. In recognition of the potential negative effect that state and local taxation could have on the growth of electronic commerce, in October 1998 Congress enacted the Internet Tax Freedom Act. The Act imposed a three-year moratorium on any "new" state or local taxes on Internet access.

Subsequent legislation in 2001 and 2004 extended the moratorium on new state or local taxes on Internet access or electronic commerce through November 1, 2007. On November 1, 2007, President Bush signed H.R. 3678, the Internet Tax Freedom Act Amendment Acts of 2007, into law. The law prohibits multiple and discriminatory taxes on electronic commerce until Nov. 1, 2014.

To ensure the integrity of state tax bases, federal legislation that allows states to tax out-of-state companies that have an economic presence, but no physical presence, may be required. One solution was the *factor presence* nexus standard for business activity taxes, adopted by the MTC in 2002. The MTC urged Congress to repeal P.L. 86-272 for states that adopted the new standard. Under this proposal, nexus determinations would be based on the same property, payroll and sales factors used to apportion corporate income.

Specifically, an out-of-state corporation would have nexus if, during the tax year, its in-state activity exceeded any of the following thresholds:

1. $50,000 in property
2. $50,000 in payroll
3. $500,000 in annual sales [Factor Presence Nexus Standard for Business Activity Taxes, Oct. 17, 2002]

Another potential solution is more uniform and simplified state and local tax systems. In fact, the states have initiated a major effort to simplify and modernize sales and use tax collection and administration through the Streamlined Sales Tax (SST). The SST now includes 19 full member states (Arkansas, Indiana, Iowa, Kansas, Kentucky, Michigan, Minnesota, Nebraska, Nevada, New Jersey, North Carolina, North Dakota, Oklahoma, Rhode Island, South Dakota, Vermont, Washington, West Virginia, Wyoming) and 3 associate member states (Ohio, Tennessee, and Utah).

The goals of the project are to:

- Create common definitions for key items in the sales tax base
- Restrict the number of tax rates that a state may impose
- Provide for state-level administration of local sales taxes
- Create more uniform sourcing rules for interstate sales

- Simplify the administration of exempt transactions
- Develop uniform audit procedures
- Provide partial state funding of the system for collecting tax

The Streamlined Sales Tax Project website can be found at **www.stream-linedsalestax.org**

STUDY QUESTIONS

15. Which of the following statements is *not* true?

 a. Treaty permanent establishment provisions are not binding for state nexus purposes

 b. The Internet Tax Freedom Act allows "new" state or local taxes on Internet access

 c. Federal legislation that allows states to tax out-of-state companies that have an economic presence but no physical presence is one potential solution to ensure the integrity of state tax bases

 d. None of the above

MODULE 2: SALES AND USE TAXES — CHAPTER 5
Sales and Use Tax Base

This chapter discusses the imposition of sales and use taxes—including rates, items and transactions that are subject to sales and use taxes, and the broad categories of exemptions. It also explains how to determine the taxable sales price in a transaction.

LEARNING OBJECTIVES

Upon completing this chapter, the student will:

- Understand which items are generally subject to sales and use tax
- Be familiar with the Streamlined Sales Tax uniform definitions
- Identify which transactions are generally subject to sales and use tax
- Know the broad categories of exemptions
- Understand how the components of sales price are determined

OVERVIEW

Forty-five states and the District of Columbia impose a *sales tax* on retail sales of tangible personal property and selected services and a *use tax* on the use or consumption of tangible personal property and selected services.

Moreover, the legislatures of a number of states have granted the power to levy a local sales tax to their localities—including cities, towns, school districts, counties, and many other taxing jurisdictions.

One state (Alaska) does not impose state-level sales and use taxes, but a number of local jurisdictions do impose sales and use taxes. Recent estimates place the number of jurisdictions imposing tax in excess of 7,000.

Sales tax is typically imposed on the retail sale of tangible personal property—that is, the tax does not apply until a sale is consummated with the ultimate consumer of the product. State sales tax may be imposed on the sale, transfer, or exchange of any taxable item or the performance of a taxable service within the taxing jurisdiction.

The tax may take the form of a *privilege tax*, imposed directly on the seller for the privilege of engaging in the sales activity, or it may take the form of a *consumer tax*, imposed on the sale or purchase transaction itself. In either case, the seller is responsible and liable for payment of tax to the state, whether or not tax is collected or reimbursement is obtained.

States that impose a sales tax also impose a *complementary use tax* on the privilege of storing, using, or otherwise consuming taxable property or services within the taxing jurisdiction. In addition, virtually all states permit a credit for sales tax paid to other states if the tax was legally imposed and due. This complementary system of taxation was designed to result in the imposition of a sales or use tax on the purchase of all consumer goods, and to protect in-state merchants from inequitable competition from out-of-state sellers. The credit mechanism required by the Constitution attempts to prevent the imposition of a double tax. However, the application of the diverse state tax imposition statutes and credit provisions may result in double taxation in certain situations.

All states impose identical rates for state sales tax and use tax. This is to ensure the constitutionality of the taxing system and to avoid placing an undue burden or hardship on purchases from outside the tax jurisdiction.

The most recent attempt to impose different levels of sales and use tax was in Missouri. That system imposed an additional 1.5 percent local tax on purchases subject to use tax, and was struck down in 1994 by the U.S. Supreme Court in *Associated Industries v. Lohman* [114 US 1815 (1994)].

At the local level, jurisdictions that impose a local sales tax do not always enact a local use tax. Therefore, the applicable rate may vary depending upon whether the goods were purchased and shipped from a vendor located within the jurisdiction or from a vendor located outside the jurisdiction.

PLANNING POINTER

Taxpayers operating in a multistate environment need to consider carefully the rate that should be imposed on transactions. As a general rule, the rate imposed should be the rate in the destination where:

- The goods come to rest
- The goods are placed into service
- The goods are used
- The service is performed

Many taxpayers incorrectly impose other rates on transactions, such as the rate in the jurisdiction where the vendor-taxpayer or its headquarters is located, or in some other location.

STUDY QUESTION

1. A seller is responsible for payment of sales tax to the state, whether or not tax is collected. *True or False?*

ITEMS SUBJECT TO SALES TAX

Overview

Sales tax is imposed on the sale of tangible personal property and certain specifically enumerated services in most states. Because each state—and, sometimes, each local government jurisdiction—may have its own sales tax system, many variations exist in the types of items subject to sales tax.

Most local jurisdictions tax the same items taxed by the state, inasmuch as their authority to tax is granted by the state legislature. Accordingly, in many states, the state administers and collects both state and local sales taxes. Under the *Streamlined Sales Tax*, a compact of states designed to assist states in administering a simpler and more uniform sales and use tax system, the state serves as the collection agent for all local jurisdictions as a way of streamlining the filing process.

The distinction between items *subject to* sales tax and items that are *exempt from* sales tax (or *nontaxable*) is mainly the result of the politics and the economy of each state. For example, a state that has a strong manufacturing base, or wants to encourage one, might exempt manufacturing machinery and equipment from tax, and a state that has an agricultural base might enact exemptions for farming machinery and equipment.

Generally, all sales of tangible personal property are considered taxable, unless a specific exemption applies. Therefore, sellers should almost always default to collecting tax unless the purchaser provides the seller with a properly executed exemption certificate or other evidence that the transaction is tax exempt.

Virtually all states have enacted exclusions for specific items. Many states exclude items of necessity from sales tax, while taxing items of discretionary consumption or luxury items. Excluding basic necessities from tax reduces the regressivity in the tax system by placing the burden of taxation on those who can afford to purchase items that are not necessities.

Hence, many states do *not* tax groceries or prescription drugs, but they do tax prepared foods, restaurant meals, furniture, and art. Such distinctions have led to some confusion for grocery and convenience stores. For example, prepared foods purchased at the deli in the grocery store may be considered taxable, since they are readily consumable, but the same items purchased in an unprepared form would be treated as exempt groceries.

Several states tax food and beverages, including water, when they are sold at a shopping mall, because it is assumed that their consumption at the mall is for the convenience of the purchaser. Generally, these items sold at a grocery store would not be taxable. Other states tax water if it is flavored or carbonated or sold in a bottle, but not when it is sold by the local utility for residential consumption. Therefore, taxpayers operating grocery and convenience stores need to exercise caution in determining their taxable and nontaxable sales classifications.

States also use sales tax exemptions as incentives to encourage certain types of purchases. For instance, some states exempt employee safety equipment or first-aid supplies as a means of reducing the costs of those items to employers. A number of states exempt purchases of manufacturing equipment from sales tax if the equipment is used in the production process.

Other states have broadened the manufacturing exemption to include equipment used in research and development activities in an attempt to increase the rate of capital formation in the state, create new jobs, and develop new technology. States that do not provide such exemptions are seeing the effects as businesses relocate to states that do offer them.

Most states aggressively seek to expand their manufacturing base because of the positive impact on their economy. States often bid against each other for a new plant or the relocation of an existing plant. If all nontax factors are equivalent, the state able to deliver the greatest tax relief and other incentives is generally awarded the facility. An exemption for manufacturing machinery and equipment is often an important component of a state's tax incentive package.

Other Issues

The *true object* of the sale is typically the key in determining whether or not and to what extent a transaction is subject to tax. This test looks through the transaction and determines if the intent of the purchaser was to acquire tangible personal property or if the tangible personal property was incidental to the rendering of a service.

Advertising Brochures. Some states apply the sales tax to the transfer of mass-produced advertising brochures but not to charges for creative services used in the production of such brochures. Such a shift makes the materials used in providing creative services taxable to the provider of those services, and it makes the provider of the brochures exempt from tax on the materials used to create the brochures. However, it obligates the provider to collect sales tax on their sale to the end-user.

Complications can arise when the same party provides both the creative effort and the finished piece of tangible personal property. In such a case, most states will deem the entire transaction to be subject to tax—including the creative work that might otherwise be exempt.

Building Materials. The sales tax treatment of building materials can be complicated by the way in which the materials are used. If they are purchased for use in making improvements, repairs, or modifications to real estate by the owner of the real estate or a construction contractor, the materials are generally taxable to the purchaser in almost every state and, in most states, to the contractor as the consumer of the materials purchased.

If the materials are used by the contractor to make, modify, or repair tangible personal property that is then sold by the contractor, the materials can be exempt as items purchased for resale. The contractor is then required to collect sales tax from the ultimate purchaser of the property.

If the materials are used by the purchaser to make, modify, or repair tangible personal property owned by the purchaser, the materials used by the purchaser are taxable at the time of purchase.

Shipping Supplies. Several states vary their sales tax treatment of shipping containers and packaging materials, depending on whether the item is returnable or nonreturnable. Returnable containers or packaging materials are generally taxable. Nonreturnable containers or packaging materials are exempt from tax.

In addition, some states distinguish taxable and nontaxable packaging based on whether the packaging accompanies the product purchased to the ultimate consumer. Under that criterion, packaging used to transfer the product to a distributor would be taxable. In states that tax returnable containers, tax would apply to the repair and maintenance of the items as well.

Publications. Many states also differentiate between magazines and newspapers purchased singly in a store from those purchased via subscription, by providing an exemption for the subscription amount. In a few states, additional tests are applied to determine taxability of subscriptions.

For example, for the subscription to qualify as exempt, the publication must be of the type that would typically be sold to the general public at a newsstand or similar place of sale. Therefore, special-interest publications or publications of organizations and associations would *not* qualify for the exemption if purchased by subscription.

Streamlined Sales Tax (SST) Uniform Definitions for Tax Base. Uniform definitions represent one of the most fundamental components of the Streamlined Sales Tax (SST). The SST developed a glossary of uniform definitions from which a state would define its tax base. The glossary includes those items or services that could be taxed by a state. Legislatures still determine what is taxable or exempt but must agree to use the uniform definitions. Because American businesses now operate in a borderless and even global economy, uniform definitions would simplify multistate compliance by providing a common base for all jurisdictions. In fact, tax software could be coded based on a matrix of states, defined property and services, and taxability determinations by the state.

An SST state is expected to adopt all items specifically mentioned in a definition. A state may *not* vary from that definition, except as provided in the agreement between the states.

For example, the SST has defined food and food ingredients and various subcategories of food, including candy, dietary supplements, soft drinks, and prepared food. A state may choose to tax all food and food ingredients, which include candy, dietary supplements, soft drinks, and prepared food.

On the other hand, a state may choose to exempt food and food ingredients as defined by the SST but tax one or more of the subcategories as defined by the SST. A state may not, however, choose to tax a subcategory such as candy and exempt a particular kind of candy that falls within the subcategory.

The SST has also defined five mutually exclusive categories of clothing:

1. Clothing
2. Fur Clothing
3. Clothing accessories
4. Sport or recreational equipment
5. Protective equipment

A state may tax or exempt any or all of these categories but may not vary from the definitions of these categories. So, for example, a state may not choose to exempt one item within the category of protective equipment.

The SST has also defined purchase price, retail sale, sales price, delivery charges, bundled transactions, telecommunications non-recurring charges, and direct mail.

Other definitions include but are not limited to those for tangible personal property, computer, computer software, delivered electronically, electronic, load and leave, prewritten computer software, prosthetic devices, durable medical equipment, mobility enhancing equipment, prescription, over-the-counter drugs, grooming and hygiene products, and lease or rental.

In addition, the SST has definitions for digital products, food and food products, healthcare, telecommunications, and sales tax holidays.

> **PLANNING POINTER**
>
> To maximize their opportunities for tax exemption, taxpayers need to consider both the nature of the item and its use. An item may be taxable as a general category of purchase, but, if it can be reclassified as something else, it may be considered exempt.
>
> For example, if clothing is purchased as wearing apparel, it is considered to be taxable in many states. However, If clothing is purchased for employee safety or to protect a manufactured product from contamination, it may be considered to be an exempt part of the manufacturing process.

> **CAUTION**
>
> Under the rules of statutory construction in most states, *all* sales of tangible personal property are deemed to be taxable—unless some specific exemption or exclusion applies.
>
> Taxpayers need to inform their vendors of the tax status of their purchases, particularly if they could make both taxable and nontaxable purchases. In addition, taxpayers should have self-assessment procedures in place to remit use tax voluntarily when vendors fail to bill the tax at the time of purchase.

STUDY QUESTION

> **2.** Many states exclude which one of the following items from sales tax?
> **a.** Luxury items
> **b.** Items of discretionary consumption
> **c.** Items of necessity
> **d.** Restaurant foods

TRANSACTIONS SUBJECT TO SALES AND USE TAXES

Overview

Sales taxes were first imposed in the United States in the 1930s. Many early sales and use taxes were generally levied on a narrow list of goods. In most states, goods were exempt unless a specific provision made them taxable.

Sales taxes were designed to apply principally to tangible personal property, but, as the need for funds grew at the state and local levels, the base on which the taxes were imposed was steadily broadened. Sales taxes have been expanded in most states to apply to *all* sales of tangible personal property and certain services, especially services involving the transfer of tangible personal property. Under the general rules of statutory construction in most states, sales tax applies to all tangible personal property sold, unless a specific exemption applies.

Over the past several decades, the importance of sales and use taxes as a source of state revenue has increased. Currently, 45 states and the District of Columbia impose broad-based sales and use taxes. The only states that do *not* impose such taxes are Alaska, Delaware, Montana, New Hampshire, and Oregon.

As mentioned previously, many of the local jurisdictions in Alaska impose sales taxes. Delaware imposes a tax on leases of tangible personal property. In addition, certain other taxes may apply to specific services or sales in those five states. For example, New Hampshire imposes a tax on communications services.

In recent years, sales and use taxes have been expanded to include in their scope a significant portion of the service sector of the economy. Thirty years ago, the service sector made up only a small portion of the U.S. economy, but the economy has evolved from a manufacturing-based economy to a service economy. Afraid of losing their tax base, states responded to that change by gradually increasing the services that are subject to tax. Most states have been hesitant to impose a general tax on all services after the unsuccessful attempts by Florida (in 1987) and Massachusetts (in 1991). Both states were forced to rescind the general sales and use tax on services shortly after they were enacted.

With the rapid growth of the Internet, states are beginning to look at transactions that flow through that medium to determine whether any taxable transactions are occurring or any new categories of transactions that would be taxable are being created. Just as controversy arose from computerization, several states were expected to aggressively apply taxation rules to the Internet until the moratorium on imposing new state and local taxes on electronic commerce was enacted by Congress and then extended through November 1, 2014.

Application of Sales Taxes

Some states, such as Hawaii and New Mexico, levy a sales tax that somewhat resembles a gross receipts tax, which applies to most economic activity occurring in the state. Even in these states, the tax is, for the most part, designed to be passed on to the ultimate consumer.

In addition to the sale of tangible personal property, sales and use taxes may apply to certain service charges made in connection with the sale of tangible personal property. An example is the freight charge accompanying the sale of tangible personal property. In some states, this charge is considered taxable as part of the sale of the tangible personal property to which it relates. In other states, this charge is not taxable if it is stated separately.

Shipping and Handling Charges. The taxation of *shipping and handling* charges can also be complex. Most states take the position that a charge for shipping and handling is taxable, presumably because that charge is tainted by the handling component.

Handling may be characterized as a service that is integrally related to the underlying sale of tangible personal property. Many states do not tax a separately stated charge for shipping alone, provided title to the property being sold passes at the seller's location and the goods are sent by common carrier. Some states also impose their sales tax on trade discounts or early payment discounts.

Installation Charges. Installation charges are another example of service charges that may be taxable as part of the sale of tangible personal property. In many states, ancillary services such as installation are not taxable if the charges for them are stated *separately* from the sale of the tangible personal property.

Mixed Transactions. Transactions involving the sale of both tangible personal property and services (i.e., mixed transactions) can be difficult to analyze. If a lump-sum charge is listed on the invoice, many states take the position that the entire invoice amount—including the otherwise nontaxable services—are subject to sales and use taxes.

A few states have taken the position that if even a small amount of tangible personal property accompanies a nontaxable service, the entire transaction is taxable; however, many states are less strict in their treatment of such transactions.

To determine taxability, those states generally use a test commonly referred to as the *true object test*. Under that test, if the true object desired by the customer is the nontaxable service rather than the tangible personal property, the transaction is not taxable. However, if the true object desired by the customer is the tangible personal property, then the entire transaction is taxable.

> **EXAMPLE**
>
> In the case of a contract drafted by an attorney, the true object desired by the client is the attorney's professional services rather than the paper on which the contract is written.

When dealing with mixed transactions, it is important to carefully consult the state's statutes, cases, and rulings. The distinctions that are made are often very fine and the questions may not always be answered by the application of logic.

As discussed above, the determination of taxability or exemption depends on:

- Category of persons or businesses
- Type of transaction
- Type of goods or services at issue

In many states that levy a sales and use tax, the incidence of taxation falls on the ultimate consumer or user. Accordingly, most states grant a resale exemption to the seller of tangible personal property because, by definition, any vendor who resells the tangible personal property cannot be the final consumer.

A number of states also have an exemption for transfers of tangible personal property that occur in a liquidation, merger, or acquisition. These exemptions are carefully circumscribed; therefore, it is prudent to carefully examine the statute or regulation and the transaction at issue before concluding that the exemption applies.

Leases. Many states afford similar treatment to purchases by a lessor for lease to a third party. Such exemptions are narrowly construed, with jurisdictions distinguishing, for example, between a *true lease,* in which the lessee returns the property to the lessor at the end of the lease term, and other leases involving an option to purchase at the end of the lease term or that provide both equipment and operating personnel. In the case of pure rentals, the lessor generally acquires the property without the imposition of a sales and use tax, but the rental stream is subject to the tax.

Casual and Isolated Sales. Many states provide an exemption for casual and isolated sales. This sort of exemption is generally provided for a person who is not normally in the business of making sales, or who is not normally in the business of making sales of the type for which the exemption is sought.

Not all states have a casual or isolated sale exemption, and many that do impose several restrictions on it. A common restriction is the number of sales per year for which the exemption may be claimed. For example, if a taxpayer has three such sales in a year in a state that allows the exemption for only two sales, it is possible that the exemption will not apply to *any* of its sales that year.

Computer Software. Computer software is typically licensed rather than sold, but most states treat licensing transactions as the sale of the underlying goods and include licensing within the definition of sales. Off-the-shelf, or canned, software generally is taxable, while the licensing or sale of custom-designed software is normally treated as a sale of services or intangible property and is, therefore, not subject to tax.

Several commentators have suggested that all software sold should be treated as the sale of an intangible because the tangible material that is transferred on the disk or tape is inconsequential—the true object desired by the customer is the intangible. Most states have not chosen to follow this line of reasoning, analogizing the sale of software to the sale of a book, which is *always* taxable. A number of states, however, have agreed that computer software that is transferred electronically is not subject to sales or use tax because no tangible property exists on which to impose tax.

Telecommunications. Most states apply their sales taxes to the sale of telecommunications. Many states tax only intrastate telecommunications, but a number of states tax both intrastate and interstate telecommunications.

A dilemma has arisen over how to tax prepaid telephone cards through which the customer buys a fixed number of minutes to use on long-distance calls. When this product first became available, most states taxed the underlying telephone service, but this service is difficult to track. It is much easier for sellers and the states to tax the cards at the point of sale. Consequently, over the last several years most states have enacted legislation or promulgated regulations to tax the cards at the point of sale—in the same way that all other tangible personal property is taxed.

Warranty Contracts. Warranty or service contracts covering equipment have become increasingly common. In recent years many states have enacted legislation governing the taxation of these contracts and the services provided under them.

A state that does not tax the repair of tangible personal property would not tax a warranty contract covering repairs of equipment. Among the states that do tax repairs, almost all of them have chosen to tax either the sale of a warranty contract or repairs made under such a contract. Only a few states tax both the sale of the warranty and any subsequent repairs made under it.

Other Transactions. Credit and conditional sales often involve the transfer of tangible personal property that would be subject to tax. The consideration given is a 'promise to pay,' rather than the actual payment.

Of particular interest in such transactions is the treatment of the interest component or financing charge, which is usually exempt when separately stated. Such treatment differs from the treatment of the interest component in a leasing transaction, which is usually *not* separately stated and is generally taxable in states that tax the lease stream payments.

Barter transactions are exchanges of tangible personal property in which the consideration given is something other than cash. Nevertheless, most states treat such transactions as sales that are subject to sales and use tax.

Most states treat intercompany sales as purchases from a third party, regardless of whether or not the seller and buyer are members of the same consolidated group for federal or state income tax purposes. Accordingly, if the selling affiliate has nexus in the state in which the property is transferred, it must collect and remit sales tax on the transaction. If the selling affiliate does not have nexus, the purchasing affiliate must self-assess use tax on the purchase.

Use Taxes

Use tax is generally imposed on the storage, use, or other consumption of a taxable item within a state. It does not apply if the state has previously imposed a sales tax on the same item, unless a subsequent taxable use is made of the item by another taxpayer.

When one state has imposed a sales tax on the sale of a taxable item that is subsequently imported into a second state, the second state may impose a use tax on that item. All states that impose a use tax in such a situation permit the taxpayer to claim a credit for the sales tax properly paid to the other state or legally imposed by the other state. If the first state's sales tax rate is greater than the second state's use tax rate, the purchaser owes no additional use tax. If the first state's sales tax rate is *less* than the second state's use tax rate, the user will owe the net amount to the second state.

A state's credit statute should be carefully reviewed to ensure that it provides for a credit against the particular tax paid. A few states allow a credit only against another state's sales tax and not another state's use tax. Another important caveat is that the first state's tax must have been lawfully imposed and paid.

> **EXAMPLE**
>
> If the Commerce Clause would have prevented the first state from imposing tax on the transaction, the second state will probably *not* allow the credit against tax paid to the first state.

Broad Interpretations. Many states interpret their use taxes quite broadly to apply to any physical manipulation of, or the exercise of any right or power over, tangible personal property. If a person or business makes *any* use whatsoever of tangible personal property in a state, the language of the state's definition of *taxable use* might cause the person to be liable for use tax on the value of the property.

> **CAUTION**
>
> The mere storage of an item in most states triggers a use tax liability.

> **EXAMPLE: USE TAX**
>
> In *Cole Bros. Circus v. Huddleston* [Tenn. Ct. App. 1993], a circus was found liable for use tax on equipment used in a state for only 29 days. Since there generally is no statutory mechanism to apportion use tax according to the time property is used in a state, the taxpayer must pay use tax on the full value of the property.
>
> However, if the circus had previously paid a sales or use tax on its equipment to another state, a credit for that tax would have been available. Also, if used out-of-state for six months or more, the item is *not* taxable if introduced into a subsequent state for use in that state.

EXAMPLE: USE TAX

A merchant mails catalogs to another state. The catalogs are printed by a commercial printer and mailed by a third-party into the taxing state. Though the merchant never actually touches the catalogs, it has repeatedly been assessed use tax on the value of the catalogs.

The rationale for upholding tax on these catalogs is that the merchant has used them in its business.

EXAMPLE: SAMPLE MERCHANDISE

A seller of goods gives away free samples of merchandise. The seller must generally remit use tax on that merchandise because the seller is considered to have used that merchandise in its business.

States vary as to the tax base of sample goods. Some states tax only the cost of materials, but some also include the cost of labor or overhead in the tax base of samples.

As noted above, almost all use taxes are applied to the storage of tangible personal property. Some states, however, have enacted an exemption for goods that are stored in and subsequently exported from the state.

Exemptions

When a sale or transfer is made, taxability depends on the transaction's purpose or effect. States have ordinarily employed broad definitions in determining taxable subjects and transactions. Generally, all transfers are considered taxable unless a specific exemption applies. Whether an exemption exists is largely a result of the political and economic issues affecting the state.

Exemptions generally fall into the following four broad categories:

1. **Identity of the purchaser.** An example is the federal government, which is exempt from a direct tax imposed by the states. Another example is a charitable organization, which in many states is exempt from sales and use tax.
2. **Character of the item sold.** Included in this category are food, clothing, and prescription drugs, which are exempt from tax in many states.
3. **Use to which the product will be put.** Examples include goods purchased for resale, which all of the states exempt from tax, and manufacturing machinery, which is exempt from sales and use tax in many states.
4. **Nature of the transaction.** Many states exempt from sales and use tax certain transactions, such as casual or isolated sales, incorporations, and nontaxable reorganizations.

PLANNING POINTER

Failure to self-assess use tax is a common sales and use tax audit adjustment. Many taxpayers fail to implement a use tax procedure on purchases from unregistered and out-of-state vendors. By implementing a simple procedure to review all ex-tax purchases where the vendor failed to bill tax on otherwise taxable purchases, taxpayers can substantially reduce their audit exposure.

Generally, the review involves isolating purchases where the seller failed to bill tax despite a purchase order stating that the transaction was taxable. Regular review and correct disposition of such purchases can greatly reduce exposure to audits and audit deficiencies.

CAUTION

Controversies often arise regarding whether a sale is a sale of a service or of tangible personal property. The implications regarding the imposition of tax on the buyer and seller in these instances may be substantial.

Generally, the courts apply a true object test to establish the intent of the parties in the transaction. If the seller is performing a service (unless the service is specifically enumerated as a taxable service), tax will be imposed on the materials and supplies used by the provider of the service but *not* on the gross receipts of the seller.

Conversely, if the sale is deemed to be a sale of tangible personal property, the seller's purchase of supplies and materials used is exempt from tax as a purchase for resale. However, unless the customer was exempt, the seller would be obligated to collect tax on the gross receipts from the performance of the contract.

STUDY QUESTIONS

3. Which one of the following would *not* be subject to sales tax in most states?
  a. Shipping and handling
  b. Custom-designed software
  c. Canned software
  d. Prepaid phone cards

---

4. Which one of the following is true?
  a. Many states provide an exemption for casual or isolated sales.
  b. Most states do *not* tax barter transactions.
  c. A use tax may *never* be imposed on an item for which a sales tax has been imposed.
  d. Exemptions generally fall into five broad categories.

DETERMINATION OF SALES PRICE

In general, sales and use taxes are imposed on the total sales price of a taxable sale. The rule applies whether the sale is of tangible personal property or of taxable services. The basis of measuring the sales or purchase price on which to calculate sales and use tax varies among the states and often is a disputed subject. The items included in the sales and use tax base are usually specified in detail in the states' statutes and are, therefore, generally construed narrowly by the courts. Most statutes include in the sales and use tax base all costs incurred before the transfer of title.

In most situations, the tax is computed on the amount of consideration received for the taxable item or service. In barter transactions, the value of property or services received in exchange for taxable items or services typically determines the sales price.

Coupons, Rebates, and Discounts. The treatment of coupons, rebates, and discounts usually varies among states, and even within each state.

Cash discounts are generally excluded from the sales price subject to tax if paid by the seller rather than by a third party and if paid as part of the sales transaction. As a result, for example, manufacturer rebates generally do *not* reduce the sales price subject to tax.

Trade-in allowances are treated differently from state to state—some states impose sales tax only on the difference between the total sales price and the amount allowed for trade-in, while others impose tax on the total sales price and disregard the trade-in value.

Excise or Import Taxes. Generally, no reduction in sales price is allowed for excise or import taxes paid by the seller. It is important to consult the rules of each state, however, because specific taxes may be given special treatment. For example, in *U.S. Sprint Communications Co. v. Commissioner* [No. C5-97-1993 (Minn. May 21, 1998)], the Minnesota Supreme Court ruled that the federal excise tax collected by Sprint from its customers is *not* part of the gross receipts received from sales of long-distance telephone service and therefore is not included in the tax base upon which the sales tax is imposed.

Credit Transactions. The sales price subject to tax usually does *not* include interest charged for credit if it is separately stated. If the debt arising from a credit sale becomes worthless, the seller is normally allowed a reduction in taxable receipts or a tax credit or a deduction—depending on the time of worthlessness, as well as the reporting period and other rules of the state in question.

A debt does not necessarily become worthless merely because the property sold on credit is repossessed. On the other hand, if a seller cancels a sale by refunding the purchase price and accepting the property as a return, whether it was originally a credit or cash sale, the return *does* generally give rise to a reduction in taxable receipts or a tax credit or deduction—although a particular state may impose time limits or other restrictions on such allowances.

Shipping Charges. If separately stated, shipping charges imposed after the sale takes place are often excluded from the sales price subject to tax. Still, fees identified as being for shipping and handling typically are taxable, even when the fee relates solely to shipping charges. Absent commercial considerations, sellers should always separately state shipping charges as a protective measure. Consult the rules of the state in question to see if the exclusion is available.

Labor, service, or installation charges may be treated in the same manner as shipping charges in many states—that is, some states do not impose sales and use taxes on them if such charges are separately identified on the invoice. However, several states do tax such services when they relate to the purchase of taxable tangible personal property.

Mixed Transactions. When a transaction involves the provision of nontaxable services in connection with a taxable sale, the charge for the nontaxable services may not be subject to tax if separately stated. When a single charge is made for the entire transaction, however, most states will require a determination of whether the transaction was primarily a taxable sale with an incidental provision of nontaxable services or primarily the provision of nontaxable services with an incidental transfer of tangible personal property. In the former case, if the charge for nontaxable services is not separately stated, sales tax will be imposed on the total charge. In the latter case, tax will not be imposed on the total charge, but the service provider will be considered the end user of the incidental tangible personal property involved and sales or use tax will be imposed on the cost of such property.

As for sales of taxable services, a few states take the position that the service provider is liable for the collection of sales and use tax from customers on the total itemized charges for performing the taxable service—including any expenses incurred by the service provider's employees (e.g., mileage costs, auto rental charges, hotel bills).

Many states exempt separately stated freight and installation or repair charges, so taxpayers wishing to minimize sales tax on customers' purchases should separately state freight and installation or repair charges on their invoices.

Vendors including these charges in the selling price of the item purchased are forcing their customers to incur unnecessary tax expense. Ideally, the separately stated charges should represent the actual costs charged to the purchaser and not some overall estimate based on average costs.

CAUTION

To reduce the administrative costs associated with taxes, taxpayers dealing in a multistate environment often make the mistake of applying one state's rules on selling price inclusions to all taxable sales—regardless of the state of destination.

Unfortunately, because any two states are the same in all respects when it comes to determining the sales price that is subject to tax, taxpayers applying this treatment to all their sales increase their audit exposure.

Some of the common differences in state tax rules include the following:

- Cash and trade discounts
- Trade-in allowances
- Freight charges
- Bad debts
- Installation charges
- Repair charges

STUDY QUESTION

5. Which of the following generally is *not* included in the total taxable sales price?

   a. Interest charged for credit, separately stated
   b. Excise taxes
   c. Manufacturer rebates
   d. All of the above are generally included in the sales price

MODULE 2: SALES AND USE TAXES — CHAPTER 6
Pre-Audit Strategies and Opportunities

This chapter discusses strategies and opportunities that could reduce audit exposure when a taxpayer is preparing for a sales and use tax audit.

LEARNING OBJECTIVES

Upon completing this chapter, the student will:

- Understand the issues involved in scheduling an audit
- Know when and how to negotiate with an auditor
- Comprehend how to control the information flow between the taxpayer and the auditor
- Be familiar with confirmation letters
- Understand when a taxpayer should agree to a waiver of the statute of limitations
- Understand how and why self-audits and reverse audits should be performed, and how they differ
- Be familiar with refund claim procedures and record retention issues
- Understand how to respond to audit and nexus questionnaires
- Be familiar with voluntary disclosure agreements and available amnesty programs

INITIAL AUDIT CONTACT AND THE AUDIT TONE

Overview

The initial contact in an audit is extremely important, as it sets the tone for the remainder of the audit. The challenge in the early stages of the audit is to take steps that will help a taxpayer gain a measure of control over the audit process. Although it is not possible to completely control the audit process, communicating to the auditor an intention to be cooperative and professional but also firm and knowledgeable can contribute to the success of the audit.

State statutes confer broad authority on the state to audit a taxpayer's records. In a system that relies heavily on voluntary compliance, the state must have substantial authority to audit taxpayers so that compliance can be verified. A weak state audit function would likely result in large-scale evasion.

> **CAUTION**
>
> Auditors generally have administrative subpoena powers that give them the authority to compel taxpayers to produce information. However, this authority is rarely exercised. It is generally reserved for extremely unco-operative taxpayers.

Scheduling the Audit

Understanding the audit plan, as well as the time constraints that it places on an auditor, can have significant implications for the outcome of the audit. For example, delaying the discussion of a difficult topic until later in the auditor's visit may result in less focus on sensitive details due to the auditor's haste to wrap up the audit. Likewise, providing an auditor with a refund schedule toward the end of an audit may result in a more limited review of the refund claim. Therefore, taxpayers should carefully consider the timing of the disclosure of important transactions or activities.

Depending upon the taxpayer and the level of activity in a particular jurisdiction, an audit can take anywhere from a few days to several months, or even years to complete.

Most auditors have a limited amount of time to complete the audit. Time limits are used to measure their efficiency. In addition, constraints related to travel can limit the amount of time an auditor has to spend on an audit.

For example, states frequently purchase nonrefundable airline tickets for their auditors. This makes it difficult for an auditor to expand the scope of his or her review without returning for an additional period of time. If an additional period cannot be scheduled for several weeks or months, the audit will remain open the entire time. Consequently, auditors must evaluate whether there are sufficient issues to warrant another trip.

Of course, the scheduling issue is not a factor in every audit. Auditors often have great latitude in the scheduling and execution of their audit. Therefore, each audit must be evaluated early in the process and an appropriate decision made regarding the auditor's time to complete the audit.

As mentioned above, an audit can take anywhere from a few days to a few years to complete. Several factors that can affect the duration of an audit:

- Size of the taxpayer
- Relative operations in the state
- Scope of activities in the state

> ### EXAMPLE
>
> Auditing a large manufacturing operation will take considerably longer than auditing a sales office because of the significantly greater number of potentially taxable transactions that have to be reviewed and the complexity of the transactions.

The greatest amount of time will be spent from the point of sample selection and transaction review through the providing of a preliminary assessment. This portion of the audit is time consuming because it involves the manual review of the transactions on an individual basis and the negotiation of the final taxable amounts with the auditor.

An auditor can question hundreds or even thousands of transactions. Each one must then be reviewed by the taxpayer and a determination made as to whether tax is due or an exemption applies.

> ### PLANNING POINTER
>
> When scheduling an audit, you must allow time to respond to the auditor's requests for information and resolve open issues. It may not be prudent to schedule one audit immediately following another if you will not have the opportunity to resolve questions from the earlier audit.

Arguably, there is never a convenient time to undergo an audit. The intense scrutiny and the exposure to additional expense make the situation stressful under the best of circumstances. However, as an audit may not be delayed indefinitely, the issue is when it will be least disruptive to the taxpayer's schedule.

While auditors have a great deal of authority regarding the timing of an audit, taxpayers have rights to exert as well.

> ### EXAMPLE
>
> A taxpayer who knows that the first quarter is the busiest time of year in the tax department can refrain from scheduling an audit during this time. A taxpayer who is fully scheduled with audits can suggest a later date that is more convenient.

Although there may be pressure to hastily schedule an audit, doing so can be unwise. Not being able to devote the necessary time to resolving audit issues can aggravate the auditor and impact the final assessment. Delaying the start of an audit because of workload constraints may be preferable to impeding the auditor during the course of the audit.

PLANNING POINTER

The following factors should be considered when scheduling an audit:

- Anticipated effort required to complete the audit
- Availability of personnel to work on the audit
- Workload of individuals who will be assigned to the audit
- Auditor's schedule and anticipated length of stay
- Company position on the issuance of a waiver of the statute of limitations if the auditor requests one in exchange for a delay in the start of the audit
- Prior audit experience with the state

Additional factors can enter into a decision regarding the scheduling of an audit. A situation that can create urgency to schedule an audit is a visit by an auditor who rarely comes to a particular locale.

Auditors sometimes visit an area for a period of time with no plans of returning. In such a case, it is more difficult to refuse a request for audit scheduling or delay the commencement of an audit due to taxpayer inconvenience. The taxpayer's convenience is generally subordinated to the state's right to perform the audit because of the scheduling problem that would ensue if the auditor were unable to perform the audit while in the vicinity of the taxpayer. Therefore, in scheduling an audit with an out-of-state auditor, the taxpayer must determine whether the auditor is under this time constraint. If so, it may not be possible to refuse the audit appointment, unless the auditor's request is unreasonable. The auditor will insist that he or she be allowed to perform the audit, unless it is absolutely impossible, which is generally not the case.

CAUTION

It is rarely impossible to accommodate a request for an audit, particularly if the request is made several weeks or months in advance. Since auditors possess the threat of a jeopardy assessment, taxpayers can be forced to schedule the audit, even if the timing is not optimal from their perspective.

To reduce the scope of the audit when time constraints exist, a taxpayer should use the following strategies:

- **Compress fieldwork through the use of assist reports and systems support.** Companies can often provide special reports to augment the auditor's review or to assist the taxpayer in responding to requests.

- **Forward records to the auditor after some preliminary review to allow the auditor to complete portions of the fieldwork at the office.** This approach can pose risks for the taxpayer by providing the auditor with unlimited time to review transactions and contact vendors, and it should only be used in areas where the taxpayer anticipates limited exposure.

- **Have the taxpayer perform some portion of the work, subject to auditor review.** This approach, sometimes called a *managed audit*, is an emerging concept in state and local tax auditing. Ohio has adopted a managed audit program that allows interest and penalty relief in exchange for assistance in executing the audit. The taxpayer and auditor agree to the areas of review after some preliminary analysis by the auditor. The taxpayer then reviews the transactions in areas identified by the auditor and prepares a summary of errors for the auditor. Once the errors have been agreed upon by both parties, an audit assessment is prepared. Taxpayers choosing approaches such as this need to be aware of the legal implications. Failure to identify transactions or areas of exposure in a voluntary program could have serious consequences. In addition, many taxpayers have expressed concern about the additional workload that would be required for them, rather than the state auditor, to complete the audit. For these reasons, it appears that many companies are relying on the traditional approach and requiring the auditor to perform the fieldwork, despite the incentives granted by the state.

- **Identify transactions that may be excluded from review for some reason and propose the exclusions to the auditor.** Very often, certain classes of transactions, such as those involving office supplies, shop supplies, or advertising materials, can be audited using alternative procedures because of the way the transactions are recorded on the books of the taxpayer. Eliminating the detailed review of these transactions by voucher and auditing by an allocation or distribution procedure or report can eliminate a substantial amount of work. For taxpayers that have special procedures in place to handle certain transactions, the risk of duplicate assessment is reduced by using these procedures.

- **Employ greater use of sampling to reduce the amount of transactional review.** If possible, suggest an alternative sampling methodology to the auditor that will reduce the effort required to complete the audit and still provide a valid result. One common criticism of state audit samples is that they over-sample to obtain a result that the taxpayer will accept. A sample of several thousand transactions achieves the same audit result as a sample of several hundred transactions in a properly constructed sample.

Note that some of the strategies discussed above may not apply in all situations. An auditor is likely to agree to alternative procedures only when the risk presented by unaudited transactions is minimal. Furthermore, the state may be unwilling to deviate from its established sampling techniques regardless of the reasons. When a taxpayer's only activity in the state is a sales office with few assets or other purchases, the auditor might be inclined to shorten the review time through the use of an alternative procedure.

STUDY QUESTIONS

1. Which of the following statements is true?

    a. Taxpayers should *never* delay the discussion of a difficult topic until late in the auditor's visit.

    b. An auditor can only question a *limited* number of transactions.

    c. An audit must *always* be completed within a year.

    d. A taxpayer that is fully scheduled with audits can suggest a later date for the audit that is more convenient.

2. To reduce the scope of the audit when time constraints exist, a taxpayer should generally do all of the following *except:*

    a. Compress fieldwork through the use of assist reports

    b. Forward records to the auditor after some preliminary review in areas where the taxpayer is concerned about exposure

    c. Perform a managed audit

    d. Employ greater use of sampling

Negotiations

The majority of negotiation activity occurs in the latter stages of the audit fieldwork, but taxpayers should be attuned to opportunities for negotiation in all phases of the audit. In the pre-audit phase, taxpayers may have the opportunity to negotiate in the areas discussed below.

Audit Period

While the audit period is generally set by statute, taxpayers have decisions to make regarding the granting of a waiver of the statute of limitations. In the pre-audit stage, auditors will occasionally propose audit periods that are outside the statute of limitations without discussing the necessity of securing a waiver. Taxpayers need to be aware of their right to grant or not grant a waiver as they deem appropriate under the circumstances. The mere fact that an auditor proposes an audit period does not mean that the auditor has the authority, without taxpayer approval, to execute the audit for that period of time.

Auditors sometimes assume that the taxpayer will automatically agree to grant a waiver. However, the taxpayer should always weigh an auditor's request for a waiver carefully. If the taxpayer can provide a good reason for not granting the waiver, the auditor may drop the issue.

For example, many taxpayers refuse to grant waivers before the audit fieldwork has begun. As long as the taxpayer can schedule the audit within a reasonable time period, it is difficult for the auditor to force the taxpayer to sign the waiver, or for the auditor to issue a jeopardy assessment. Taxpayers can always argue that the jurisdiction did not contact them soon enough to complete the audit within the statutory period.

Sampling Methodology

Auditors often seek agreement from the taxpayer on the sampling methodology to be used in the audit. This usually occurs during a preliminary telephone conversation with the taxpayer. These conversations are an opportunity for taxpayers to advance proposals that are in their interest. Auditors sometimes use these conversations as an opportunity to fulfill statutory requirements that an agreement be reached with the taxpayer on sampling. Therefore, taxpayers should be wary of making any quick, over-the-phone agreements on sampling.

It is highly recommended that the auditor make all sampling proposals in writing, so that they can be studied before any firm agreement is reached. On the telephone, taxpayers should go no further than providing some assurances that a sample is an acceptable audit methodology, subject to a formal review of the state's sampling technique.

CAUTION

Although some states, such as New York and Ohio, have statutes that require taxpayer approval or that attempt to obtain taxpayer approval of the sampling methodology, the majority of states give the state the authority to impose a sampling methodology on the taxpayer, whether the taxpayer agrees or not.

PLANNING POINTER

Even though most states are *not* required to obtain taxpayer agreement on the sampling methodology, they do not want to contest sampling issues on appeal. Therefore, the state may be willing to accommodate a taxpayer's special sampling request as long as it does not compromise the overall audit and does not require any significant additional effort on the part of the state.

Scope of Review

In the early stages of an audit, the auditor is generally open to discussing issues involving the scope of the audit. Taxpayers should freely discourage the auditing of transactions that they feel may not be necessary. Although auditors may be skeptical of the taxpayer's motives, they can sometimes be convinced to restrict the scope of certain reviews.

Even if the auditor does not agree to forgo auditing certain transactions, he or she may be persuaded to modify the scope of the review, subject to further verification. Any time the audit fieldwork time is reduced, the taxpayer's exposure is reduced as well.

> **EXAMPLE**
>
> If the taxpayer has a special accounting procedure for marketing materials, the auditor may agree to audit the distribution reporting procedure rather than the specific purchases of marketing materials, which may not be traceable to any state from the voucher records. This can save time for both the auditor and taxpayer.

Entities Subject to Audit

Early in an audit, the auditor will be uncertain about which entities have nexus in the tax jurisdiction and should be included in the audit. If some of the taxpayer's entities have nexus and others do not, the taxpayer should *refuse* to allow the auditor to audit the books or transactions of entities *without* nexus.

> **NOTE**
>
> The auditor's authority to audit an entity is predicated upon that entity's doing business in the state. If the entity does not have nexus, the state and the auditor have no authority to exert over that entity.

> **CAUTION**
>
> Fraud or misrepresentation of the facts to an auditor is never an acceptable audit strategy, but taxpayers do have the right to highlight only those facts that support their position. They are *not* required to volunteer any information; the burden is on the auditor to ask the right questions.

Timing of the Audit

Taxpayers should be able to negotiate the timing of the audit with the auditor in the early stages of discussions. The taxpayer should not hesitate to suggest alternatives if the timing desired by the auditor does not fit the taxpayer's schedule. Closing schedules, vacations, medical leaves for key employees, or special projects can hinder a taxpayer's ability to conduct an audit. While rescheduling an audit for the taxpayer's convenience may raise waiver questions, taxpayers should not let that deter them from negotiating a more appropriate time for the audit.

The Audit Contact Person

In the early stages of an audit, it is important to designate one or two individuals who will serve as the audit contact person(s). Maintaining control over the auditor's contact with the taxpayer's personnel provides several safeguards for the taxpayer.

Many companies require the auditor to check in with the contact person upon arrival and departure for the day. This gives the company greater control over the auditor's presence at its location. Check-in procedures also afford the contact person the opportunity to briefly discuss the progress of the audit with the auditor.

Use of a contact person also assures continuity and consistency in providing data and responding to auditor requests. Other reasons for limiting the auditor's contact with taxpayer personnel include the following:

- The taxpayer needs to know exactly what information has been provided to the auditor and what the auditor has been told about various positions taken by the taxpayer on its tax returns. As the number of individuals involved in the audit increases, it becomes virtually impossible to maintain consistency in responses to information requests and explanations of positions taken on the return.
- Auditors sometimes attempt to communicate with individuals who are readily available to answer their questions, such as clerical employees in accounts payable or purchasing. While this is understandable from the auditor's viewpoint, it can have undesirable consequences for the taxpayer.

> **CAUTION**
>
> Most employees do not understand the complexity and delicate nature of tax positions. As a result, they may provide inaccurate, misleading, or unnecessary information that could seriously undermine a position taken by the taxpayer.
>
> Providing conflicting or inconsistent responses can damage the taxpayer's credibility and the working relationship between the taxpayer and the auditor. This can manifest itself during the negotiation stage of the audit or at the conclusion of the audit, when the taxpayer is forced to provide additional evidence to support its positions.

Designating one contact person allows that individual to focus on audit issues and take ownership of the audit results. This should result in more thorough preparation and more successful negotiation during the audit.

PLANNING POINTER

The auditor may attempt to bypass the designated contact person. Some suggestions for keeping the auditor from doing so include the following:

- Tell the auditor that you expect all questions to be addressed to the contact person.
- Locate the auditor in an area where there is little opportunity for contact with others, such as an office in the manufacturing department.
- Warn employees of the auditor's visit and discourage them from responding to the auditor's questions without prior approval.
- Regularly keep track of the auditor's whereabouts with surprise visits and phone calls.

Written Communications

As early as possible in the audit, the taxpayer needs to stress to the auditor the importance of written communications. Generally, auditors only put communications that are important to the state in writing, unless the taxpayer requests written communications for all significant issues.

Reasons to require written communications in an audit include the following:
- Establishes a written, formal record of the audit
- Documents questions that have been raised and responses that have been provided, so there can be no dispute about what was said
- Provides less likelihood of misunderstanding and misinterpretation
- Forces the questioner to be concise and reduces the likelihood of follow-up conversations; may also eliminate some questions because they will be forgotten or deemed not worth the effort required

Taxpayers are obliged to respond to written questions in writing, but the extra effort may prove worthwhile by responding with only the necessary information. This forces the auditor to come back with yet another request if the expected answer was not received. Although auditors are often skilled questioners, they are not always skilled at writing questions.

Written communication should be stressed throughout the audit, but the personal touch of verbal communication should *not* be overlooked. Taxpayers should not hesitate to verbally engage the auditor on minor issues or issues unrelated to the audit. Much insight about the auditor can be gained through casual conversation.

Limits need to be placed on the use of written communication to avoid unnecessarily burdening the auditor or taxpayer. Generally, written communications are appropriate for questions that involve major issues or positions in the audit. They are also appropriate for outlining scope issues and audit procedures.

Written communications are *not* appropriate if the auditor is requesting technical assistance about how to read a report or attempting to understand a company's filing system. The more appropriate way to deal with questions of this nature is to meet regularly with the auditor to resolve these issues informally.

Controlling Information

Controlling the information provided to an auditor is critical to successful audit administration. Therefore, it is important to establish a detailed record or log to track what information has been provided to the auditor and how long the auditor has had it.

Suggested data to retain in an information log includes:
- Description or copy of information provided
- Date the information was provided
- Date the information was returned
- Reference to the question in response to which the information was provided
- Indication of whether the auditor must return the information or may keep it

The date the information was provided can be particularly critical if the taxpayer feels that the auditor should have completed his or her work with the information. Taxpayers should request that information be returned when it is no longer needed. This will both:

1. Force the auditor to efficiently use data that has been provided and discourage him or her from "fishing" for something
2. Assist the taxpayer in maintaining control over the records for use in other audits as required.

When giving information to an auditor, the taxpayer should evaluate the auditor's right to see the information and determine whether the auditor will be allowed to keep or copy it as part of a permanent audit file. Auditors have broad authority to examine taxpayer records, but they do *not* have carte blanche to examine everything. They must be able to show that the record requested relates to the audit.

> **CAUTION**
>
> Care should be exercised in disputing an auditor's authority to examine certain records, as auditors have subpoena powers to compel a taxpayer to turn them over.

It is prudent for the taxpayer to require that as much information as possible be returned. Although auditors are required to treat taxpayer records with confidentiality, they generally should not be allowed to remove business records from the taxpayer's premises.

In addition to keeping a log, it is advisable to make copies, where feasible, of all data provided to the auditor. This assures that the taxpayer will have an exact duplicate of any information that the auditor has in his or her possession.

Questions can arise as to whether the taxpayer provided certain data in a timely fashion or ever provided it at all. By maintaining a log of the information provided, the taxpayer will be in a stronger position to refute any accusations that the progress of the audit was impeded by slow responses to requests for data.

An additional use of the data log is to assist the taxpayer in maintaining a log of the time spent on the audit by the auditor and the taxpayer. This information can be useful in the event questions about the taxpayer's cooperation arise. It is also useful when making waiver or waiver extension decisions to have some objective measure of the time the auditor has spent on the audit.

STUDY QUESTIONS

3. Which of the following statements is true?

    a. Taxpayers should make agreements on sampling over the phone if necessary.

    b. Taxpayers should always grant a waiver if requested by the auditor.

    c. Taxpayers should discourage the auditing of transactions they feel may be unnecessary.

    d. Taxpayers should allow the auditor to audit the books or transactions of entities without nexus.

4. Ways to keep the auditor from bypassing the designated contact person include all of the following *except:*

    a. Locate the auditor in an area near as many employees as possible.

    b. Discourage other employees from responding to the auditor's questions without prior approval.

    c. Keep track of the auditor's whereabouts.

    d. Tell the auditor you expect questions to be addressed to the contact person.

CONFIRMATION LETTER FROM AUDITOR

In follow-up to the initial contact and scheduling of an audit, the auditor will usually send the taxpayer a confirmation letter that outlines the audit and any agreements that have been made for its conduct. This *boilerplate* letter will also contain a broad delineation of records or information that the auditor may wish to have available on the first day of the audit.

Confirmation letters generally contain a standard set of information and are more of a form letter than many taxpayers realize. The states use this boilerplate approach to assure that proper notification has been given to the taxpayer in the event that a subpoena of certain records is necessary.

Confirmation letters usually contain the following information:

- The name(s) of the taxpayer(s) under audit and their appropriate identification numbers
- A statement regarding the period under review. If the taxpayer has agreed to provide a waiver of the statute of limitations, a request to complete the waiver will usually be included as part of the letter.
- The taxes that the auditor will be reviewing
- Dates of any fieldwork scheduled with the taxpayer
- A list of records, returns, and other documentation that the auditor may deem to be material in the course of the audit. Items typically requested include copies of the sales and use tax returns for the entire audit period; supporting work papers and other data used to prepare the returns; general ledgers, supporting journals, and journal entries; copies of other tax returns, such as a federal income tax return, state income tax return, and property tax return; exemption certificates if exempt sales are made; purchase orders or other purchase contracts and lease agreements; accounts payable files; sales invoices and supporting documentation; listing of capital assets; and any other relevant information that the auditor may need during the conduct of the audit
- A statement documenting any agreements that have been reached regarding the scope or conduct of the audit. An example would be an agreement that has been reached to audit fixed assets in detail and to sample expense purchases using a block sample.

The taxpayer usually will not have to respond to the letter, unless there is an error regarding the dates of the fieldwork or the conduct of the audit. If an error is discovered, the auditor should be notified as soon as possible.

The auditor may submit a questionnaire for the taxpayer to complete and forward or have available on the first day of the audit fieldwork. These questionnaires frequently contain questions about nexus-creating events, and they may also contain requests for information about taxpayer operations in the state. Taxpayers should exercise care in responding to such requests, as they frequently serve as a basis for initiating expanded audit procedures. For example, the auditor may decide to expand the scope of the audit or audit a customer in the state if he or she believes important information can be gained about the nature of the taxpayer's activities. Taxpayers should delay responding to these requests as long as possible. Providing information of this nature at the early stages of an audit rarely benefits the taxpayer.

> **PLANNING POINTER**
>
> Taxpayers that provide written audit guidelines to the auditor might wish to respond to the confirmation letter by providing a copy of the guidelines. Even if guidelines are provided in this manner, they should be reviewed with the auditor at the start of the audit.

Another issue that these letters raise is whether the taxpayer must have all the information that the auditor has requested available on the first day of the audit. In general, this is not necessary. By listing all the information in the letter, the auditor is requesting everything that could possibly be needed, but this does *not* mean all the information will actually be used. And here lies an important point that taxpayers need to consider: Can the auditor achieve the desired results by reviewing some other document in lieu of the one requested?

For example, rather than providing the auditor with copies of the general ledger, can the taxpayer satisfy the auditor's need for verification of the data through the use of a specially created assist report that summarizes the information in a way that is useful to the auditor? Taxpayers must evaluate whether it is better to provide the auditor with the requested information or force the auditor to achieve the desired result through some other means.

> **EXAMPLE**
>
> The auditor may request copies of the taxpayer's federal tax return to verify the sales that have been reported on the sales tax return. If the taxpayer has some other documentation available, such as a sales reconciliation that shows all the sales broken out by state, it might be preferable to provide that report rather than the federal income tax return. Similarly, it generally would be easier to provide a listing of fixed assets in the location than to provide copies of the property tax returns and attempt to reconcile the returns to the fixed-asset schedules.

STUDY QUESTION

5. In general, it is **not** necessary for the taxpayer to have all the information requested in the confirmation letter on the first day of the audit. **True or False?**

WAIVER OF STATUTE OF LIMITATIONS

The agreement to extend the statute of limitations is referred to as a waiver of the statute of limitations, or *waiver*. A waiver means that the taxpayer and the tax jurisdiction have entered into an agreement to jointly waive, or set aside, their legal rights under the state's statute and extend the period of assessment to some other date, which is generally three to six months beyond the expiration date.

CAUTION

The statute of limitations in all states is based on the filing of a return. If the taxpayer fails to file a return, the statute of limitations never begins to toll. Therefore, taxpayers that are not filing returns are open as far back as the state can establish some business connection with the state.

Deciding whether to grant the state a waiver is one of the more difficult issues that can arise in the early stages of an audit. It might seem that taxpayers would never want to grant the state a waiver, since it only prolongs the time period for the state to issue its assessment. However, under certain circumstances, a taxpayer may have no other choice. Generally, if the audit is being delayed beyond the statutory assessment period for the taxpayer's convenience or benefit, the taxpayer will be forced to issue a waiver to avoid a jeopardy assessment. The threat of a jeopardy assessment, and its related burden of proof, frequently forces a taxpayer to sign a waiver at the beginning of the audit.

Jeopardy Assessments

Jeopardy assessments are issued by a state when the taxpayer has failed to provide sufficient information for the state to make a reasonable determination of audit deficiency. A key aspect of the jeopardy assessment is that the state can base the assessment on the best available information. This allows the state to become creative in the basis for its assessment.

EXAMPLE

The state might base a sales tax deficiency on typical assessments for similar taxpayers or on a limited amount of information that is provided to the auditor or is publicly available.

The states tend to err on the high side when making assessments of this nature. Once a jeopardy assessment is made, the burden of proof rests with the taxpayer. This means the taxpayer must demonstrate that the jeopardy assessment is *not* correct to receive relief. The taxpayer may have to do a detailed review of its records to support some other assessment amount.

Waiver Timing

Before granting a waiver at the beginning of an audit, the taxpayer should carefully evaluate the timing of the auditor's request. Auditors frequently contact taxpayers just prior to the expiration of the statute of limitations and request an audit or a signed waiver that will allow them to audit the expired period at a later date.

> **EXAMPLE**
>
> An auditor might contact a taxpayer late in the year to request an audit appointment before the end of the year. For many taxpayers, an audit at this time of the year would be inconvenient, and they would be justified in refusing to grant the waiver. On the other hand, if the auditor contacted the taxpayer earlier in the year to request an appointment, the taxpayer might be forced to grant the waiver if the taxpayer could not meet the auditor's schedule. Most states take the position that when an audit extension is granted for the convenience of the taxpayer, the taxpayer should be willing to sign a waiver to extend the expiring periods.

There is frequently pressure to issue a waiver in the closing stages of an audit. Since audits are often done in the final year of the statute of limitations, the presence of unresolved issues in the latter stages of the audit can delay its completion beyond the statutory period for assessment.

> **PLANNING POINTER**
>
> In circumstances where the taxpayer is working with the auditor on concluding issues that the taxpayer reasonably believes can be resolved through additional research of the law or facts or through negotiation, the taxpayer *should* grant the waiver to the auditor. Failing to grant the waiver in these circumstances will result in a greater assessment and the need to appeal the unresolved issues, which can be expensive and risky.

Taxpayers must also evaluate the impact that granting a waiver will have on any refunds they might request as part of the audit. While it might be logical to assume that any time the right of the state to issue an assessment is extended, the right of the taxpayer to request a refund of any overpaid tax is also automatically extended, that is not the case. Although some states grant the same extension to refunds and assessments, many others, such as North Carolina, do not. Taxpayers need to be aware of each state's treatment and, if possible under the statute, modify the wording of the waiver so that it includes an extension of time for the filing of refund claims as well as the issuing of assessments. Modifying the waiver in some states, such as Florida, will have no impact on a taxpayer's ability to receive a refund after the statute has expired.

In instances where the state bars refunds in the period under waiver, the *doctrine of equitable recoupment,* or *equitable offset,* allows a taxpayer to receive partial relief in the years under waiver. Under this doctrine, taxpayers may apply for refunds from that time period, otherwise statutorily barred, against any deficiency assessed for the period. In this way, taxpayers may recover some of their lost refunds.

> **NOTE**
>
> The taxpayer must still provide proof to establish the validity of the claim with the tax jurisdiction.

> **CAUTION**
>
> Most states require that the waiver be signed by the taxpayer or a corporate officer. An employee or representative of the taxpayer may *not* sign a valid waiver in most jurisdictions. In addition, the waiver must be executed by both the taxpayer and the state prior to the expiration date of the statute of limitations.

STUDY QUESTION

> **6.** In which of the following situations would a taxpayer be justified in *not* granting a waiver of the statute of limitations?
>   **a.** The audit is being delayed for the taxpayer's convenience.
>   **b.** The auditor contacts the taxpayer to request an audit appointment late in the year that the statute of limitation ends.
>   **c.** The taxpayer is working with the auditor to conclude issues that the taxpayer believes can be resolved through additional research.
>   **d.** None of the above

PERFORMING SELF-AUDITS

Overview

All taxpayers that make taxable and exempt sales or purchases should have a regular self-audit program in place to detect errors and procedural breakdowns prior to an audit. Taxpayers that do not have an ongoing self-audit procedure in place should consider performing a self-audit prior to the commencement of the audit fieldwork. If there is not sufficient time or staffing to perform a complete self-audit prior to the auditor's arrival, a limited review should be performed to identify obvious areas of exposure. These areas would include incomplete or missing exemption certificates and failure to self-assess use tax on capital or expense purchases.

In a *self-audit*, the taxpayer identifies breakdowns in compliance procedures and filing practices that could result in underpayments of tax. In a *reverse audit*, the taxpayer identifies errors that result in an overpayment of tax. Thus, the self-audit seeks to identify and correct underpayment errors before the auditor reviews the books, while the reverse audit looks for overpayment errors that will generate a refund of tax.

Exemption Certificates

Exemption certificates are a common source of problems in sales and use tax audits. If the seller does not have an exemption certificate for each exempt sale, the auditor will assess the tax otherwise due against the seller. Therefore, having either a strong exemption certificate procedure or an exemption certificate self-audit procedure in place will reduce audit exposure.

Most sellers are missing at least some certificates at the time of an audit, which can translate into increased audit exposure, particularly when a sample is performed. Samples tend to increase exposure because of the projection of error over the entire audit period. However, depending on the sampling methodology to be used in the audit, the taxpayer may be able to secure many missing exemption certificates in advance, thereby reducing the audit exposure.

If nonstatistical samples are to be used in the audit, the sample test period will generally be established during the initial contact with the auditor. The *test period* is established by selecting representative months from the audit period for review. Once the sample period has been selected, the taxpayer can begin to review for missing exemption certificates by focusing on the test periods.

If a statistical sample is to be performed, the transactions tested will come from the entire period, and it will be more difficult to anticipate which transactions will be reviewed. A general review for missing exemption certificates would be more appropriate in the case of a statistical sample. In a general review, the taxpayer would look for exemption certificates from major customers.

Most internal accounting systems can provide sales by customer. Reports such as this can be used to screen for sales to exempt customers. Cross-checking exemption certificates against the report of exempt sales should provide an indication of missing certificates.

If a specific sample period has been established for sales, a review can be performed to test the adequacy of exemption certificate files for exempt sales in the test period.

> **PLANNING POINTER**
>
> Customers should be contacted to request replacements for certificates that are missing or incomplete. Many states require that certificates be renewed at periodic intervals, typically from three to five years. Therefore, even complete certificates must be refreshed regularly to remain in force.

Because the auditor is likely to ask that replacements for any missing, incomplete, or inaccurate certificates be obtained, requesting replacement certificates prior to the auditor's arrival should not result in any wasted effort by the taxpayer. The effects on the audit of having complete certificates on file can be dramatic. If an auditor observes that many certificates are missing or incomplete, he or she might react by being very particular about any replacement certificates that are obtained.

In addition, any decision made by an auditor that is documented in the work papers is subject to challenge by the auditor's superiors or an audit review panel, so auditors are usually cautious about accepting replacement exemption certificates. On the other hand, if the taxpayer has obtained valid exemption certificates for virtually all the exempt sales in the test periods, the auditor is more likely to feel confident that the taxpayer has diligently complied with the tax laws. When only one or two certificates are missing or incomplete, the auditor might deem this an immaterial level of error that does not require an assessment.

A decision must be made regarding the *effective date* of a replacement certificate obtained from a customer. If the customer signs and currently dates the certificate, the auditor may determine that the certificate is not valid for purchases prior to the date of signature. In this case, the taxpayer would need to obtain another certificate from the customer. Therefore, it is advisable to put a statement on the certificate that it is effective with the first day of the audit period or the date of first sale to the customer. That way, even if the customer signs with a current date, an argument can be made that the certificate is valid for all prior purchases that are part of the audit.

Missed Transactions

A major area of exposure that needs to be addressed in the self-audit process is taxable purchases on which the vendor failed to bill tax and/or no self-assessment was made. For many companies, this is the greatest area of exposure in an audit. Taxpayers have difficulty adequately monitoring purchases for the correct payment of tax because of the diversity and complexity of these transactions. Therefore, taxpayers should have a self-audit program in place to look for missed transactions and make the appropriate corrections before the auditor reviews the purchases.

While the states have become sophisticated in their use of sampling to determine audit deficiencies, most states do not allow taxpayers to make self-assessments based on a sample determination without some prior agreement. Therefore, taxpayers must review all purchases in detail to properly determine their tax liability.

> **CAUTION**
>
> Self-assessment payments must be made within the audit period or on amended returns within the period. If payment is made outside the audit period, the auditor will assess the tax paid as a deficiency in the audit.

Taxpayers with self-audit procedures in place should review their last self-audit to determine if the months preceding the audit require review. It may not be possible to complete the review before the beginning of the audit.

Self-assessment procedures for purchases generally involve a review of purchase invoices or vouchers to determine whether tax was self-assessed at the time the item was purchased.

> **PLANNING POINTER**
>
> In most computerized accounts payable systems, there are support programs that can be run to generate specific purchases for review. In many systems, the amount of sales tax paid to the vendor or self-assessed can also be isolated as a separate data field.

Once assist reports have been created, the process becomes an audit activity. The taxpayer reviews the selected purchases and determines whether tax has been properly paid. For a transaction in which the tax is *underpaid*, the taxpayer should self-assess and report the tax on its return. If the tax is *overpaid*, a refund claim should be filed.

Taxpayers must decide whether to file an amended return to report any self-assessments. If a significant amount of tax is unpaid, the taxpayer should file an amended return to capture the appropriate amount of interest due with the underpayment. Taxpayers self-assessing on purchases that are older than three to six months would generally be expected to file an amended return.

> **CAUTION**
>
> The regular filing of amended returns may attract more audit scrutiny, so every effort should be made to incorporate self-assessments at the time the item is purchased.

For both assets and expenses, an evaluation of the item's ultimate use must be made. Making an informed decision about the taxability of a purchase may require communication with operations personnel. If the item is used in a taxable manner and no tax has been paid or self-assessed, the taxpayer should voluntarily self-assess.

The focus of a self-audit is on the individual transaction level. However, the taxpayer should also seek to identify broader procedural breakdowns.

> **EXAMPLE**
>
> The review may disclose that a particular buyer is incorrectly coding a taxable purchase as exempt. The buyer should be notified of the incorrect procedure so that it can be corrected.

Once the review of all the transactions has been completed, the results of the review should be summarized and maintained for future reference. Adequate records must be retained for future reference.

It does little good to go through all the effort to perform the self-audit and then neglect to retain the files necessary to prove which purchases have been self-assessed. Most state audit procedures require that the taxpayer prove the self-assessment was made on a particular transaction by showing the transaction on a report or listing and reconciling it to a summary schedule.

Sampling

While most states require that taxpayers perform the self-audit review in detail, some states allow taxpayers to estimate their tax liability through sampling, using state approved sampling procedures. Generally, arrangements must be made with the state to self-assess using sampling. The state will review the procedures used by the taxpayer to make certain that a sound basis exists for them.

Of particular interest are the state's procedures to avoid a duplicate assessment. When a self-assessment is made without the use of sampling, it is easy to relate the self-assessment to a particular transaction. However, when payments are made on the basis of a sample, the issue of which transactions were covered by the self-assessment can arise. Before a self-audit sample is performed, the taxpayer should reach an agreement with the state regarding how the results will be reflected in an audit.

A common approach is to ignore the self-assessment at the individual transaction level and, instead, reflect the total amount paid against the entire amount of the audit deficiency and net the results as an overpayment or underpayment. If expenses have been sampled on a self-assessment basis, care must be exercised so that there is no duplication in the assessment. Particular note should be taken of the accounts that form the basis of the self-assessment or deficiency.

For accounts that have been self-audited using a satisfactory sampling methodology, the focus of review should be the sampling methodology, not the individual transactions. If the sampling methodology used by the taxpayer has validity, *all* transactions that were sampled should be covered under the sample self-assessment. For the sample to have statistical validity, it must be conducted using a method of statistical sampling.

CAUTION

A nonstatistical sample, such as a block sample, does *not* have the same validity as a statistical sample and, therefore, would not be appropriate for this purpose.

STUDY QUESTIONS

7. Which of the following statements is true regarding missing exemption certificates?
   a. Sampling tends to *decrease* exposure.
   b. A replacement certificate should contain a statement that it is effective on the date it is signed.
   c. A general review for missing certificates would be more appropriate in the case of a statistical sample.
   d. Requesting replacement certificates before the auditor's arrival is *not* advisable.

8. If a taxpayer determines that a significant amount of tax is unpaid due to a self-assessment, the taxpayer should *not* file an amended return because it will attract more audit scrutiny. *True or False?*

REVERSE AUDITS AND REFUND REVIEWS

Overview

Taxpayers that are focused solely on the negotiation and analysis of vouchers and invoices selected for potential assessment by the auditor are missing substantial opportunities. In most self-assessment and tax-payment models, taxpayers are as likely to make an *overpayment* as they are to make an *underpayment*. Therefore, taxpayers need to regularly review transactions for the overpayment of tax. Ideally, the reverse audit should be undertaken before commencement of the audit so the refund can be a part of the audit settlement.

The object of a *reverse audit* is to recover tax incorrectly paid to the taxing jurisdiction. It is called a reverse audit because of its focus on generating a refund rather than an assessment. Taxpayers need to consider each state's treatment of refund waivers when planning their reverse audit activity. Priority should be placed on completing reverse audits in states that refuse to grant extensions on refund claims.

Most auditors concentrate on underpayment errors and only give cursory attention to overpayment errors. Taxpayers must seize the refund initiative for themselves by performing a reverse audit or hiring an outside firm to perform one.

Billing Errors

The nature of the relationship between the seller and purchaser is such that overpayment errors are usually quickly identified by the purchaser and corrected with a revised invoice or credit.

However, billing errors may occur, and the focus of the sales review should be in these three principal areas:

1. Incorrect tax status of purchaser or transaction
2. Incorrect application of tax to items sold
3. Incorrect tax rate applied to the items purchased

Tax Status of Purchaser or Transaction

The tax status of the purchaser should be reviewed to determine if tax was properly billed. Generally, a review of taxable invoices is performed by cross-checking the invoices against the exemption certificate files. In addition, a logic check may be performed against any taxable invoices billed to challenge whether the transaction is taxable. For example, a sale to a wholesaler or distributor or to a local government would typically *not* be subject to tax.

After a preliminary review of sales, potentially exempt transactions should be segregated and the customers contacted to determine their status with regard to exemption. If any of the sales are subsequently determined to be tax-exempt, a refund claim should be filed with the state.

> **CAUTION**
>
> When a properly executed exemption certificate is received, the customer's tax status should be corrected so the error is not perpetuated.

Improper Application of Tax

Correctly billing the sales tax requires that the seller properly classify the billing elements on the invoice and then apply the tax to the charges. Sellers frequently have difficulty doing this correctly, particularly in a multistate environment, which can result in an overpayment of tax. For example, if the tax jurisdiction does not charge tax on separately stated freight charges, and the seller unbundles the price, it is important to segregate those charges and not bill the tax. Sellers should periodically verify that the sales tax is being correctly charged on the taxable elements of their sales.

> **EXAMPLE**
>
> A number of states, including California, exempt the installation labor associated with tangible personal property if it is separately stated on the invoice. Sellers that bill in this manner need to review each state to verify that they have properly exempted the installation labor. If they have overcharged their customers, refund claims should be filed. Follow-up action may also be required to make certain that the billing error is corrected on future billings.

Incorrect Rate Applied

Many sellers have difficulty determining the proper local taxes to apply to a purchase. Therefore, the reverse audit procedure for sales should include a review of the rates applied to various invoices during the audit period. If it is determined that incorrect rates have been applied to certain sales invoices, a refund claim should be filed and procedures should be modified so the problem is avoided in the future.

In some states, sales tax that is refunded to the seller must, by statute, be returned to the customer that ultimately paid the tax. While such statutes represent a well-intentioned attempt by the states to assure that all refunds are returned to the customers, they can serve as a barrier to refund claims on past sales. Sellers adopt the attitude that they do not want to invest time and effort recovering tax that must be returned to the customer. In addition, sellers may be concerned about the potential fallout of admitting to customers that sales tax billing errors were made. Therefore, before undertaking a reverse audit of the sales area, taxpayers should determine what their refund policy will be.

Overpayments on Purchases

The greatest opportunities for refunds are on purchases. The inherent complexity of state tax law, combined with the ever-changing nature of business operations, makes the purchase and capital addition reverse audit a fertile ground for refunds.

Most purchasing and accounts payable systems are not designed to handle the complexities of sales and use tax law. In addition, individuals who work in these areas are generally not motivated to learn basic tax concepts, as they are measured on other factors, such as cost savings and transaction processing speed. This lack of knowledge, combined with the tremendous volume of purchases in most companies, makes it difficult for taxpayers to designate the correct tax status of purchases.

The steps to perform in a reverse audit of purchases include the following:

1. Identify likely transactions for the incorrect payment of tax by reviewing charts of account, return work papers, and supporting schedules.
2. Capture the activity in the identified accounts for the period under review, isolating transactions that are tax-paid.
3. Review applicable exclusions from tax and look for potential overpayment errors.
4. Review exemptions from tax. In particular, look for purchases that are unique to the manufacturing process (in states that offer a manufacturing exemption) that may have been taxed in error.
5. Review purchases shipped to other jurisdictions for misapplication of tax.
6. Review any other transactions that may be eligible for special treatment under the statute.

PLANNING POINTER

The key to success in reverse audits is to learn to assertively apply the tax laws to individual transactions in much the same way that an auditor applies the laws in an audit.

For example, there might be a requirement in the manufacturing process to have temperature and humidity controls to protect the product from damage. The taxpayer could argue that these controls are required for manufacturing and not employee comfort, and the heating and air conditioning system is therefore exempt.

Another example is the taxability of employee clothing such as gloves and gowns. Many states that otherwise tax these items will exempt them if it can be demonstrated that the clothing is required for product quality purposes.

Areas that may afford opportunities for assertive application of *manufacturing tax exemptions* by the taxpayer include the following:

- Identifying custom manufacturing activities that frequently take place outside the manufacturing departments and making sure they are treated as tax-exempt in states with a manufacturing exemption
- Isolating the beginning and ending points in the manufacturing process to make sure that all eligible items are included in the manufacturing exemption
- Treating material handling throughout the manufacturing process as exempt if the state follows the integrated plant doctrine
- Applying the manufacturing exemption to items purchased for some unique aspect of the manufacturing process, such as clean rooms or worker apparel used to prevent contamination of the product
- Applying the manufacturing exemption to specialized temperature and humidity controls required for product quality
- Applying the manufacturing exemption to items used in the in-house print shop

In addition to reviewing purchases for exemption from tax, it is important to look at exclusions from tax. An exclusion from tax refers to an item that the statute does not reach for imposition of tax. When reviewing exclusions, the focus should be on the manner in which the invoicing is executed and how that might impact the tax status of the purchase.

As mentioned previously, there are a number of states that exclude tax on installation of tangible personal property when the installation charge is separately stated. A taxpayer reviewing transactions in such a state would look for purchases that were billed or self-assessed in this manner.

CAUTION

For multistate taxpayers, there can be confusion regarding which state's tax to apply. This happens when vendors set up a single master account for all purchases. The account is generally identified for tax purposes to the main location of the taxpayer's business. For purchases shipped to another state, the vendor's invoicing system does *not* recognize that another state's tax should be applied.

The problem is compounded when the purchasing company's accounts payable or purchasing system also does not recognize that some other tax rate should be applied. This situation can actually result in two errors:

1. The wrong state's tax has been paid
2. A liability to the state of use has been underpaid. Unfortunately, when tax is paid in error, there is no offset allowed for the correct amount of tax when it is paid.

This can result in a duplicate payment of tax:

- Once for the wrong state
- Once as part of the audit assessment

STUDY QUESTIONS

9. The sales review in a reverse audit may include all of the following activities *except:*

a. A review of the rates applied to various invoices during the audit period

b. A review of the tax status of purchasers

c. Verification that the sales tax is being correctly charged on the taxable elements of sales

d. None of the above

10. Which of the following statements is *not* true?

a. The greatest opportunities for refunds are on sales.

b. When performing a reverse audit, the taxpayer should apply tax laws similar to the way in which an auditor applies the laws in an audit.

c. State statutes that require sales tax refunds to be refunded by the seller to its customers can serve as a barrier to refund claims on past sales.

d. None of the above

Refund Claim Procedures

After identifying all the errors, the taxpayer must determine the correct way to proceed with the refund claim. If the overpayments have been made to a vendor, the taxpayer should either request a refund from the vendor, or request that the vendor sign an assignment of its rights to receive the refund so the taxpayer can request the refund directly from the state.

Such assignments include provisions that prohibit the seller from claiming the refunds in the future. For very large taxpayers, this can be an attractive option, as it eliminates dealing with vendors on the details and reasons for the refund claims. This approach also removes the vendor as a middleman in the transaction and allows the taxpayer to deal directly with the state.

> **CAUTION**
>
> Vendor refunds should *not* be claimed as an adjustment to the next month's self-assessment or treated as a return offset to sales tax due. In virtually all states, netted refunds such as this will be disallowed by an auditor. If the statute of limitations has expired when the refunds are disallowed as offsets, the taxpayer will not be able to recover the lost adjustment.

If the taxpayer has merely overassessed in error, the correct procedure is to take an offset against use tax due on a future return, unless the adjustment is substantial in amount.

Once the data has been summarized and supporting documentation has been gathered to substantiate the refund claim, the next step in the reverse-audit procedure is to file a refund claim or amended return with the appropriate state.

The necessary supporting documentation for a refund claim is a copy of the invoice from the seller that includes the tax and some substantiation to show that the tax has been paid. This might include a copy of the check or voucher to show the amount of the payment. If the refund claim is field audited, it is reasonable to expect that the auditor will test some of these transactions to verify that the erroneous payments have been made.

In addition to providing documentation supporting the refund claim, it will be necessary to explain why the transaction in question is *not* subject to tax. This may involve explaining the use of the item or indicating why the transaction falls under a particular statute or court case as exempt. Explanations for each category of purchase are generally provided in an attachment that accompanies the filing.

States have varying administrative procedures for refund claims. Depending on the state, one of the following may be required:

- An amended return
- A special refund claim form
- Or a letter noting the issues in the refund claim may be required

> **CAUTION**
>
> Before filing a claim, be sure to check on the particular state's filing requirements. Failure to properly file the claim can result in disallowance of some or all of the claim.

When a taxpayer files a refund claim as part of an audit, special procedures may be required for the refund claim to be processed along with the assessment. Generally, these procedures require that the auditor promptly receive the refund claim so that it can be reviewed in conjunction with the audit.

> **PLANNING POINTER**
>
> A taxpayer under audit should notify the auditor that it intends to file a refund claim before the fieldwork is completed and request that the refund be processed as part of the overall audit settlement.

After determining the proper procedure to follow in requesting the refund, the taxpayer must decide on the content of the refund claim. Most state refund processing procedures require that a limited review in the form of an office audit occur before the refund claim is processed or denied. The purpose of the review is to substantiate the refund and review the taxpayer's account for underpayments before the refund is issued. If the taxpayer is currently under audit, the office audit procedure will be modified to accommodate the field auditor's review.

Taxpayers should expect that processing a refund claim will take at least three months from the time it is filed. In many states, the goal is to process the refund claim and notify the taxpayer within one year. Other states and local jurisdictions, such as Louisiana parishes and cities, are open-ended as to when they must respond to refund claim requests.

Taxpayers filing refund claims should attach sufficient documentation to the claim so that the reviewer can determine the basis of the claim. For large refund claims involving many transactions, the state may grant the refund claim, contingent upon a subsequent field audit and review by the refund office staff.

Taxpayers need to follow the refund claim judiciously, as it is processed by the state department of revenue. Failure to keep track of the progress of the refund claim could result in a loss of important appeal rights. Each state has specific appeal procedures that provide taxpayers with certain statutorily set periods for appealing the denial or reduction of any refund claim.

> **CAUTION**
>
> Failure to meet an appeal deadline can result in denial of the claim. In addition, at the office review level, taxpayers are frequently given deadlines for responding to queries regarding the refund claim. Failure to respond or provide the additional documentation requested can result in a partial or complete disallowance of the refund claim.

Using Outside Consultants

In recent years, the performance of reverse audits by outside consultants has been a growing trend. As corporations have downsized, the pressure on internal tax departments to do more with less has led to the outsourcing of a substantial amount of tax work. For companies that are faced with the prospect of not being able to recover any tax because they don't have the personnel to perform a reverse audit, outsourcing is a logical solution.

Taxpayers need to carefully evaluate the expertise of the firm proposing to perform the work, as not all outsourcing options are equal.

Questions that should be addressed before employing an outside firm to do refund recovery work include the following:

- Does the taxpayer have final veto over any refund claims filed?
- Who bears the cost of appeal or litigation expenses?
- Is the outsourcing firm willing to enter into a confidentiality agreement?
- Does the outsourcing firm require support personnel from the taxpayer?

Final Veto

Outsourcing firms frequently encourage taxpayers to take extremely aggressive positions. It is advisable for taxpayers to have final authority over any refund claims submitted on their behalf to reduce the possibility of having a filing position jeopardized through an ill-advised refund claim.

Appeal or Litigation Expenses

A refund claim may be denied by the state if, in the state's view, granting it could create an undesired precedent or undermine a position that the department of revenue is attempting to defend in court.

> **EXAMPLE**
>
> Taxpayers and states with a manufacturing exemption have engaged in disputes over the scope of the exemption. If a state is litigating a particular issue, it would not be wise for the state to grant a refund claim based upon a lower court decision that is under appeal by the state.

Anytime a refund claim is filed, the possibility of litigation or appeal exists. This can be particularly true if the taxpayer is attempting an appeal based upon a recent court decision. In this situation, the issue of representation by the outsourcing firm must be addressed in any contract to perform reverse audit work. Many firms that engage in this type of work have attorneys, either on their staff or available on a retainer, to assist in any required appeal.

Confidentiality Agreements

The confidentiality of taxpayer records is an important consideration whenever a taxpayer deals with outside organizations. While attorneys may always claim the *client privilege* to withhold documents, CPAs generally are not afforded this privilege.

In general, there is the possibility of disclosure to competitors or others that could be damaging or embarrassing to the taxpayer's business or employees. Therefore, taxpayers should always insist that an outside consulting firm sign a confidentiality agreement stipulating that it will not disclose any information learned about the taxpayer during the course of its review. A confidentiality agreement provides an avenue for legal remedy in the event something is disclosed. In addition, most individuals will take their responsibility with respect to confidentiality more seriously if they are required to sign something attesting to that responsibility.

Support Personnel

Many outsourcing firms have a sufficient number of technical personnel, but they lack an adequate number of clerical personnel to complete the project in an efficient and timely manner. This can be particularly true for out-of-town engagements where the outsourcing firm is attempting to hold its costs down. The firm may look to the clerical personnel of the taxpayer to do photocopying, data entry, and other clerical tasks. Prior to the start of the engagement, an agreement should be reached on how these tasks will be done and who will bear the costs.

RECORD RETENTION ISSUES

Record retention and the timely destruction of unneeded records is an important facet of a company's tax-planning strategy. The burden of proof that a transaction is nontaxable rests with the taxpayer and not the auditor. Therefore, the taxpayer must maintain the necessary records to refute any assertions made by the auditor.

In order to prove that a transaction is exempt, it may be necessary to review original source documents for explanations regarding the use of various items. Nothing is more frustrating in an audit than to know the correct answer but not be able to prove it to the auditor because of a lack of adequate records.

Conversely, unnecessary and out-of-date records should not be retained unless there are legal reasons for retaining them, such as a lawsuit that is either anticipated or in progress. Occasionally, having too much information can be costly to a taxpayer, while if nothing is available, an acceptable compromise may be worked out with the taxing jurisdiction. Before discarding any data, however, taxpayers need to verify that the information is not needed for IRS record retention agreements or for legal reasons.

> **PLANNING POINTER**
>
> If no valid reasons exist for retaining records, they should be discarded to avoid the additional storage expense and exposure that accompanies their retention.

Increasing numbers of taxpayers are relying on personal computers as aids in the preparation of financial information and tax returns. Record retention policies need to encompass personal computer records as well as paper records. In many instances, there are no backups for this information since it exists at the workstations of individual employees. The lack of backup protection makes it all the more critical to address personal computer records in the record retention policy.

> **CAUTION**
>
> Employees should be educated as to the importance of retaining records on the personal computer. Good habits include securing the integrity of information through passwords and regularly backing up data.

STUDY QUESTIONS

11. A taxpayer that accidentally overassesses an *insubstantial* amount of sales tax from a customer should do which of the following?

   a. Claim the refund as an adjustment to the next month's self-assessment

   b. Take an offset against use tax due on a future return

   c. Treat it as a return offset to sales tax due

   d. None of the above

12. Which of the following statements is true?

   a. The burden of proof that a transaction is taxable rests with the auditor.

   b. Some states and local jurisdictions have *no* specific period for processing refund claims.

   c. When a reverse audit is outsourced, the outsourcing firm should be given final authority for refund claims.

   d. Records should be retained indefinitely since it is always uncertain what the future will bring, even if there is no particular reason for doing so.

RESPONDING TO AUDIT AND NEXUS QUESTIONNAIRES

Nexus is the minimum threshold of activity that is necessary for a state to impose its tax upon a taxpayer. Nexus issues frequently become the focal point of audit activity as states seek to force taxpayers to pay tax. For sales and use tax, the current nexus standard was established by the U.S. Supreme Court in *Quill Corp. v. North Dakota* [504 US 298 (1992)]. In *Quill,* the Court established that physical presence is required for a state to impose its sales and use tax on a particular seller. *Physical presence* is generally created when a business has employees, property or other assets, or agents of the seller in the state.

A federal statute, commonly known as Public Law 86-272, does not provide for any *protected activities* for sales and use tax purposes as it does for income tax purposes. Any physical presence greater than some *de minimis* presence creates nexus for the taxpayer and subjects the taxpayer to the state's sales and use tax.

Not surprisingly, the states aggressively enforce nexus provisions. Once a taxpayer is filing with a state, it generally continues to do so for some time. Therefore, the state's reward for securing taxpayer compliance can be substantial. The states employ a variety of techniques to ferret out nonfilers. These techniques are important to understand, as they frequently form the basis for an audit.

Some of the more common techniques employed include the following:
- Nexus questionnaires
- Nexus squads
- Information-sharing arrangements with other states
- Referrals from other taxpayer audits
- Targeting compliance of specific groups or classes of taxpayers

Nexus Questionnaires

Many states have developed questionnaires that are used to gather information necessary to determine whether a taxpayer has nexus in the jurisdiction. Taxpayers may receive a nexus questionnaire in a variety of situations. In the early stages of an audit, the auditor may request that the taxpayer complete a nexus questionnaire to assist the auditor in determining the scope of the audit.

> **CAUTION**
>
> Great care should be exercised in responding to nexus questionnaire questions. The questions are usually designed to elicit yes or no replies from the respondent. In some instances a yes or no answer may be sufficient, but further explanation is often needed to support the taxpayer's position.

Prior to any preliminary audit contact, nexus questionnaires may be mailed to the taxpayer without being addressed to a specific person in the organization. Most tax advisors suggest that when this happens, the taxpayer should *not* respond to the initial inquiry. Mailings of this nature are often done with little or no follow-up on nonrespondents, so failing to respond should not have adverse consequences.

Nexus questionnaires that are mailed to a specific company officer or employee generally *do* require a reply, as follow-up is more likely to result from noncompliance. However, even in these instances, most advisors would recommend that taxpayers not rush to respond.

> **CAUTION**
>
> The taxpayer must evaluate the state's intent in mailing the questionnaire. If it appears, based on information provided with the questionnaire, that the taxpayer has been targeted for specific reasons, the taxpayer should respond promptly. However, if it appears that the state does *not* have any particular information about the taxpayer, it might be prudent for the taxpayer to wait for follow-up from the state before responding. When it comes to responding to nexus questionnaires, taxpayers should always err on the side of caution.

Nexus questionnaires can also be provided to taxpayers as part of an audit investigation, in the pre-audit phase or once the fieldwork begins, to determine whether the taxpayer is subject to a particular tax. In an audit, the taxpayer will usually have little alternative but to respond.

Taxpayers should seek assistance if they have any uncertainty about how to respond to a nexus questionnaire. Given the seriousness of any audit-related inquiry, seeking advice is always a good idea, even if the taxpayer is relatively well informed.

In general, nexus questionnaires explore activities that, if undertaken, would support the state's position that the taxpayer is subject to tax. Many questionnaires ask about specific activities that the courts have held create nexus for taxpayers.

> **CAUTION**
>
> A common mistake that taxpayers make with nexus questionnaires is having them completed by an individual who is not familiar with the tax implications of the questions. A nexus questionnaire should always be completed by an individual who understands tax issues.

It can be extremely difficult, if not impossible, to retract a response. This is especially unfortunate if the statement could have been made in a way that would not create exposure for the taxpayer.

Nexus Squads

It has become common for a state to have a group of auditors that specialize in nexus reviews. These audit groups are sometimes called *nexus squads*. The role of the nexus squad is to engage in investigative work that is designed to identify taxpayers with undeclared nexus.

An audit is often precipitated by the work of a nexus squad. Therefore, it is important to understand their methods of operation.

In addition to using nexus questionnaires, *nexus squads* engage in the following activities to discover nonfiling taxpayers:
- Checking various taxpayer tax registrations for inconsistencies
- Reviewing advertising in local media and phone books to identify taxpayers with business activities in the state
- Contacting taxpayers suspected of engaging in nexus-creating activities

Checking Various Taxpayer Tax Registrations for Inconsistencies

Taxpayers frequently register for one tax but ignore another tax obligation that might be expected to accompany it. For example, if a taxpayer is registered for payroll tax purposes, it might be logical to conclude that the taxpayer should also be registered for sales and use tax, as it would appear that the taxpayer has an employee working in the state.

In many instances, there is a logical explanation for the seeming inconsistency. In the example cited, nexus would *not* be created for the employer if the employee merely lived in the state of withholding but worked for the taxpayer in another state.

Reviewing Advertising in Local Media and Phone Books

Nexus squads can obtain leads from advertising by the taxpayer. Advertising is a primary means by which taxpayers reach potential customers and provide information to them. Such information can provide an audit trail that can be used against the taxpayer in a nexus review. Taxpayers need to anticipate whether the auditor has information of this nature at the start of the audit and, if so, take this into consideration when responding to questions from the auditor.

EXAMPLES

The provision of a local telephone number could be an indication that the taxpayer has a place of business in the state. The solicitation of sales through advertisement could be an indication that employees of the taxpayer are engaging in revenue-generating activities within the state.

> **PLANNING POINTER**
>
> It is possible that, through planning, activities may be structured in a manner that reduces or eliminates the exposure for the taxpayer but still accomplishes the revenue-generating activity that the taxpayer is seeking. For example, it may not be necessary to provide a local phone number as a contact number. An out-of-state toll-free line may accomplish the same results without exposing the taxpayer to further nexus inquiries.

Tax planning may, however, interfere with business objectives. For example, a taxpayer may need a local contact for competitive reasons, despite the fact that it creates nexus and other tax consequences.

CONTACTING TAXPAYERS SUSPECTED OF ENGAGING IN NEXUS-CREATING ACTIVITIES

As mentioned earlier, taxpayers frequently receive nexus questionnaires addressed to the company but to no particular individual. These questionnaires are often sent by a nexus squad. They may be a form of cold-calling by which the state is attempting to identify a new taxpayer through the answers provided, or they may be the result of the state having some additional information about the taxpayer's activities. While it not likely that a substantial number of taxpayers are identified in this manner, the effort required for the state to generate periodic mailings of this nature is relatively low. Therefore, it seems likely that this type of activity will continue.

STUDY QUESTION

> **13.** If a nexus questionnaire is mailed to a taxpayer but **not** addressed to any particular person, and the mailing includes **no** indication that the taxpayer has been targeted for specific reasons, the taxpayer should do which of the following?
>
> **a.** Respond immediately
> **b.** Respond, but *not* immediately
> **c.** Not respond, unless there is follow-up from the state
> **d.** Not respond, even if there is follow-up from the state

Information Sharing

A number of states engage in information-sharing agreements and compacts with other states. As a result, taxpayers should expect the auditor to have received advance information about their activities. The Great Lakes Regional Compact and the Southeastern States Compact are examples of information-sharing agreements between the states.

The member states of these organizations assist each other by sharing information gathered during audits. Member states may request that taxpayers complete questionnaires similar to the nexus questionnaires discussed in the previous section. In addition to requesting information regarding the taxpayer's activities in the state under audit, these questionnaires request information about the taxpayer's activities in other states. The taxpayer's responses are made available to the members of the compact.

PLANNING POINTER

Taxpayers confronted with these questionnaires in an audit should be cautious about providing the information requested. As a general rule, states participating in information-sharing arrangements have little or no authority to compel the taxpayer to complete the questionnaire.

In most instances, if the taxpayer refuses to provide the information, the auditor will not pursue the issue any further, although the auditor may note on the questionnaire that the taxpayer refused to complete it. In limited circumstances, the auditor may attempt to complete the questionnaire based upon his or her knowledge of the taxpayer's operations. However, there is little motivation for the auditor to complete the questionnaire, as the information requested does not relate to the audit at hand.

The largest and most sophisticated of the information-sharing groups is the Multistate Tax Commission (MTC). A number of states rely on the MTC to perform some portion or all of their audit function. For taxpayers that are selected by the MTC for audit, this can be an overwhelming experience, as the auditor could be auditing on behalf of numerous states rather than just one. While the audit techniques are often the same, the assessment can be substantially greater due to the number of states engaging in the audit.

CAUTION

Although the extent of MTC audit work has diminished in recent years, taxpayers selected for MTC audit should be particularly cautious in dealing with the auditor or providing any nexus information in response to a request from the MTC.

In the course of completing an audit, auditors frequently gather evidence about the tax practices of other taxpayers. For example, in reviewing vouchered invoices for purchases from other companies, auditors observe what types of activities are being billed by the vendors, in addition to information about the billing practices of the seller. If the auditor sees something that does not appear to be correct or properly billed for tax purposes, a referral can be made for the state to audit the vendor. Also, if it appears that the seller is performing services in the state but has failed to register for sales and use tax, the auditor could make a referral based upon these observations.

> **CAUTION**
>
> Referral audits can result from any audit, so vendors always need to be cognizant of the tax positions that are reflected through their invoicing and other activities in a state. Taxpayers need to be particularly aware of these issues when dealing with customers that are more frequent audit candidates. Generally, these would be the larger taxpayers in a state.

Profiling

States frequently develop profiles of certain industries or types of businesses for auditors to use as a guide. For example, states know that taxpayers in the same trade or business tend to make similar purchases and, as a result, they can develop a profile of business purchases. Taxpayers can also benefit from such information if the state prepares a guideline that is published for taxpayer guidance on purchases.

Some states have even used this information to develop a self-audit list for taxpayers to complete on their own. This allows the state to perform a quasi-audit without having to devote all the personnel that would be required to perform a field audit. In addition, states that engage in these industry self-audits can achieve a higher level of future compliance through the educational process that occurs as part of the overall review.

Harsh Consequences

For a taxpayer discovered through the nexus process, the consequences can be particularly harsh if the taxpayer has been operating in a state for several years. Since the statute of limitations in all states only begins to run with the filing of a return, a taxpayer that has never filed a return has not begun to toll the statute of limitations. The taxpayer is therefore open to assessment as far back as the state can establish a connection between the taxpayer and the state. This could be many years beyond what the statute of limitations would otherwise allow.

In addition to the tax assessed for these open periods, the taxpayer would also owe various late-filing penalties, late-payment penalties, and potential negligence penalties. Some states provide additional penalty interest, over and above the normal interest, that is assessed in these situations. Such taxpayers, rather than waiting to be caught, may wish to proceed under a voluntary disclosure agreement with the state as a means of mitigating their exposure.

Voluntary Disclosure

A taxpayer that has a sound basis for not filing in a particular state may be able to negotiate a settlement with the state that minimizes the penalties and the number of years that the state goes back for assessment. Under a voluntary disclosure program, a taxpayer generally agrees to pay the tax due for the agreed-upon years, plus interest and possibly penalties. In addition, the taxpayer agrees to begin filing going forward. Such agreements benefit both the taxpayer and the state. The taxpayer may begin filing without being liable for the entire period of noncompliance. The state derives an adjustment for the open years and has a compliant taxpayer going forward.

Taxpayers wishing to make voluntary disclosure generally work through a third party to reach an agreement with the state before beginning to file. The states are not under any obligation to accept an offer, so premature disclosure by a taxpayer could have significant consequences.

Taxpayers may also wish to consider voluntary disclosure if there is little or no support for the position that they have taken. This could be the result of negligence or evasion on the taxpayer's part or erosion of a position as a result of a court case or legislation.

Generally, once the auditor has contacted the taxpayer and initiated the preliminary phases of a nexus review, the taxpayer will *not* be able to participate in a voluntary disclosure program. Therefore, it is important for taxpayers to anticipate these problems and stay ahead of the states' nexus squads.

PLANNING POINTER

Taxpayers not wishing to be part of a voluntary disclosure program may also consider voluntarily complying on a prospective basis. However, many states require that taxpayers complete questionnaires about the extent of their prior business activities in the state. Responding to these questions truthfully can be difficult if the taxpayer has a lengthy history of noncompliance.

Amnesty Programs

Generally, states may offer amnesty under provisions enacted by their legislature. Such amnesty programs are usually offered for a limited period of time and provide a "no questions asked" opportunity for taxpayers to address past lapses in compliance.

Amnesty for sales tax is also provided through the Streamlined Sales and Use Tax Agreement. A state that wishes to become a member of the Agreement must certify that its laws, rules, regulations, and policies are substantially in compliance with each of the requirements of the Agreement. The requirements of the Agreement include an amnesty for uncollected or unpaid tax for sellers that register to collect tax, provided they were not previously registered in the state.

Taxpayers wishing to avail themselves of this amnesty must register within 12 months of a state's participation in the Agreement. To obtain amnesty, taxpayers must agree to register in all full-member states while registration in associate-member states is optional. In addition, a member state may allow amnesty on terms and conditions more favorable to a seller than that required by the Streamlined Sales and Use Tax Agreement.

> **NOTE**
>
> Amnesty under the Agreement does *not* include use tax that may be due upon purchases.

STUDY QUESTIONS

14. Which of the following statements is true?
- **a.** A taxpayer that has never filed a return is open to assessment as far back as the state can establish a connection between the taxpayer and the state.
- **b.** Under a voluntary disclosure program, a taxpayer generally agrees to pay tax due for the agreed-upon years, but pays *no* interest or penalties.
- **c.** The largest and most sophisticated of the information-sharing groups are *nexus squads.*
- **d.** The requirements of the Streamlined Sales and Use Tax Agreement include an amnesty for uncollected or unpaid tax for sellers that were previously registered in the state.

15. As a general rule, states participating in information-sharing arrangements have authority to compel the taxpayer to complete a questionnaire similar to a nexus questionnaire. ***True or False?***

MODULE 2: SALES AND USE TAXES — CHAPTER 7

Construction Contractors and Manufacturers

This chapter discusses construction contractors and how their varying roles can affect their sales and use tax liability. It also discusses the sales and use tax treatment of manufacturers and tax exemptions that are available to them.

LEARNING OBJECTIVES

Upon completing this chapter, the student will:

- Understand how a construction contractor's varying roles can affect their sales and use tax liability
- Know how to distinguish between real and tangible property
- Recognize when contractors act as retailers
- Understand the implications of contractors acting as retailers for contractors and their customers.
- Understand the treatment of the construction contractor when the contractor performs a contract for a tax-exempt entity
- Be familiar with the treatment of contractor repair transactions
- Be aware of available exemptions for manufacturing equipment and the requirements for eligibility
- Understand the treatment of materials and labor used in the production process and in making repairs
- Be familiar with the tax implications of making inventory withdrawals

TREATMENT OF CONSTRUCTION CONTRACTORS

Overview

The *sales and use tax* treatment of a construction contractor is complicated by the varying roles that a contractor may assume in fulfilling a contract or performing a job. Generally, contractors can act as either retailers or consumers, depending on the nature of the work involved in a particular project. Contractors act as *retailers* of tangible personal property when they resell tangible personal property in its present state without transforming it into real estate. Contractors acting as retailers are required to collect tax on their sales of tangible personal property.

On other projects, contractors install or apply tangible personal property as a real property improvement and are treated as the consumers of the incorporated materials. As *consumers* of the materials incorporated into the project, the contractor is subject to tax on their cost.

Contractors may also perform repairs to either real or tangible personal property with varying tax consequences, depending on the state's treatment of the labor associated with real and tangible personal property. In addition, contractors may perform a project management function, where they oversee the work of various other contractors in the completion of a project. As stated above, each of these activities has an impact on the sales and use tax treatment of the contractor.

In a few taxing jurisdictions, the type of contract (lump-sum contract or time and materials contract) can affect the tax treatment of the contractor.

In addition to imposing sales and use taxes on contractors, many states impose special excise or gross receipts taxes on contractors' sales. Therefore, contractors need to exercise caution when dealing with sales and use taxes and other local taxes to avoid incurring unnecessary or unwarranted tax liabilities that cannot be passed along to their customers.

Distinction Between Real and Tangible Property

In most jurisdictions, the key to understanding the treatment of a construction contractor is to understand the distinction that is made between *real* and *tangible personal property*. Although states can have varying criteria for making this determination, most states consider the following three factors:

1. Actual physical annexation of an item to the real property
2. Application or adaptation of an item to the purpose to which the real property is devoted
3. An intention on the part of the person making the annexation to make a permanent accession to the real property

Actual Physical Annexation of an Item to the Real Property

Generally, the tax jurisdiction evaluates the degree of attachment of an item to the real property and whether its removal would cause irreparable damage to the real estate. If the degree of annexation of an item is sufficient to cause irreparable damage to the real estate on the item's removal, the item installed or applied is more *real* property than tangible personal property. By contrast, if *tangible personal property* is easily removed from the real estate without damaging its function or use that would generally be evidence that the item installed or applied retained its character as tangible personal property.

Application or Adaptation of an Item
to the Purpose to Which the Real Property is Devoted

The more integrated an item is into the overall function of the real estate, the more it tends to assume the characteristics of the real estate. If the item is more independent of the real estate in function, it tends to retain its character as *tangible personal property*. For example, a large machine may be attached to a building for its safe operation, but it functions independently from the real estate. Therefore, once installed, it is *not* considered part of the real estate.

Intention on the Part of the Person Making the Annexation to Make a Permanent Accession to the Real Property

This is a more difficult factor to assess, since it deals with the presumed intent of the person making the annexation to real property. Generally, it involves applying a *prudent person* standard to the facts and circumstances to make a reasonable determination of the person's intent, based on the person's actions.

Contractors as Retailers

Contractors frequently act as *retailers* when they resell tangible personal property without installing it or by installing it in such a way that it retains its character as tangible personal property. When contactors act as retailers, they are required to collect tax from their purchasers unless exempt, just like any other retail vendor.

An example of when a contractor acts as a retailer would involve the sale of an item, such as a refrigerator that retains its character as tangible personal property when resold. Contractors acting as retailers may purchase the item being resold as exempt for resale by providing their suppliers with an appropriate exemption certificate.

PLANNING POINTER

Contractors operating as both *consumers* (performing real property improvements) and *retailers* (reselling tangible personal property) need to carefully segregate their purchases so that the purchases are afforded the proper sales tax treatment. Failure to do so can result in an unwanted and unnecessary tax bill.

To determine whether contractors are engaging in real property improvements or reselling tangible personal property, contractors should apply the rules discussed above for distinguishing real property from tangible personal property.

Tax-Exempt Entities

Another issue that often arises involves the treatment of the construction contractor when the construction contractor is performing a contract for a tax-exempt entity or organization. If the construction contractor is performing a contract for a real property improvement in a state that considers the contractor to be the *consumer* of any tangible personal property incorporated into the real estate, the treatment of the contractor performing real property improvements for tax-exempt entities or organizations may vary.

In some jurisdictions, contractors performing real property improvements for tax-exempt entities or organizations are allowed to assume the exempt status of the tax-exempt entity or organization in making purchases of tangible personal property for incorporation into the real estate of the tax-exempt entity or organization.

In other states, the contractor is taxed as a consumer of the materials incorporated into the real estate of a tax-exempt entity or organization.

In states that allow the pass-through of the tax-exempt status, the contractor may purchase the tangible personal property incorporated into the real estate as if the tax-exempt entity or organization had purchased the materials directly and, therefore, may avoid incurring this additional cost.

Repair Transactions

In many instances, the contractor acts as a *repairer* of property. When the contractor repairs real estate, in most states, the contractor is treated as the consumer of materials and owes tax on the cost of materials used for the project. The labor associated with the repair of real estate is typically *not* subject to tax.

However, the contractor acts as a *retailer* of the property when the contractor repairs tangible personal property. In such instances, the contractor's purchase of the parts consumed in performing the repairs *would* be exempt as a purchase for resale. If the state taxes labor, the contractor would charge tax on the cost of labor used to perform the repair and on the parts transferred in connection with the repair—unless the customer is exempt.

Further complexities exist in some states because certain items of real estate are deemed to retain their character as tangible personal property for repair purposes. In some jurisdictions, such items are referred to as *quasi-tangible personal property fixtures.*

For contractors working in a multistate environment, this can introduce a significant complexity into the proper taxation of repair transactions. These real estate components are typically items such as:

- Water heaters
- Water softeners
- Dishwashers
- Furnaces
- Air conditioners

When a contractor repairs such items, even though they are real estate in nature, their repair is treated as a repair of *tangible personal property.* The contractor is therefore required to charge tax on the labor if it is taxed in the state and on the material charges for repair of the items, unless the customer is tax exempt.

PLANNING POINTER

In states that will *not* allow the tax-exempt entity or organization to pass through its tax-exempt status to the construction contractor, it may be possible for the tax-exempt entity or organization to purchase the materials directly and then to contract with the construction contractor separately to install or apply materials purchased. Because the majority of states do not impose tax on the *labor* to install or apply materials sold, the tax-exempt entity would effectively avoid tax that would otherwise be incurred without careful planning.

PLANNING POINTER

Construction contractors must consider the use tax that might be due on supplies and equipment that they purchase for their own use in performing construction contracts. Many construction contractors will purchase supplies or equipment that are not consumed or incorporated into the real estate of their customer.

For example, supplies or equipment that is purchased by the contractor is generally taxable to the construction contractor in the jurisdiction where it is being stored or used. If the contractor has stored or used the item in another jurisdiction and paid tax there, the contractor may be eligible for a credit for the tax paid in that jurisdiction.

CAUTION

Contractors engaged in multistate activities need to carefully consider the sales and use tax treatment of the state in which the contractor's customer is located. Many contractors make the mistake of assuming that all states treat contractors the same and apply the tax rules from their home state to transactions in another jurisdiction.

When bidding on a project, contractors must carefully consider the state sales and use tax treatment of their transactions to avoid over or underbidding the project.

Contractors need to carefully evaluate the nature of their activities in a tax jurisdiction and determine whether they need to be registered as a retailer, a contractor, or both.

STUDY QUESTIONS

> **1.** Contractors frequently act as _____ when they resell tangible property without installing it.
>   **a.** Consumers
>   **b.** Subcontractors
>   **c.** Retailers
>
> **2.** A large machine, attached to a building that is used in manufacturing, would be considered part of the real estate once it is installed. ***True or False?***

TREATMENT OF MANUFACTURERS

Materials, Machinery, and Equipment Overview

State statutes often grant sales and use tax exemptions or reduced rates for manufacturing machinery and equipment as an incentive for manufacturers to relocate to, expand in, or remain in a state. Generally, industrial machinery and equipment are exempt from tax if certain limitations or requirements are met.

Many sales and use tax statutes exempt sales of tangible personal property becoming an ingredient or component part of tangible personal property that is resold. An exemption certificate typically is required to claim any type of exemption.

Production Machinery

Most states provide for an exemption from sales/use tax for machinery and equipment used in the manufacturing or processing of tangible personal property. However, manufacturing encompasses so many diverse activities that its definition varies among states. There is no universal rule, and each state determines its own standards and statutory definitions or has its own judicial interpretations.

To qualify for the machinery and equipment exemption, a company must typically be a *manufacturer* or be *engaged in manufacturing*. Normally, a *manufacturing operation* is defined as an operation or process in which raw materials are changed, converted, or transformed into a new article with a different form, use, name, and function.

Most states require that machinery and equipment be *directly* and *exclusively* used in the manufacturing operation for the exemption to apply.

The definition of *direct use* varies among states. Some states require machinery to come into direct contact with, or be directly involved in the formation of, the item being produced to qualify for the exemption. Other states merely require that the equipment be essential to the production process or contribute to the change.

Exclusive use is generally defined as 100 percent utilization in the manufacturing process, but oftentimes allows for a *de minimis* nonmanufacturing use of up to 5%.

Primary or predominant use ordinarily means greater than 50 percent utilization in the production process.

Materials

Sales and use tax is imposed on the ultimate consumer of the property subject to taxation. Accordingly, sales to manufacturers and processors are generally *not* subject to sales tax if the property purchased becomes or is made a part of a product that is to be sold by the manufacturer.

In some states the material exemption is expanded to include property that is used and either consumed or destroyed in processing.

The criterion for exempting materials and supplies differs from state to state. Therefore, the statutes and regulations of each state should be examined for the appropriate rules. In order for the materials and supplies that are consumed or destroyed to qualify for the exemption, most states require that the item produced be resold.

Shipping Containers and Packaging Materials

Many states provide exemptions for shipping containers and packaging materials that are used to ship products to the consumer and are sold with the products. This includes items such as:

- Wrapping material
- Bags
- Cans
- Twines
- Gummed tapes
- Boxes
- Bottles
- Drums
- Cartons

> **NOTE**
>
> Taxpayers need to exercise care in this area, since many states draw subtle distinctions in what qualifies as exempt shipping containers or packaging materials.

> **EXAMPLE**
>
> Many states distinguish between returnable and nonreturnable shipping containers and packaging materials—imposing tax on returnable shipping containers and packaging materials, such as pallets, but not on nonreturnable shipping containers and packaging materials, such as the product package or carton. Other states provide a broader exemption, allowing materials that are used to ship the product to the customer, such as shipping pallets, to be exempt.

Recognizing the crucial role that shipping containers and packaging materials play in the delivery of goods to purchasers, most states do not impose tax on all shipping containers and packaging materials.

In general, states differentiate between *taxable* and *nontaxable* shipping containers and packaging materials as follows:

- The lowest threshold for exemption requires only that the item be either a shipping container or packaging material.
- Many states impose one or two additional requirements for the item to be exempt. The shipping containers or packaging materials must be:

   1. Used to transfer the purchased product to the end-user
   2. Nonreturnable

Exemptions from tax are a matter of legislative grace. Therefore, the burden of proof rests on the taxpayer claiming an exemption. Most states tend to interpret exemption provisions narrowly. In recent years, however, it appears that judicial bodies are moving toward broader interpretations of the scope of exemptions.

Transfer to Purchaser

Taxpayers often misapply the treatment afforded to shipping containers and packaging materials to shipping aids used to facilitate the transfer of products to the purchaser.

In states that exempt shipping containers and packaging materials, the qualifying items must usually be incorporated into the packaging in such a manner that the item becomes a part of the product sold. This means the item must be within the product packaging or affixed to the packaging in such a way as to make it an integral part of the product.

Items in this category that would *not* qualify for the exemption include:

- Blocking, shoring, and bracing outside the product package to stabilize the load while it is in transit
- Items used to facilitate the transfer that may be returnable, such as:
   - Insulating blankets
   - Tie-downs
   - Protective pads

Even in states that provide exemptions for nonreturnable and/or returnable shipping containers or packaging materials, these items do not typically qualify for the exemption.

Repair and Maintenance

Whether the cost of materials and labor for the repair and maintenance of taxable shipping containers, packaging materials, and shipping aids is subject to tax depends on the treatment of labor to repair tangible personal property in the state and whether the underlying item is taxable. Even in states that exempt certain shipping containers and packaging materials, tax may be imposed on their repair and maintenance.

PLANNING POINTER

In states that impose tax on returnable shipping containers, it may be possible to purchase the shipping containers and ship them to states that exempt returnable shipping containers. After the shipping containers have been used for a year or so, they can often be transferred to taxable states as used equipment that is not subject to tax.

CAUTION

Even in states that exempt returnable and nonreturnable shipping containers and packaging materials, the repair and maintenance of shipping aids is usually subject to tax. Shipping aids generally include items that are used to facilitate the transfer of tangible personal property but that are not transferred to the end-user or consumer, such as protective pads.

STUDY QUESTIONS

> **3.** Which of the following statements is true?
>   **a.** Most states exempt industrial machinery and equipment from sales tax if certain limitations or requirements are met.
>   **b.** Most states require that industrial machinery be used directly or indirectly in the manufacturing process for an exemption to apply.
>   **c.** Most states require that machinery and equipment be used at least 40 percent in the manufacturing process to be exempt from sales tax.
>   **d.** Many states impose sales tax on nonreturnable shipping containers *not* on returnable shipping containers.

4. Which of the following statements is **not** true?
  a. The burden of proof rests on the taxpayer claiming an exemption.
  b. It appears that judicial bodies are moving toward narrower interpretations of the scope of exemptions.
  c. In states that exempt shipping containers and packaging materials, shipping aids used to facilitate the transfer of products to the purchaser must usually be incorporated into the packaging such that it becomes a part of the product sold in order to be exempt.
  d. Even in states that exempt certain shipping containers and packaging materials, tax may be imposed on their repair and maintenance.

Pollution Control Exemption Overview

In recent years, as people have become more environmentally conscious, concern has increased about potential pollution of the air, ground water, and surface water. New laws have been enacted and enforced to punish businesses for polluting the environment and other steps have been taken to monitor the quality of the environment. At the same time, governments have responded with requirements for businesses to curb pollution.

As is often the case with enacted tax laws, exemptions have been enacted in many states to ease the cost of purchasing pollution abatement related equipment, supplies and facilities and to provide an incentive for businesses to make such purchases. While the specifics of these exemptions vary from state-to-state, pollution control exemptions generally exempt purchases of equipment used to reduce or eliminate pollution of the air, ground water or surface water.

In addition, states often provide an exemption for the cost of constructing and equipping a pollution control/abatement facility. Such facilities are typically used by manufacturers to treat effluents from the manufacturing process before the contaminated water is reintroduced into the environment.

EXAMPLE

Many spray painting processes utilize a waterfall to reduce the overspray from the painting process. The contaminated water is then cleansed through a series of filters before it is discharged into the city sanitation system. This process protects the environment from harmful chemicals and additives that might otherwise be introduced into the environment if the contaminated water were not treated before it was discharged into the municipal system.

PLANNING POINTER

The manufacturing or industrial processing exemption, as it applies to machinery and equipment as well as consumable items, is usually limited to equipment used or items consumed during the manufacturing process. Thus, a determination of when a manufacturing process begins and ends must be made.

There are often disputed areas of manufacturing activities that may fall within or outside the exemption, depending on the state. Those marginal activities include:

- Shipping and receiving
- Intraplant movement and storage of goods
- Waste removal
- Research and development
- Quality control
- Safety
- Plant heating
- Lighting
- Air conditioning
- Repair or maintenance

The scope of manufacturing often depends on the function of the equipment and its physical proximity to the remainder of the manufacturing process.

Some states also offer an exemption for the equipment used in pollution control or tangible personal property used to construct a pollution control facility and any chemicals or supplies used in the pollution control process.

As a prerequisite for exempting pollution control equipment and facilities, most states require that the equipment or facility used in pollution control be certified by the state department of natural resources or similar agency in order for it to be eligible for the exemption.

States with such requirements provide a form for taxpayers to file with the state department of natural resources or similar agency that describes the equipment or facility and its intended use. Once the pollution control equipment or facility has been certified, future purchases are exempt as provided under that particular state's statutes. Taxpayers in states with these requirements must retain their certification documents for future audit use.

> **CAUTION**
>
> To qualify for the pollution control exemption in some states, the tax must be paid to the seller and then a claim for refund must be filed along with the state application.

Use Tax on Self-Constructed Machinery Overview

The use tax is designed to complement the sales tax. *Sales tax* is imposed on the retail sale of tangible personal property, and *use tax* is imposed on the taxable use of an item that was not taxed in a sales tax transaction. Sales tax is collected by the seller as an agent for the tax jurisdiction. Use tax on a transaction is remitted by the purchaser when the purchaser files its sales and use tax return.

In a typical purchase, the use tax due is measured by the purchase price of the property. Therefore, the cost (or fair market value) of the item serves as the tax base. However, complications arise if the taxpayer constructs the machinery or equipment for his or her own use.

The taxpayer not only must determine whether the property is taxable but also must determine the amount that is subject to tax. Typically, there are three possible ways of measuring taxability:

1. Full cost
2. Fair market value
3. Material cost

Although the majority of states impose a use tax on self-constructed machinery, a number of states offer exemptions that could apply to equipment of such a nature. The most common exemption that would apply to self-constructed machinery is the exemption for manufacturing machinery and equipment. The first step in determining taxability is to establish whether an exemption that would eliminate the tax on self-constructed equipment is available.

Use Tax Base

If there is no appropriate exemption, the next step is to establish a taxable measure for the item. Because the use tax complements the sales tax, some states base the use tax on the fair market value of the self-constructed asset. Other states look to the material cost of the self-constructed item, and still other states tax the total cost of the item, including the labor applied to manufacture the item.

If the machinery is unique or cannot be purchased, the valuation process can become even more complicated. In such situations, many states accept the allocated costs from the accounting records.

For machinery that is purchased and modified for another use, valuation becomes an issue if the state attempts to tax the fair market value of the machinery. Some states tax only the materials used to construct the machinery or the allocated costs per the accounting records. Most of those states include component parts used in the construction in the tax base at cost, rather than at retail value.

Labor Costs. If the taxpayer's employees are used in the construction process, allocated labor costs are generally not included in the value for use tax purposes.

Overhead Charges. Applied overhead charges are also usually excluded from the tax base. Therefore, it is generally not a good idea to rely solely on the asset or accounting records to determine the taxable value of self-constructed machinery. Some analysis of the cost elements making up the valuation can result in a significant tax savings.

Equipment and Tools. Another issue that can complicate the valuation of self-constructed machinery and equipment is the treatment of the equipment and tools that are used to manufacture the self-constructed items. In states that do not provide a manufacturing exemption, those equipment and tools are taxable. However, in states that provide a manufacturing exemption, the equipment and tools used to self-construct production equipment may or may not be covered under the scope of the exemption.

Generally, states have adopted one of two approaches to the taxation of these items:

1. The narrow application is that the manufacturing machinery and equipment exemption includes *only* those items used directly or exclusively in the manufacturing process or those items that directly contribute to the changes in raw materials that occur as part of the manufacturing process (depending on the qualifying definition of manufacturing in the state statute).
2. The broad application is that the machinery and equipment exemption includes machinery or equipment that is used to manufacture production machinery or equipment that is then used in an exempt way in the manufacturing process (often referred to as the *use-on-use* exemption).

Being aware of whether a state statute allows for the narrow or broad scope of the manufacturing exemption can have a substantial impact on the tax liability associated with self-constructed assets.

PLANNING POINTER

Taxpayers that have self-constructed machinery should establish procedures to identify self-constructed assets and to analyze the costs associated with them. Self-constructed assets typically comprise both of the following:

- Items transferred from inventory, which should have been purchased without payment of tax
- Machinery component parts, which may or may not have been purchased without payment of tax

Such costs generally flow through special project accounts. Therefore, additional analysis is often required for proper reporting. Care should be exercised when assessing tax on self-constructed assets—most accounting systems include internal labor cost as part of the asset's cost but many states exclude that cost from their tax base. By analyzing those accounts, taxpayers can avoid unnecessary overpayments. Having proper procedures in place to capture, review, and report those amounts is an important part of all compliance procedures to avoid additional audit assessments and penalties.

STUDY QUESTIONS

5. Which of the following statements is **not** true regarding certification for a state pollution control exemption?

   a. Some states require that pollution control equipment be certified by the state department of natural resources or similar agency for it to be eligible for an exemption.

   b. States with certification requirements provide a form for taxpayers requesting a description of the equipment.

   c. States with certification requirements provide a form for taxpayers requesting information regarding the intended use of the pollution control equipment.

   d. After certification, future pollution control purchases must also be certified.

6. Which of the following is ordinarily included in the use tax base for machinery that is purchased and modified for another use?

   a. Materials

   b. Labor

   c. Overhead

   d. None of the above

Inventory Withdrawals

Most businesses are aware that a *use tax* is due when an item is purchased from a vendor that is not registered to collect sales tax, and a subsequent taxable use is made of the item. To comply with this requirement, use tax procedures are put in place.

In most companies, the procedures involve either a systemic or manual review of the purchase order tax coding and the amount of any tax billed on the vendor's invoice. When the purchase order is taxable and the vendor fails to bill the tax, the tax is accrued and reported on the purchaser's use tax return.

Many taxpayers are not aware that a tax may be due on the taxable use of an item if it is purchased for inventory and subsequently used in a taxable manner—as a sample not to be resold, in research and development, or for display.

> **EXAMPLE**
>
> When a manufacturer purchases inventory to manufacture a product, the manufacturer's intention is to resell the item purchased as an ingredient or component part of the item being manufactured. If the manufacturer makes a subsequent use of the item, either as a sample or in research and development, then a tax is usually due.

For most taxpayers, capturing the information to report use tax on these purchases requires a procedure that goes beyond the accounts payable procedure outlined above. That is because when the items are initially purchased and entered into the accounts payable system, the intention is that they are going to be used in manufacturing. It is a subsequent decision that removes the item from its intended use and makes it taxable. Therefore, procedures must be implemented to capture the items at their point of inventory withdrawal.

For many taxpayers, cost accumulation reports capture the inventory transfers to research and development or sales and marketing uses, such as samples or display items. Therefore, taxpayers can rely on these reports in many instances to give them the information needed for tax compliance purposes.

In a survey of the states, the majority of states indicated that transfers of inventory items to uses such as samples, research and development, and display or demonstration are subject to tax. While a few exceptions were listed by some states, most states indicated that these uses of inventory items would be subject to tax. None of the states responding to this question indicated that inventory withdrawals would not be taxed. Therefore, taxpayers engaging in such transfers should be aware that tax is due on these uses of inventory items.

If a tax is due on the use of the item, the three values that could potentially be used for reporting the tax liability on inventory transfers are as follows:

1. **Selling price**—the equivalent of the fair market value of the item used or consumed if it were sold in an arm's-length transaction
2. **Full inventory cost**—the manufactured cost of the item that would generally be the sum of material, labor, and overhead costs for the item
3. **Material cost**—the cost to acquire the material content of the item when purchased into inventory (*This is the only value that should be used*).

> ### CAUTION
>
> When using internal reports to capture the information required for use tax compliance, care should be exercised so that the correct value is used. While internal reports can be useful in capturing the items used in a taxable manner, they may not contain the value that should be used for tax reporting purposes. Taxpayers facing this problem may have to adjust the amounts on their reports to get to the correct taxable amount for compliance purposes.

> ### PLANNING POINTER
>
> When taxable transfers out of inventory are made, and the item is used in a taxable manner for a period of time and then returned to inventory and resold, most states will allow the taxpayer to take a credit for the tax on the value of the item when it is returned to stock.

Items Consumed or Destroyed in the Manufacturing Process

In addition to machinery and equipment exemptions in some states, most states allow an exemption on purchases of tangible personal property that becomes an ingredient or component part of tangible personal property that is offered for sale by the manufacturer.

In some states, the material exemption is expanded to include property that is used and either consumed or destroyed in the manufacturing process. The criteria for exempting *consumed or destroyed* materials and supplies often differ from state to state.

STUDY QUESTIONS

> **7.** Which one of the following is the value that should be used to report the tax liability on inventory transfers ?
>
> **a.** Full inventory cost
> **b.** Selling price
> **c.** Labor cost
> **d.** Material cost

> **8.** Inventory withdrawals for research and development are ***never*** taxable. ***True or False?***

Printers

States offering production machinery exemptions often include printers in their definition of manufacturers qualifying for the exemption. However, the sales and use tax treatment of printers can be complicated by the varying services that printers provide.

Many printers perform a service when they use materials provided by their customers to produce their finished products. In this case, the printer is transformed from a manufacturer to a service provider and this has a significant impact on the printer's tax obligations.

Printers function as *manufacturers* when they produce a printed document from raw materials. In such instances the printer is transforming tangible personal property from one form to another by a process that many states consider to be manufacturing.

In other instances, however, the customer may provide paper, ink, or other raw materials for the printer to use in producing the printed document. The customer may do that to coordinate color, texture, or appearance with some other document that will be displayed with the printed piece. In addition, the customer may be able to obtain a substantially discounted price for the supplies because of other commercial relationships with the vendor that may not be transferable to the printer.

In many states, when the printer produces a printed document using materials provided by its customer, the printer is viewed as a *service provider*. Performing this service can result in a loss of the sales tax exemption for machinery and equipment that is otherwise available to the printer, because the printer has stepped outside the role of a manufacturer. In addition, the tax treatment of the supplies provided may be impacted.

When the printer acts as a *manufacturer*, it is selling tangible personal property and is required to collect sales tax on the transaction. When the printer acts as a *service provider*, it may or may not have an obligation to collect the tax, depending on whether the state taxes the services performed by the printer.

State statutes often grant exemptions or reduced rates for manufacturing machinery and equipment as an incentive for manufacturers.

Generally, industrial machinery and equipment are exempt from tax if certain limitations or requirements are met. In addition, many sales and use tax statutes exempt sales of tangible personal property that become an ingredient or component part of tangible personal property that is resold.

CAUTION

Many companies have in-house print shops that create internal publications, advertising materials, etc. In states allowing a manufacturing exemption, the printing equipment will usually qualify for the exemption. However, any supplies used in the production of materials that are given away will *not* qualify as tax exempt. Most states have an additional requirement that the item be resold for the materials consumed in order to qualify for the exemption.

Integrated Plant Doctrine

In states that offer a manufacturing exemption, the state has the option of viewing the manufacturing exemption narrowly or broadly. The narrower view of manufacturing requires that the manufacturing machinery and equipment come into direct contact with the product being manufactured and/or contribute to the transformation in some direct way.

The broader view of manufacturing, or the Integrated Plant Doctrine, does not view each manufacturing task separately, but rather looks to whether the equipment is part of a synchronized system that is engaged in manufacturing. For example, under the Integrated Plant Doctrine, a conveyer that moves raw materials and work-in-process from one workstation to another within the plant would be considered part of a synchronized system engaged in manufacturing.

Under the narrower view of manufacturing, the conveyor would likely *not* qualify for exemption, since it does not directly contribute to the change in the product being manufactured—it merely moves the product and raw materials from one point in the process to another point in the process. This distinction can be crucial when evaluating whether a particular piece of equipment should be considered exempt as manufacturing machinery and equipment.

Utilities Used in Manufacturing

For many manufacturers, the cost of fuel and electricity used in the manufacturing process represents a substantial expense—particularly in recent years, as the cost of fuel and other energy commodities have increased dramatically.

To help reduce those costs and to level the competitive playing field, many states have enacted exemptions for fuel and electricity consumed in the manufacturing process. The exemption can cover virtually all forms of energy that might be purchased for use in manufacturing, or the exemption can be broad enough to cover virtually every type of fuel that might be used or consumed in the manufacturing process.

Freight and Shipping Charges

The growth of the mail-order and the electronic commerce purchase of tangible personal property has heightened taxpayer awareness of the sales and use tax treatment of freight and shipping charges. This growth in remote purchasing has led to greater confusion for vendors and customers alike, because of the conflicting treatment afforded freight and shipping charges by the states.

There are several issues that can impact the taxability of freight and shipping charges.

As a general rule, many states impose sales and use tax on all charges that are incurred prior to the passage of title from the vendor to the customer. Despite that general rule, many states do not include separately stated freight and shipping charges in the tax base.

In many states, the treatment of freight and shipping charges varies depending on whether the charges are billed by the vendor to the purchaser or by a freight carrier directly to the purchaser. In some states, even if the freight or shipping charge is separately billed by the seller, it is subject to tax.

Conversely, if the freight or shipping charge is billed by the freight company directly to the purchaser, it is *not* subject to tax in most states, even if it is incurred in connection with the delivery of tangible personal property and would be taxable if billed by the vendor. It can be viewed either as a cost incurred after the passage of title or as a charge for a nontaxable service, regardless of the tangible personal property aspect of the transaction.

The following questions are integral in making the determination of taxability of freight and shipping charges. Are the charges subject to tax:

- Even if separately billed?
- If included in the selling price?
- If billed directly by a carrier?

PLANNING POINTER

If possible, a transaction should be structured so that either the freight and shipping charges are billed separately or the freight company directly bills the purchaser for the cost of the freight and shipping charges.

Many states exempt separately stated freight and shipping charges. Therefore, structuring the purchase in such a manner avoids the unnecessary payment of tax. Since the majority of states do not impose tax on freight and shipping charges billed directly by the freight company, handling the transaction in this manner can even further reduce exposure to additional taxes.

> **CAUTION**
>
> In states that impose tax on freight and shipping charges, even postage can be subject to tax when billed to the purchaser as a freight or shipping charge.

STUDY QUESTIONS

9. When a printer acts as a service provider, which of the following is **not** true?

  a. It may or may not have an obligation to collect sales tax.

  b. The tax treatment of supplies provided by the customer may be impacted.

  c. It is selling tangible personal property and is required to collect sales tax on the transaction.

  d. None of the above

10. Which of the following statements is **not** true?

  a. Many states do *not* include separately stated freight and shipping charges in the tax base.

  b. Under the narrower view of manufacturing, a conveyor that moves raw materials and work-in-process from one workstation to another within the plant would probably qualify for an exemption.

  c. Under the *Integrated Plant Doctrine*, if a conveyer moves raw materials and work-in-process from one workstation to another within the plant, that would be considered part of a synchronized system engaged in manufacturing.

  d. Many states have enacted exemptions for fuel and electricity consumed in the manufacturing process.

CPE NOTE: When you have completed your study and review of chapters 4-7, which comprise Module 1, you may wish to take the Quizzer for this Module.

For your convenience, you can also take this Quizzer online at **www.cchtestingcenter.com.**

Answers to Study Questions

MODULE 1 — CHAPTER 1

1. d. Correct. South Dakota is one of the four states that do not levy a corporate income tax.
a. Incorrect. Alabama is one of the 46 states that impose some type of income-based tax.
b. Incorrect. The California corporate franchise tax is computed essentially in the same manner as an income tax.
c. Incorrect. The Florida corporate franchise tax is computed essentially in the same manner as an income tax.

2. d. Correct. All of the above are limitations of P.L. 86-272.
a. Incorrect. This is a limitation of P.L. 86-272. Public Law 86-272 provides no protection against the imposition of a sales tax collection obligation, a tax based on gross receipts, or state franchise taxes imposed on a base other than income.
b. Incorrect. This is a limitation of P.L. 86-272. Public Law 86-272 does not protect activities such as leasing tangible personal property, selling services, selling or leasing real estate, or selling or licensing intangibles.
c. Incorrect. This is a limitation of P.L. 86-272. If a salesperson exercises authority to approve orders within a state, or performs non-solicitation activities, such as repairs, customer training or technical assistance, the company does not qualify for protection under P.L. 86-272.

3. a. Correct. Conformity with federal provisions simplifies tax compliance for multistate corporations. The states that do not tie the computation of state taxable income directly to a corporation's federal tax return typically adopt the majority of the federal provisions governing items of gross income and deduction in defining the state tax base.
b. Incorrect. This is a disadvantage of state conformity to federal tax provisions. States must be wary that changes to the federal tax law could significantly affect state tax revenues.
c. Incorrect. This is a disadvantage of state conformity to federal tax provisions. Complete conformity would allow the federal government to determine state tax policy.
d. Incorrect. One of the above is an advantage of state conformity to federal provisions.

4. c. Correct. This is not a true statement. Under the UDITPA approach, a taxpayer apportions a percentage of its business income to each state in which it has nexus, but specifically allocates the entire amount of any nonbusiness income to a single state.

a. Incorrect. This is a true statement. UDITPA has been adopted, at least in part, by most states.

b. Incorrect. This is a true statement. Business income is defined as income arising from transactions and activity in the regular course of the taxpayer's trade or business and includes income from tangible and intangible property if the acquisition, management, and disposition of the property constitute integral parts of the taxpayer's regular trade or business operations. Nonbusiness income is all income other than business income.

d. Incorrect. One of the above is not a true statement.

5. False. Correct. Assigning more weight to the sales factor tends to reduce the tax on *in-state* corporations that have significant amounts of property and payroll in the state, but sales nationwide.

True. Incorrect. Assigning more weight to the sales factor than to the property or payroll factor tends to *increase* the percentage of an out-of-state corporation's income that is subject to tax, because the out-of-state corporation's principal activity in the state—sales of its products—is weighted more heavily than its payroll and property activities.

6. b. Correct. This is known as the destination test.

a. Incorrect. This only applies to sales to the U.S. government, which are assigned to the state from which the goods are shipped, and in the case of throwback.

c. Incorrect. Certain types of nonbusiness income, such as nonbusiness interest and dividend income, is assigned to the state of commercial domicile.

d. Incorrect. One of the above determines where the sales are assigned.

7. a. Correct. Arizona is one of the states that requires members of a unitary business group to compute their taxable income on a combined unitary basis.

b. Incorrect. Delaware is one of the four states that requires separate-company returns.

c. Incorrect. Maryland requires separate-company reporting. In contrast, most states require or permit some type of consolidated or combined reporting.

d. Incorrect. Wisconsin requires separate-company reporting as do three other states.

8. False. *Correct.* Inclusion in a state consolidated return generally requires 80 percent or more ownership, which piggybacks on the ownership threshold for inclusion in a federal consolidated return.
True. *Incorrect.* Inclusion in a combined unitary report generally requires more than 50 percent ownership; however, inclusion in a state consolidated return generally requires 80 percent or more ownership.

9. a. *Correct.* Non-solicitation activities are not protected by P. L. 86-272, and generally create income tax nexus.
b. *Incorrect.* Solicitation activities are protected by P. L. 86-272, and generally do not create income tax nexus..
c. *Incorrect.* Providing a sales representative in that state with an office allowance rather than an actual office may avoid nexus if maintaining a formal corporate office in that state creates an undesired nexus.
d. *Incorrect.* One of the above is not a way to avoid nexus in a state.

10. a. *Correct.* Wisconsin is not a popular location for an intangible property holding company because it imposes a 7.9 percent corporate income tax.
b. *Incorrect.* Delaware is a popular state for intangible property holding companies because it does not tax the income of a corporation whose only activity in the state is the maintenance and management of intangible property.
c. *Incorrect.* Nevada is a popular state for intangible property holding companies because it does not levy a corporate income tax.
d. *Incorrect.* One of the above is not a popular state for intangible property holding companies.

MODULE 1 — CHAPTER 2

1. d. *Correct.* Affiliates organized in a foreign country generally are *not* included in a state consolidated return. However, states can require the inclusion of foreign country affiliates in a combined unitary report.
a. *Incorrect.* Combined unitary reporting is not so much a type of return as the name given to the calculations (akin to a spreadsheet) by which a unitary business group apportions its income.
b. *Incorrect.* Inclusion in a state consolidated return generally requires stock ownership of 80 percent or more, but inclusion in a combined unitary report generally requires stock ownership of more than 50 percent.
c. *Incorrect.* To be included in a combined report, an affiliate must be engaged in the same trade or business as the other group members, as exhibited by such factors as functional integration and centralized management.

2. c. *Correct.* A primary disadvantage of both consolidated returns and combined unitary reporting is that they can prevent a taxpayer from creating legal structures and intercompany transactions that shift income from affiliates based in high-tax states to affiliates based in low-tax states.

a. *Incorrect.* The ability to offset the losses of one affiliate against the profits of other affiliates is an *advantage* of both consolidated returns and combined reporting. The deferral of gains on intercompany transactions is another major advantage of both consolidated returns and combined reporting.

b. *Incorrect.* The elimination of intercorporate dividends is a major *advantage* of both consolidated returns and combined reporting.

d. *Incorrect.* One of the above is a disadvantage of both filing options.

3. b. *Correct.* About 20 states—including California, Illinois and Michigan—require members of a unitary business group to compute their taxable income on a combined basis.

a. *Incorrect.* Fewer than 30 states require members of a unitary business group to compute their taxable income on a combined basis.

c. *Incorrect.* Roughly 15 states generally allow commonly controlled corporations to file separate company returns, but they also require or permit a combined unitary report, if certain conditions are satisfied.

d. *Incorrect.* More than 10 states require members of a unitary business group to compute their taxable income on a combined basis.

4. a. *Correct.* Whether it is beneficial for a taxpayer to make a water's-edge election depends on the facts and circumstances. A major advantage of making a water's-edge election is that it avoids the compliance burden of a worldwide combination, which can be substantial, particularly if the unitary business group includes a large number of foreign affiliates.

b. *Incorrect.* If the unitary business group includes no foreign affiliates, a water's-edge election is not an issue.

c. *Incorrect.* A water's-edge election may increase the taxpayer's state tax if the taxpayer's U.S. operations are more profitable than its foreign operations.

d. *Incorrect.* One of the above is a situation where it may be beneficial for a taxpayer to make a water's-edge election.

5. d. *Correct.* Factors of profitability include functional integration, centralization of management, and economies of scale.

a. *Incorrect.* Under the three-unities test, a unitary business exists if unity of ownership, unity of operation, and unity of use are present.

b. *Incorrect.* Under the contribution or dependency test, a unitary business exists if "the operation of the portion of the business done within the state is dependent upon or contributes to the operation of the business without the state."

c. Incorrect. Under the flow-of-value test, a parent corporation and its subsidiary are unitary if there is some sharing or exchange of value beyond the mere flow of funds arising out of a passive investment or a distinct business operation.

6. False. Correct. A conglomerate may or may not be considered unitary, depending on whether there is strong centralized management, as exhibited by a centralized executive force and shared staff functions, as well as economies of scale in the form of common employee pension and benefit plans, common insurance policies, etc.

True. Incorrect. A conglomerate is *not* always considered to be unitary. Factors that will determine if it is unitary include whether there is strong centralized management and economies of scale.

7. a. Correct. Joint participation of corporate directors and officers in management decisions that affect different business units is an indication of centralized management.

b. Incorrect. Common distribution systems are an example of functional integration.

c. Incorrect. Centralized administrative functions are an example of economies of scale.

d. Incorrect. Centralized purchasing is an example of economies of scale.

8. b. Correct. New York provides the following tests for determining whether related corporations satisfy the substantial intercorporate transactions requirement: substantial intercorporate receipts, substantial intercorporate expenditures, multi-year tests and substantial intercorporate asset transfers.

a. Incorrect. Unity of operations is a factor in applying the three-unities test for determining the existence of a unitary business.

c. Incorrect. Unity of use is a factor in applying the three-unities test for determining the existence of a unitary business.

d. Incorrect. Functional integration is a factor in applying the factors of profitability test for determining the existence of a unitary business.

9. d. Correct. All of the states listed use an 80/20-type test in determining which members should be included in a combined report.

a. Incorrect. California permits a unitary group to make a water's-edge election. A water's-edge group includes unitary members whose average property, payroll, and sales factors in the United States is 20 percent or more.

b. Incorrect. For Illinois tax purposes, a unitary business group does not include an 80/20 corporation, which is a corporation whose business activity outside the United States, as measured by payroll and property factors, is 80 percent or more of the member's total business activity.

c. Incorrect. For Texas tax purposes, a taxable entity that conducts business outside the United States is excluded from the combined report if 80 percent or more of its property and payroll are assigned to locations outside the United States.

10. False. Correct. California has *not* adopted a statutory definition of a unitary business. However, California regulations provide guidelines on what a unitary business is.

True. Incorrect. California has *not* adopted a statutory definition of a unitary business. However, California regulations state that determination of whether two or more commonly controlled corporations are unitary depends on the facts in each case, and there is a strong presumption that the taxpayer's operations are unitary if any of the following factors is present: 1) same type of business, 2) steps in a vertical process, or 3) strong centralized management.

MODULE 1 — CHAPTER 3

1. c. Correct. A domestic corporation must make an S corporation election by filing federal Form 2553.

a. Incorrect. To be eligible to make an S corporation election, a domestic corporation must have only one class of stock.

b. Incorrect. To be eligible to make an S corporation election, a domestic corporation must have no more than 100 shareholders.

d. Incorrect. For a domestic corporation to be eligible to make an S corporation election, all of its shareholders must be either individuals who are U.S. citizens or resident aliens, estates, or certain types of trusts.

2. a. Correct. States generally conform to the federal pass-through treatment of S corporations if the corporation has filed a valid S corporation election for federal tax purposes.

b. Incorrect. Most, but not all states provide that the filing of a federal S corporation election automatically qualifies the corporation as an S corporation for state tax purposes.

c. Incorrect. Only a handful of states require taxpayers to comply with special procedures in addition to federal procedures in order to make a valid S corporation election.

d. Incorrect. One of the statements is correct.

3. True. Correct. Most states treat S corporations as pass-through entities. However, some states impose a corporate-level tax in addition to a shareholder-level personal income tax.

False. Incorrect. Although a number of states impose entity-level taxes on S corporations, most states treat S corporations as pass-through entities.

4. c. *Correct.* New Jersey previously imposed an income tax on S corporations, most recently at 0.67 percent. The tax does *not* apply for tax years ending on or after July 1, 2007.
a. *Incorrect.* Kansas imposes a franchise tax on S corporations that is scheduled to be phased out by 2011.
b. *Incorrect.* Michigan repealed its single business tax effective December 31, 2007, and replaced it with a business income tax and modified gross receipts tax. Both taxes apply to S corporations.
d. *Incorrect.* S corporations are subject to both the Tennessee corporate excise tax and the Tennessee corporate franchise tax.

5. d. *Correct.* All of the above are ways states may promote tax compliance by nonresident shareholders.
a. *Incorrect.* One technique for promoting compliance on the part of nonresident shareholders is to require the S corporation to withhold and remit any taxes due on the shareholders' distributive shares of S corporation income.
b. *Incorrect.* To foster compliance, states require S corporations to file an annual informational returns (similar to federal Form 1120S) and issue K-1s for shareholders.
c. *Incorrect.* One method of enhancing compliance is to require or permit an S corporation to file a composite return on behalf of the nonresident shareholders. A composite return is a single filing in which the participating shareholders report their distributive shares of the S corporation's income and the S corporation pays the state tax on behalf of the nonresident shareholders.

6. b. *Correct.* In a limited partnership, the limited partners generally do *not* take part in the management of the partnership. The general partner(s) manage the partnership.
a. *Incorrect.* In a general partnership, each partner has unlimited liability for the partnership's debts and each partner generally has the right to participate in the management of the partnership.
c. *Incorrect.* In a limited liability partnership, partners of certain types of professional service firms are able to reduce their exposure to lawsuits but operate as a general partnership. In a general partnership, each partner has the right to participate in the partnership's management.
d. *Incorrect.* Only one of the types of partnerships does not allow every partner to participate in the partnership.

7. d. Correct. All of the statements are true.

a. Incorrect. An entity's owners can merely check a box on federal Form 8832 to determine an eligible entity's classification, but if Form 8832 is not filed, default classification rules determine an eligible entity's classification for federal income tax purposes.

b. Incorrect. Under the federal check-the-box regulations, the default classification for a domestic limited liability company that has two or more members is a partnership.

c. Incorrect. Most states do treat partnerships as pass-through entities. However, a number of states impose entity-level taxes on partnerships.

8. False. Correct. Virtually all of the states conform to the federal classification rules for partnerships.

True. Incorrect. In the vast majority of cases, an entity that is treated as a partnership for federal tax purposes is also treated as a partnership for state income tax purposes.

9. b. Correct. In asserting that an out-of-state corporation has nexus solely by virtue of its ownership interest in a partnership doing business in the state, states rely primarily on the *aggregate theory* of partnership, which holds that a partnership is the aggregation of its owners, rather than an entity that is separate and distinct from its owners.

a. Incorrect. The types of contacts that create nexus for a partnership are determined partially, but not primarily, by applicable state statutes.

c. Incorrect. The types of contacts that create nexus for a partnership are determined partially, but not primarily, by Public Law 86-272.

d. Incorrect. The types of contacts that create nexus for a partnership are determined partially, but not primarily, by U.S. constitutional law.

10. a. Correct. Under *partner*-level apportionment, the partner computes its state apportionment percentage by combining its share of the partnership's property, payroll, and sales with its other apportionment factors.

b. Incorrect. Under the partnership-level apportionment approach, the corporate partner's distributive share of partnership income is independently apportioned to the state by multiplying the distributive share of partnership income by the partnership's apportionment percentage.

c. Incorrect. Under the partnership-level apportionment approach, the corporate partner's state tax base is determined by combining the apportioned partnership income with any other income that the corporate partner allocates or apportions to the state by virtue of its other (non-partnership) activities.

d. Incorrect. Partnership-level apportionment treats the corporate investment in the partnership as a separate trade or business. The corporate partner's distributive share of partnership income is apportioned to the nexus state based solely on the property, payroll, and sales of the partnership.

11. c. Correct. Some states, including Georgia and Pennsylvania, require partner-level apportionment, regardless of whether there is a unitary relationship between the partner and the partnership.
a. Incorrect. California is one of a number of states that require partner-level apportionment if the activities of the corporate partner and the partnership constitute a unitary business, but require partnership-level apportionment if the corporate partner and partnership are not unitary.
b. Incorrect. New Jersey is one of a number of states that require partner-level apportionment if the activities of the corporate partner and the partnership constitute a unitary business, but require partnership-level apportionment if the corporate partner and partnership are not unitary.
d. Incorrect. One of the states listed requires partner-level apportionment, regardless of whether there is a unitary relationship between the partner and the partnership.

12. d. Correct. The default classification for an LLC that is organized in the United States and has two or more members is partnership. Different default classification rules apply to an LLC organized in a foreign country.
a. Incorrect. If all the members of a *foreign* LLC have limited liability, the default classification is corporation.
b. Incorrect. The default classification for an SMLLC is a branch if the single member is a corporation.
c. Incorrect. The default classification for an SMLLC is a sole proprietorship if the single member is an individual.

13. c. Correct. Texas subjects LLCs to its margin tax. Prior to 2007, LLCs were subject to the Texas corporate franchise tax.
a. Incorrect. Illinois imposes a personal property replacement tax on LLCs classified as partnerships.
b. Incorrect. Michigan imposes a business income tax and a modified gross receipts tax on LLCs.
d. Incorrect. Washington subjects LLCs to its business and occupation tax.

14. False. Correct. States in which the member does *not* reside tax a nonresident member's distributive share of LLC income *only* if the LLC has nexus in the state, and then only to the extent the nonresident member's distributive share of income is attributable to sources within the state.

True. *Incorrect.* The state in which a member *resides* generally taxes the entire amount of a resident member's distributive share of LLC income, regardless of where the income was earned.

15. b. *Correct.* The primary method for establishing a substantial business purpose is to satisfy a natural business year test. A *natural business year* is one in which at least 25 percent of the taxpayer's gross receipts are received in the last two months of the 12-month period.

a. *Incorrect.* Twenty-five percent of the taxpayer's gross receipts can be received in more than just the last month of the 12-month period.

c. *Incorrect.* If a partnership, S corporation, or PSC can establish to the satisfaction of the IRS that there is a substantial business purpose for adopting a different tax year, an exception applies to the requirement of using a calendar year. The last three months is *not* the period of time in which at least twenty-five percent of the taxpayer's gross receipts must have been received in order to qualify for the exception.

d. *Incorrect.* The period in which 25 percent of the taxpayer's gross receipts must be received to establish a natural business year is shorter than four months.

MODULE 2 — CHAPTER 4

1. c. *Correct.* In *Wrigley,* the U.S. Supreme Court dealt with whether the taxpayer's activities in Wisconsin caused it to have income tax nexus with the state.

**a. *Incorrect. National Bellas Hess* is a use tax case.

**b. *Incorrect. Quill* is a case dealing with use taxes.

d. *Incorrect.* One of the cases dealt with whether the taxpayer was subject to state income taxes.

2. a. *Correct.* With respect to nexus, the Supreme Court has interpreted the Commerce Clause as prohibiting a state from taxing an out-of-state corporation unless that company has *substantial nexus* with the state.

b. *Incorrect.* With respect to nexus, the Supreme Court has interpreted the Due Process Clause as prohibiting a state from taxing an out-of-state corporation unless there is a *minimal connection* between the company's interstate activities and the taxing state.

c. *Incorrect.* P.L. 86-272 allows taxpayers to engage in certain protected activities without triggering the imposition of income tax.

d. *Incorrect.* One of the answers is what prohibits a state from taxing an out-of-state corporation unless that company has *substantial nexus* with the state.

3. c. Correct. The Supreme Court found that storage of inventory (in this case, gum) within the state was *not* ancillary to Wrigley's solicitation activities.

a. Incorrect. This activity was considered entirely ancillary to solicitation by the Court because it served no purpose, apart from facilitating requests for purchases.

b. Incorrect. The Supreme Court considered this activity as falling within its definition of solicitation, which encompassed "those activities that are entirely ancillary to requests for purchases—those that serve no independent business function apart from their connection to the soliciting of orders."

d. Incorrect. The use of hotels and homes in the state for sales-related meetings was considered by the Supreme Court to be an activity that was ancillary to the solicitation of sales.

4. b. Correct. Although solicitation of orders by a salesperson is considered a protected activity, order approval by a salesperson in the state is unprotected.

a. Incorrect. Solicitation of orders is a protected activity under P.L. 86-272.

c. Incorrect. Replacing damaged or returned property is considered a protected activity under the MTC's policy statement.

d. Incorrect. One of the activities is considered "unprotected" under the MTC's policy statement regarding the proper allocation of P.L. 86-272.

5. a. Correct. Solicitation of orders is a protected activity under P.L. 86-272.

b. Incorrect. Although solicitation of orders by a salesperson is considered a protected activity, order approval by a salesperson in the state is unprotected.

c. Incorrect. Repossessing property is considered an unprotected activity under the MTC's policy statement.

d. Incorrect. One of the activities is considered "protected" under the MTC's policy statement regarding the proper allocation of P.L. 86-272.

6. True. Correct. Court decisions indicate that the relative value of a company's in-state property, the number of in-state employees, or the relative amount of sales made in the state may not be determinative if the company is otherwise found to have activities in the state that are more than *de minimis*.

False. Incorrect. The U.S. Supreme Court noted in *Quill* that the slightest presence in the state does not meet the substantial nexus requirements of the Commerce Clause, but did not define how much physical presence is necessary to establish substantial nexus.

7. d. Correct. The position taken in the bulletin is based on the Supreme Court's decisions in *Scripto* and *Tyler Pipe,* both of which dealt with the use of independent sales representatives, as opposed to independent service providers.
a. Incorrect. The bulletin takes the position that this type of activity does create nexus.
b. Incorrect. Only a handful of states, including California, have taken a position contrary to that in Nexus Bulletin 95-1.
c. Incorrect. The position taken in the bulletin is not based on *Quill.* In *Quill,* the Supreme Court upheld the bright-line physical presence test.

8. d. Correct. *J.C. Penney National Bank,* the Tennessee Court of Appeals rejected the affiliate nexus argument because the in-state retail stores did not conduct any activities that assisted the affiliated out-of-state bank in maintaining its credit card business in Tennessee.
a. Incorrect. In *Borders Online,* the California Court of Appeals ruled that an out-of-state online retailer had substantial nexus in California for sales tax purposes because an affiliated corporation, which sold similar products in stores in California, performed return and exchange activities for the online retailer.
b. Incorrect. In *Reader's Digest Association,* the California Court of Appeals held that Reader's Digest had income tax nexus with California because of solicitation activities performed by its wholly owned in-state subsidiary.
c. Incorrect. In *Dillard National Bank,* the Tennessee Chancery Court ruled that an out-of-state subsidiary corporation that issued proprietary credit cards for use in a chain of in-state department stores that were operated by the parent corporation had income tax nexus in Tennessee.

9. a. Correct. The Supreme Court also noted in the *Scripto* decision that "to permit such formal 'contractual shifts' to make a constitutional difference would open the gates to a stampede of tax avoidance."
b. Incorrect. *Reader's Digest Association* is a California case in which the Court of Appeals held that an out-of-state parent corporation had nexus as a result of solicitation activities performed by its wholly owned in-state subsidiary.
c. Incorrect. *Kmart Properties Inc.* is a New Mexico intangible holding company case.
d. Incorrect. *Share International Inc.* is a Florida case in which the state Supreme Court upheld a district court's *insufficient nexus* decision.

10. c. *Correct.* Also, the Texas Comptroller of Public Accounts has held that a taxpayer could claim immunity from the earned surplus portion of the Texas franchise tax under P.L. 86-272 even though the taxpayer delivered tangible personal property into Texas using company-owned trucks.
a. *Incorrect.* This is also known as back-hauling and is likely *not* protected under P.L. 86-272.
b. *Incorrect.* Activities of a delivery truck driver such as collecting payments is likely *not* protected under P.L. 86-272 because it exceeds solicitation of sales.
d. *Incorrect.* One of the activities is generally protected under P.L. 86-272.

11. d. *Correct.* In this case, the Missouri Supreme Court ruled that two trademark holding companies were not subject to the Missouri corporate income tax because they did not have any activity in Missouri in the form of payroll, property, or sales.
a. *Incorrect.* In this case, the South Carolina Supreme Court held that a trademark holding company that licensed its intangibles for use in South Carolina had nexus for income tax purposes despite the lack of any tangible property or employees in South Carolina.
b. *Incorrect.* In this case, the North Carolina Court of Appeals held that licensing intangibles for use in North Carolina was sufficient to establish income tax nexus for an out-of-state trademark holding company.
c. *Incorrect.* In this case, the Oklahoma Court of Civil Appeals ruled that licensing intangibles for use in Oklahoma was sufficient to establish income tax nexus for a Delaware trademark holding company, even though the holding company had no physical presence in Oklahoma.

12. True. *Correct.* However, many states provide targeted exemptions for selected activities that would otherwise create nexus.
False. *Incorrect.* The statement is true. However, states must provide the protections afforded taxpayers under the U.S. Constitution and P.L. 86-272.

13. c. *Correct.* For leased mobile property (e.g., airplanes and other transportation vehicles), many states provide that an isolated landing or trip through the state will not create nexus.
a. *Incorrect.* In addition to the presence of property, another factor that helps to support nexus is the negotiation or execution of the lease agreement in the state.
b. *Incorrect.* Nexus may be established for the lessor because of the in-state presence of owned business property. Another factor that helps to support nexus is the receipt of the rental payments in the state.

d. Incorrect. In the case of leased property that is immobile, the creation of nexus generally is easy to identify because the lessor is informed of the state in which the property is expected to be located during the rental period.

14. a. Correct. In *Bandag Licensing Corp. v. Rylander,* the Texas appeals court determined that under *Quill,* a state may *not* constitutionally impose its corporate franchise tax on an out-of-state corporation that lacks a physical presence in the state.
b. Incorrect. In *Kelly-Springfield Tire Co.* (1993), the *Connecticut* Supreme Court also ruled that the authority to do business does *not* deny a corporation the protections afforded by P.L. 86-272.
c. Incorrect. In *Kelly-Springfield Tire Co.* (1994), the *Massachusetts* Supreme Judicial Court ruled that the authority to do business in a state is *not* a separate business activity that creates nexus.
d. Incorrect. In *LSDHC Corp.,* the *Ohio* Board of Tax Appeals ruled that registration to do business was *not,* by itself, sufficient to create nexus for purposes of Ohio's corporate franchise tax on net income.

15. b. Correct. The Internet Tax Freedom Act imposed a three-year moratorium on any "new" state or local taxes on Internet access. Subsequent legislation extended the moratorium.
a. Incorrect. This statement is true. Treaty permanent establishment provisions are *not* binding for state nexus purposes because income tax treaties generally do not apply to state taxes.
c. Incorrect. This statement is true. Another potential solution is more uniform and simplified state and local tax systems.
d. Incorrect. One of the statements is *not* true.

MODULE 2 — CHAPTER 5

1. True. Correct. A seller is responsible and liable for payment of tax to the state, whether or not tax is collected or reimbursement is obtained.
False. Incorrect. State sales tax may take the form of a privilege tax imposed directly on the seller for the privilege of engaging in the sales activity, or it may take the form of a consumer tax imposed on the sale or purchase transaction itself. In either case, the seller is responsible for payment of tax to the state, whether or not tax is collected or reimbursement is obtained.

2. c. Correct. Excluding basic necessities from tax reduces the regressivity in the tax system by placing the burden of taxation on those who can afford to purchase items that are not necessities.
a. Incorrect. Most, if not all, states tax luxury items such as art.

b. Incorrect. Most, if not all, states tax items of discretionary consumption such as furniture.

d. Incorrect. Most, if not all, states tax prepared foods and restaurant meals.

3. b. Correct. The licensing or sale of custom-designed software is normally treated as a sale of services or intangible property and is *not* subject to tax.

a. Incorrect. Most states take the position that a charge for shipping and handling is taxable, presumably because that charge is tainted by the handling component.

c. Incorrect. Off-the-shelf, or canned, software generally is taxable.

d. Incorrect. Most states have enacted legislation or promulgated regulations to tax prepaid phone cards at the point of sale, in the same way that all other tangible personal property is taxed.

4. a. Correct. Many states do provide an exemption for casual or isolated sales. However, a common restriction is the number of sales per year for which the exemption may be claimed.

b. Incorrect. Barter transactions are exchanges of tangible personal property in which the consideration given is something other than cash. Most states treat such transactions as sales that are subject to sales and use tax.

c. Incorrect. A use tax does *not* apply if the state has previously imposed a sales tax on the same item, unless a subsequent taxable use is made of the item by another taxpayer. Also, when one state has imposed a sales tax on an item that is subsequently imported into a second state, the second state may impose a use tax on that item.

d. Incorrect. Exemptions generally fall into *four* broad categories: 1. Identity of the purchaser, 2. Character of the item sold, 3. Use of the product, and 4. Nature of the transaction.

5. a. Correct. The sales price subject to tax does *not* usually include interest charged for credit if it is separately stated.

b. Incorrect. Generally, no reduction in sales price is allowed for excise or import taxes paid by the seller. However, the rules of each state must be consulted because specific taxes may be given special treatment.

c. Incorrect. Manufacturer rebates generally do *not* reduce the sales price subject to tax.

d. Incorrect. One of the items listed is generally not included in the total taxable sales price.

MODULE 2 — CHAPTER 6

1. d. Correct. While auditors have a great deal of authority regarding the timing of an audit, taxpayers have rights to exert as well. A taxpayer who is fully scheduled with audits can suggest a later date that is more convenient.

a. Incorrect. Delaying the discussion of a difficult topic until later in the auditor's visit may result in less focus on sensitive details due to the auditor's haste to wrap up the audit.

b. Incorrect. An auditor can question hundreds or even thousands of transactions.

c. Incorrect. An audit can take anywhere from a few days to years to complete.

2. b. Correct. Forwarding records to the auditor after some preliminary review to allow the auditor to complete portions of the fieldwork at the office poses risks for the taxpayer by providing the auditor with unlimited time to review transactions and contact vendors, and should only be done in areas where the taxpayer anticipates *limited* exposure.

a. Incorrect. Companies can often provide special reports to augment the auditor's review or to assist the taxpayer in responding to requests to reduce the scope of the audit when time constraints exist.

c. Incorrect. This approach allows the taxpayer to perform some portion of the audit work, subject to auditor review.

d. Incorrect. Employing a greater use of sampling can reduce the amount of transactional review.

3. c. Correct. In the early stages of an audit, the auditor is generally open to discussing issues involving the scope of the audit. Taxpayers should freely discourage the auditing of transactions that they feel may not be necessary.

a. Incorrect. On the telephone, taxpayers should go no further than providing some assurances that a sample is an acceptable audit methodology, subject to a formal review of the state's sampling technique.

b. Incorrect. Taxpayers have the right to grant or not grant a waiver as they deem appropriate under the circumstances.

d. Incorrect. If some of the taxpayer's entities have nexus and others do not, the taxpayer should refuse to allow the auditor to audit the books or transactions of entities without nexus. If the entity does not have nexus, the state and the auditor have no authority to exert over that entity.

4. a. Correct. The auditor should be located in an area where there is little opportunity for contact with others.

b. Incorrect. Employees should be warned of the auditor's visit and discouraged from responding to the auditor's questions without prior approval.

c. *Incorrect.* A taxpayer under audit should regularly keep track of the auditor's whereabouts with surprise visits and phone calls.

d. *Incorrect.* Designating one contact person allows that individual to focus on audit issues and take ownership of the audit results. The auditor should be told to address all questions to the contact person.

5. True. *Correct.* The auditor lists all information that could possibly be needed in the confirmation letter, but this does not mean all the information will actually be used.

a. False. *Incorrect.* In general, it is not necessary for the taxpayer to have all the information requested on the first day of the audit. The auditor may be able to achieve the desired results by reviewing some other document in lieu of the one requested.

6. b. *Correct.* For many taxpayers, an audit at this time of the year would be inconvenient, and they would be justified in refusing to grant the waiver.

a. *Incorrect.* Generally, if the audit is being delayed beyond the statutory assessment period for the taxpayer's convenience or benefit, the taxpayer will be forced to issue a waiver to avoid a jeopardy assessment.

c. *Incorrect.* In circumstances where the taxpayer is working with the auditor on concluding issues that the taxpayer reasonably believes can be resolved through additional research of the law or facts or through negotiation, the taxpayer should grant the waiver to the auditor.

d. *Incorrect.* In one of the situations, it is possible that the taxpayer should *not* grant the waiver.

7. c. *Correct.* A general review, in which the taxpayer looks for exemption certificates from major customers, would be more appropriate in the case of a statistical sample.

a. *Incorrect.* Samples tend to increase exposure because of the projection of error over the entire audit period.

b. *Incorrect.* A statement should be on the exemption certificate noting that the certificate is effective with the first day of the audit period or the date of first sale to the customer.

d. *Incorrect.* Because the auditor is likely to ask that replacements for any missing, incomplete, or inaccurate certificates be obtained, requesting replacement certificates prior to the auditor's arrival should not result in any wasted effort by the taxpayer. Also, the effects on the audit of having complete certificates on file can be dramatic.

8. False. *Correct.* If a significant amount of tax is unpaid, the taxpayer should file an amended return to capture the appropriate amount of interest due with the underpayment.

True. *Incorrect.* Taxpayers self-assessing on purchases that are more than three to six months old would generally be expected to file an amended return. However, the regular filing of amended returns may attract more audit scrutiny, so every effort should be made to incorporate self-assessments at the time the item is purchased.

9. d. *Correct.* All of the activities listed may be included in a reverse audit.
a. *Incorrect.* The reverse audit procedure for sales should include a review of the rates applied to various invoices during the audit period because it is often difficult to determine the proper local taxes to apply to a purchase.
b. *Incorrect.* A review of taxable invoices should be performed by cross-checking the invoices against the exemption certificate files. A logic check may also be performed against any taxable invoices billed to challenge whether the transaction is taxable.
c. *Incorrect.* Sellers frequently have difficulty properly classifying billing elements on an invoice, which can result in an overpayment of tax.

10. a. *Correct.* The greatest opportunities for refunds are on purchases.
b. *Incorrect.* The key to success in reverse audits is to learn to assertively apply the tax laws to individual transactions in much the same way that an auditor applies the laws in an audit.
c. *Incorrect.* When such a statute exists, a seller may not want to invest time and effort recovering tax that must be returned to the customer, or admit to the customer that it made billing errors.
d. *Incorrect.* One of the statements is *not* true.

11. b. *Correct.* If the taxpayer has merely overassessed in error, the correct procedure is to take an offset against use tax due on a future return, unless the adjustment is substantial in amount.
a. *Incorrect.* Vendor refunds should *not* be claimed as an adjustment to the next month's self-assessment. In virtually all states, netted refunds such as this will be disallowed by an auditor.
c. *Incorrect.* Vendor refunds should *not* be treated as a return offset to sales tax due. This would be disallowed by an auditor in virtually all states.
d. *Incorrect.* One of the procedures should be followed when a taxpayer overassesses sales tax from a customer.

12. b. *Correct.* In many states, the goal is to process the refund claim and notify the taxpayer within one year. Other states and local jurisdictions, such as Louisiana parishes and cities, are open-ended as to when they must respond to refund claim requests.
a. *Incorrect.* The burden of proof that a transaction is nontaxable rests with the taxpayer. The auditor is *not* required to prove that the transaction is taxable.

c. Incorrect. It is advisable for taxpayers to have final authority over any refund claims submitted on their behalf to reduce the possibility of having a filing position jeopardized through an ill-advised refund claim.

d. Incorrect. If no valid reasons exist for retaining records, such as an anticipated or pending lawsuit, they should be discarded to avoid additional storage expense and exposure.

13. c. Correct. Most tax advisors suggest that when a nexus questionnaire is mailed to a taxpayer but not addressed to any particular person, the taxpayer should not respond to the initial inquiry. Mailings of this nature are often done with little or no follow-up on nonrespondents, so failing to respond should not have adverse consequences.

a. Incorrect. If it appears, based on information provided with the questionnaire, that the taxpayer has been targeted for specific reasons, the taxpayer should respond promptly.

b. Incorrect. Nexus questionnaires that are mailed to a specific company officer or employee generally require a reply. However, in these instances, most advisors would recommend that taxpayers *not* rush to respond.

d. Incorrect. If there is follow-up from the state, the taxpayer should respond.

14 a. Correct. Since the statute of limitations in *all* states only begins to run with the filing of a return, a taxpayer that has never filed a return has not begun to toll the statute of limitations.

b. Incorrect. Under a voluntary disclosure program, a taxpayer generally agrees to pay tax due plus interest and possibly penalties. The taxpayer also agrees to file going forward.

c. Incorrect. The largest and most sophisticated of the information-sharing groups is the Multistate Tax Commission.

d. Incorrect. The requirements of the Streamlined Sales and Use Tax Agreement include an amnesty for uncollected or unpaid tax for sellers that register to collect tax, provided they were *not* previously registered in the state.

15. False. Correct. States participating in information-sharing arrangements generally have little or no authority to compel a taxpayer to complete such a questionnaire.

True. Incorrect. In most instances, if the taxpayer refuses to provide the information, the auditor will *not* pursue the issue any further.

MODULE 2 — CHAPTER 7

1. c. *Correct.* Contractors frequently act as *retailers* when they resell tangible personal property without installing it or by installing it in such a way that it retains its character as tangible personal property. When contactors act as retailers, they are required to collect tax from their purchasers, unless exempt.
a. *Incorrect.* Contractors are treated as *consumers* of incorporated materials when they install tangible personal property. As consumers of the materials incorporated into the project, the contractor is subject to tax on their cost.
b. *Incorrect.* Whether a contractor is treated as a *subcontractor* is irrelevant.

2. False. *Correct.* A machine may be attached to a building but, if it performs functions independently from the real estate, it is not considered part of the real estate.
True. *Incorrect.* If the machine is independent of the real estate in function, it tends to retain its character as tangible personal property, and would not be considered part of the real estate even after installation.

3. a. *Correct.* Generally, industrial machinery and equipment are exempt from tax if certain limitations or requirements are met. An example of some state requirements is that the machinery and equipment be used directly in the manufacturing operation.
b. *Incorrect.* Most states require that industrial machinery be used directly in the manufacturing process for an exemption to apply. Indirect use usually does *not* qualify.
c. *Incorrect.* Most states require that machinery and equipment be used primarily, predominantly or exclusively in the manufacturing process to be exempt from sales tax. Primary or predominant use ordinarily means greater than 50 percent utilization in the production process. Exclusive use is generally defined as 100 percent utilization in the manufacturing process, but it oftentimes allows for a *de minimis* nonmanufacturing use.
d. *Incorrect.* The opposite is true. Many states impose sales tax on returnable shipping containers not on nonreturnable shipping containers.

4. b. *Correct.* Most states tend to interpret exemption provisions narrowly. However, in recent years it appears that judicial bodies are moving toward *broader* interpretations of the scope of exemptions.
a. *Incorrect.* Exemptions from tax are a matter of legislative grace. Therefore, the burden of proof rests on the taxpayer.
c. *Incorrect.* In states that exempt shipping containers and packaging materials, shipping aids must usually be incorporated into the packaging in such a manner that the item becomes a part of the product sold. This means the item must be within the product packaging or affixed to the

packaging in such a way as to make it an integral part of the product.

d. Incorrect. Whether the cost of materials and labor for the repair and maintenance of taxable shipping containers, packaging materials, and shipping aids is subject to tax depends on the treatment of labor to repair tangible personal property in the state.

5. d. Correct. Once the pollution control equipment or facility has been certified, future purchases are exempt as provided under that particular state's statutes. Taxpayers in states with these requirements must retain their certification documents for future audit use.

a. Incorrect. As a prerequisite for exempting pollution control equipment and facilities, some states require that the equipment or facility used in pollution control be certified by the state department of natural resources or similar agency in order for it to be eligible for the exemption.

b. Incorrect. States with certification requirements provide a form for taxpayers to file with the state department of natural resources or similar agency that describes the equipment or facility.

c. Incorrect. States with certification requirements provide a form for taxpayers to file with the state department of natural resources or similar agency that describes the intended use of the equipment or facility.

6. a. Correct. For machinery that is purchased and modified for another use, some states tax only the materials used to construct the machinery, or the allocated costs per the accounting records. Most of those states include component parts used in the construction in the tax base at cost, rather than at retail value.

b. Incorrect. If the taxpayer's employees are used in the construction process, allocated labor costs are generally *not* included in the value for use tax purposes.

c. Incorrect. Applied overhead charges are usually excluded from the tax base. Therefore, it is generally *not* a good idea to rely solely on the asset or accounting records to determine the taxable value of self-constructed machinery.

d. Incorrect. One of the above items is ordinarily included in the use tax base for self-constructed machinery.

7. d. Correct. The value that should be used for reporting the tax liability on inventory transfers is *material cost*, which is the cost to acquire the material content of the item when purchased for inventory.

a. Incorrect. *Full inventory cost*, which is the manufactured cost of the item and generally the sum of material, labor, and overhead costs for the item, is *not* the value that should be used to report the tax liability of inventory transfers.

b. Incorrect. *Selling price*, which is the equivalent of the fair market value of the item used or consumed if it were sold in an arm's-length transaction, is *not* the value that should be used to report the tax liability of inventory transfers.

c. Incorrect. *Labor cost* is *not* even potentially a value to be used in reporting the tax liability of inventory transfers.

8. False. Correct. In a survey of the states, the majority of states indicated that transfers of inventory items to uses such as samples, research and development, and display or demonstration are subject to tax.

True. Incorrect. The majority of states have indicated in a survey that transfers of inventory items to uses such as research and development are subject to tax. None of the states responding to this question indicated that inventory withdrawals would not be taxed.

9. c. Correct. When the printer acts as a *manufacturer*, it is selling tangible personal property and is required to collect sales tax on the transaction.

a. Incorrect. When the printer acts as a *service provider*, it may or may not have an obligation to collect sales tax, depending on whether the state taxes the services performed by the printer.

b. Incorrect. In many states, when the printer produces a printed document using materials provided by its customer, the printer is viewed as performing a service. This can result in a loss of the sales tax exemption for machinery and equipment and may impact the tax treatment of the supplies provided by the customer.

d. Incorrect. One of the above is not a true statement.

10. b. Correct. Under the narrower view of manufacturing, the conveyor would probably *not* qualify for exemption since it does *not* directly contribute to the change in the product being manufactured, but merely moves the product and raw materials from one point in the process to another point in the process.

a. Incorrect. Although many states impose sales and use tax on all charges that are incurred prior to the passage of title from the vendor to the customer, many states do *not* include separately stated freight and shipping charges in the tax base.

c. Incorrect. The broader view of manufacturing, or the *Integrated Plant Doctrine*, does not view each manufacturing task separately, but rather looks to whether the equipment is part of a synchronized system that is engaged in manufacturing.

d. Incorrect. To help reduce fuel and electricity costs and to level the competitive playing ground, many states have enacted exemptions for fuel and electricity consumed in the manufacturing process.

Index

A

Advertising brochures, sales
taxability of ... 122

Advertising checked by nexus squads for
nexus review ... 171–172

Affiliate nexus ... 94–100
case law for ... 94–97
MTC model statute for ... 98
state statutes for ... 97–98

Affiliated group
defined ... 16
offsetting income on consolidated
return of ... 26
state filing options for ... 16–19
structure planning in ... 25–26
substantial nexus for members of ... 95
use of most beneficial filing
method by ... 26–27

Affiliates
income shifting among ... 16, 17, 25–26, 27
out-of-state, nexus issues for ... 94–98
requirement for apportionment of
income of ... 29

Agency nexus ... 94, 100
applied to intangible property use ... 102

Agency nexus principle ... 99–100
tax applications of ... 101–104

Aggregate theory, creation of
nexus under ... 64, 74, 110

Alabama
LLC taxation in ... 70
partnership taxation in ... 60
presence of in-state retailer imputed to
out-of-state vendor in ... 97

Alaska
combined reporting and water's-edge
election in ... 35
local sales taxes in ... 119, 125
sales and use tax not imposed
statewide in ... 119, 125

Amnesty programs for sales and use
tax liability ... 175–176

Appeal deadline for refund claim ... 165

Apportionment formulas ... 10–15
alternatives listed by UDITPA
to standard ... 12
chosen by individual states ... 11

industries provided special ... 11
of partnership income ... 65–66
three-factor ... 10–11

Apportionment methodology, type of
return versus ... 30–31

Apportionment of business income
adverse consequences of ... 12
case law for ... 7–8
establishing right for ... 23–24
factors for. See Payroll factor of
apportionment, Property factor of
apportionment, and Sales factor of
apportionment
formulary ... 29
requirements for corporation to establish
right for ... 10

Apportionment of
partnership income ... 64
determining methodology for ... 66–67
partner-level ... 65, 67
partnership-level ... 65–67

Arizona, water's-edge
combination in ... 35

Arkansas, sales and use tax in ... 97

Assignment of rights to receive refunds,
vendor signature of ... 163–164

Assist reports generated in self-audit
process ... 156

Audit exposure, reducing ... 137, 144

Audit guidelines provided by taxpayer ... 150

Audit period, waivers of statute of
limitations for ... 142–143, 151–153

Audit plan, understanding ... 138

Audit procedures, expanding ... 150

Auditors
audit review panel challenges to
decisions of ... 155
authority to audit of ... 144, 147–148
check-in and -out procedures for ... 145
completion by, of part of fieldwork
prior to visit ... 141
confirmation of audit letter sent to
taxpayer by ... 149–150
controlling information provided to ... 147–148
proposing exclusions to ... 141
refund claims received by ... 165
scope of reviews by ... 143–144
subpoena powers of . 148

time constraints on ... 138, 140
written communications by ... 146–147

Audits, nexus ... 171, 175

Audits, sales and use tax ... 132, 137–176.
See also **Self-audit process**
authority to conduct ... 137
contact person designated for ... 145–146
copying data used in ... 148
duration of ... 138–139
entities subject to ... 144
exclusions from, proposal to
auditor of ... 141
fieldwork for. *See* Fieldwork in sales and
use tax audit
information log for ... 147, 148
initial contact in ... 137
negotiations in, opportunities for ... 142, 145
overview of ... 137–138
questionnaires completed prior to. *See*
Questionnaires completed by taxpayer
reducing scope of ... 140–141
retention of records related to ... 167–168
sample selection for ... 139
sampling methodology for, taxpayer's
suggestion of alternative ... 141–142, 143
scheduling ... 138–142
scope of, 140–141, 143–144, 169
timing of ... 144, 152–153
written communications for significant
issues in ... 146–147

**Authority to do business, nexus issues
related to ... 112–113**

B

**Barter transactions, sales and
use tax on ... 129**

Billing errors, review of ... 159

**Brick-and-mortar retailers, sales over
Internet versus by ... 115**

Bright-line test
of physical presence under *Quill* ... 82
for unitary business ... 43

**Building materials, sales
taxability of ... 122–123**

**Business Activity Tax Simplification
Act of 2007 ... 108**

Business income
distinguished from nonbusiness
income ... 6–9
UDITPA definition of ... 8–9

C

California
case law on unitary business in ... 40–41
combined unitary reporting in ... 18, 30

franchise tax in ... 1
guidelines on unitary business in ... 40
LLC taxation in ... 70
partnership taxation in ... 60
S corporation shareholder credit for entity
income tax in ... 57
S corporation taxation in ... 53
taxation of partner in ... 66
water's-edge election in ... 35

**Casual and isolated sales, some states'
exemption from sales tax of ... 128, 131**

**Catalogs mailed to other states, use tax
on merchant mailing ... 131**

Centralization of management
exhibition of ... 38
in unitary business ... 21

**Charitable organization, general exemption
of, from sales and use tax ... 131**

**Check-the-box regulations for classifying
partnerships ... 59–60**

Clothing
protective and
product-quality related ... 124, 161
SST types of ... 124

Code Sec. 444 election of tax year ... 77–78

**Colorado, factors of unitary
business in ... 43–44**

Combined unitary reporting ... 29–49
advantages of ... 31
consolidated returns versus ... 30–32
differences between consolidated
returns and ... 18–19
disadvantages of ... 31
inclusion of foreign country
affiliated in ... 19, 31
mandatory versus discretionary ... 32–33
overview of ... 29
states requiring ... 18, 19, 32
unitary business requirement for ... 18, 31
view of U.S. business community of ... 34
worldwide versus water's-edge ... 18–19,
33–35

**Commerce Clause of
U.S. Constitution ... 2**
actions of independent agents establishing
nexus under ... 102
imposition of tax obligation on out-of-state
corporation under ... 113
minimum connection for taxation under ... 7
substantial nexus requirement of ... 2–3,
80, 81–82, 88, 105, 107

**Compensation, employee, computed for
payroll factor ... 15**

**Complementary use tax on consumption
of property or services ... 120**

Composite returns
filed on behalf of out-of-state
LLC members ... 75
filed on behalf of
out-of-state partners ... 67–68

Computer records of financial
information and tax returns, retention
policies for ... 168

Computer software, sales or use
taxability of ... 128

Computer warranty and repair, case law
for nexus issues of ... 93–94

Confirmation letter sent to taxpayer
confirming audit ... 149–150

Conglomerate, factors in consideration as
unitary of ... 36

Connecticut, S corporation
taxation in ... 53

Consolidated returns
advantages of ... 17, 31
combined unitary
reporting versus ... 30–32
differences between combined unitary
reporting and ... 18–19
disadvantages of ... 17, 27, 31
election to file ... 16, 26–27
elective ... 16, 17
stock ownership requirement
for inclusion in ... 17, 18, 31
worldwide ... 35

Constitutional nexus ... 80, 81–82
landmark cases regarding ... 2–3
for out-of-state mail-order affiliate ... 94–98
for ownership interest in partnership doing
business in state ... 110
presence of company-owned delivery
trucks as creating ... 103

Construction contractors
performing contracts for
tax-exempt entity ... 179–180
repairs performed by ... 177–178, 180–181
as retailers versus
consumers ... 177, 179, 181
sales and use tax treatment of ... 177–181
supplies and equipment taxable to ... 181
type of contract affecting
tax treatment of ... 178

Consultants, refund claims management
by outside
aggressive positions taken in ... 166
clerical support for ... 167
confidentiality agreements
required for ... 167
taxpayer's final authority over ... 166

Consumer tax on transactions ... 119

Contractors. See Construction contractors
and Independent contractor

Contribution or dependency test of unitary
business ... 20, 37–38, 40–41

Conventions, exemption from creating nexus
for employees attending ... 109–110

Corporations, regular
double taxation of earnings of ... 51
tax rates on income of ... 76

Coupons applied to taxable sales price,
treatment of ... 133

Credit against tax paid in
another state ... 130

D

Delaware
intangible property holding
companies in ... 24
tax on leases of tangible personal
property in ... 125

Destination test for sales ... 13

Direct costs defined ... 14

Discounts applied to taxable sales price,
treatment of ... 133

Disregarded entities, LLCs
treated as ... 69–70, 73

District of Columbia
corporate income tax in ... 1
LLC taxation in ... 71
partnership taxation in ... 60
S corporation taxation in ... 53

Doctrine of equitable recoupment
or offset ... 153

Due Process Clause of
U.S. Constitution ... 2
minimal connection requirement of ... 2, 7,
80, 81, 82, 105

E

Economic nexus, case law for ... 105–108

Economic presence for nexus ... 80

Economies of scale
demonstration of ... 38
in unitary business ... 21

80/20 corporations, combined
reporting by ... 34

Electricity used in manufacturing, use tax
exemption by many states for ... 194

Electronic commerce
nexus issues for ... 115–117
taxable transactions of ... 126

Equipment and tools to manufacture self-
constructed machinery ... 189–190

Excise taxes applied to taxable sales
price, treatment of ... 133

Exemption certificates
cross-checked against report of
exempt sales ... 155
general review for missing ... 154
receipt of properly executed, correcting
customer's tax status following ... 160
replacement ... 155

F

Factor presence nexus standard for
business activity taxes ... 116

Factors-of-profitability test of unitary
. business ... 21, 38

Fieldwork in sales and use
tax audit ... 140
negotiations during ... 142
questionnaire available from taxpayer on
first day of ... 149–150
reducing time required for ... 144

Financing charge on credit or
conditional sales ... 129

Fiscal year of
pass-through entities ... 77–78

Florida
franchise tax in ... 1
general sales and use tax on services
rescinded in ... 126

Flow-of-value test of
unitary business ... 21, 38

Foreign corporations, state versus federal
nexus standards applied to ... 114–115

Franchise taxes, state ... 1–2, 53, 84
imposition of, on out-of-state corporation
lacking physical presence, 105

Freight charges
exemption from sales tax of
separately stated ... 135
taxability of ... 195–196

Fuel used in manufacturing, use tax
exemption by many states for ... 194

Functional integration
examples of ... 21
exhibition of ... 38

Functional test of business income ... 9

G

General partner in LLC, risk of limited
partners versus ... 74

General partner in limited partnership ... 59
as typically unitary with partnership ... 66

Geoffrey rules or regulations, state
adoption of ... 105

Georgia, partner-level
apportionment in ... 67

Great Lakes Regional Compact,
information sharing by ... 172

H

Horizontally integrated business
considered unitary ... 20, 36

I

Idaho, water's-edge combination in ... 35

Illinois
case law on unitary business in ... 42–43
combined reporting in ... 31
common ownership defined in ... 41
80/20 company defined for ... 34
LLC taxation in ... 71
partnership taxation in ... 60
S corporation taxation in ... 53
unitary business activity statutes of ... 42
unitary business group defined in ... 41
water's-edge combination in ... 35

Import taxes applied to taxable sales
price, treatment of ... 133

Income-producing activity
defined ... 13
examples of ... 13
performed in multiple states ... 14

Income shifting from affiliates in
high-tax states to affiliates in
low-tax states ... 16, 17, 25–26, 27

Income tax nexus ... 80–81

Independent contractor
activities of, not creating income tax nexus
for out-of-state principal ... 100
case law for income tax nexus
created by ... 100–101
defined ... 100
MTC statement regarding activities for
out-of-state principal by ... 101
payments to ... 15

Indiana, combined reporting in ... 33

Indirect costs defined ... 14

Information log kept for sales and use
audit ... 147, 148

Information-sharing arrangements
among states ... 169, 172–174

Installation charges, sales
taxation of ... 126–127, 134, 135, 162

Intangible property holding companies ... 24–25, 105–108

Integrated Plant Doctrine for manufacturing ... 194

Intercompany sales, use tax on ... 129

Interest on credit or conditional sales ... 129, 134

Internet Tax Freedom Act, moratorium on state or local taxes for Internet access under ... 116, 126

Internet sales. *See* Electronic commerce

Internet vendors, nexus issues for ... 115–117

Inventory storage for foreign corporation ... 115

Inventory withdrawals, use tax for ... 191–192

J

Jeopardy assessments, state's basis for ... 151–152

Jurisdiction of state to tax nondomiciliary corporation ... 63–64

K

Kansas
LLC taxation in ... 71
partnership taxation in ... 61
S corporation taxation in ... 53
water's-edge combination in ... 35

Kentucky
LLC taxation in ... 71
partnership taxation in ... 61
S corporation taxation in ... 53–54

L

Labor costs for self-constructed machinery ... 189

Leased property, creation of nexus for ownership of ... 110–112

Leases, sales taxability of ... 126

Limited liability companies (LLCs) ... 69–75
composite returns by ... 75
federal tax treatment of ... 69
nexus standards for ... 73–74, 75
state conformity to federal pass-through treatment of ... 69–70
states imposing entity-level taxes on ... 70–73
taxation of individual members of ... 74–75
withholding requirements for nonresident members of ... 75

Limited liability partnership ... 59

Limited partner in LLC, risk of general partner versus ... 74

Limited partner in limited partnership ... 59
unitary relationship with partnership of ... 66

Limited partnership, general and limited partners in ... 59

M

Mail-order computer vendors, case law regarding ... 93–94

Maine, water's-edge combination in ... 35

Managed audit, taxpayer performance of work in ... 141

Manufacturers
ownership of equipment or tooling for use by unrelated in-state ... 109
pollution control/abatement facilities of ... 186–188
printers as service providers versus ... 193–194
sales and use tax treatment of ... 182–196

Manufacturing exemption from sales tax ... 122, 124
assertive application of ... 162
narrow versus broad view by states of ... 194
printers eligible for, criteria of ... 193–194
for utilities used in manufacturing ... 194

Manufacturing operation defined ... 182

Massachusetts
general sales and use tax on services rescinded in ... 126
S corporation taxation in ... 54
unitary business defined in ... 44
worldwide combined reporting election in ... 35

Materials
criteria for tax exemption of ... 183, 192
packaging ... 183–185
repair and maintenance ... 185

Michigan
LLC taxation in ... 71
net income tax and modified gross receipts tax in ... 2
partnership taxation in ... 61
S corporation taxation in ... 54
single business tax in ... 84
unitary business group defined in ... 45–46

Minnesota
unitary business defined in ... 44–45
use tax collection of affiliated remote sellers in ... 97
water's-edge combination in ... 35

Mixed transaction of property and service, sales taxability of ... 127, 134–135

Montana, water's-edge
  combination in ... 35

Multistate corporate income taxation
  basic principles of ... 1–27
  introduction to ... 1–2

Multistate Tax Commission (MTC)
  application of P.L. 86-272 in policy
    statement of ... 90, 92, 101, 104
  audits by ... 173
  concept of unitary business in
    regulation of ... 21
  costs of performance defined by ... 14
  establishment in 1967 of ... 21, 39, 90
  factor nexus standard of ... 116
  income-producing activity
    regulation of ... 13
  information sharing by ... 173
  model affiliate nexus statute of ... 98
  model combined reporting statute of ... 39
  model statute reporting options for
    nonresident shareholder pass-through
    entities of ... 57–58
  Nexus Bulletin 95-1 of ... 93–94
  tests of business income
    regulations of ... 9
  unitary business concept in
    regulation of ... 39

N

Net operating losses (NOLs) ... 26

Nevada, corporate income tax not
  levied in ... 1

New Hampshire
  LLC taxation in ... 71
  partnership taxation in ... 61
  S corporation taxation in ... 54
  tax on communication services in ... 125
  water's-edge combination in ... 35

New Jersey
  corporate business tax in ... 84
  LLC taxation in ... 71–72
  partnership taxation in ... 61
  S corporation election in ... 52
  S corporation taxation in ... 54
  separate-company and consolidated
    returns in ... 19, 33
  taxation of partners in ... 66–67

New York City
  partnership taxation in ... 62
  S corporation taxation in ... 54

New York State
  combined reporting in ... 46
  nexus not created by out-of-state mail-
    order catalog company in ... 97–98
  taxpayer approval of sampling methodology
    for sales and use tax audit in ... 143

tests of substantial intercorporate
  transactions in ... 46–47

Nexus ... 79–117. *See also* Commerce
  Clause of U.S. Constitution *and* Due
  Process Clause of U.S. Constitution
  avoiding undesired ... 23
  creating beneficial ... 23
  defined ... 79, 169
  for foreign corporations ... 114–115
  landmark cases regarding ... 2–3, 79–80, 169
  for leased property ... 110–112
  limiting entities subject to sales and use
    tax audits to those having ... 144
  for LLCs ... 73–74, 75
  nexus squad techniques to detect nonfiling
    taxpayers having ... 169–172
  overview of ... 79–81
  for partnerships ... 59, 63–64, 67, 110
  questionnaires developed by
    states regarding ... 169–171
  state-specific statutory and administrative
    exemptions for ... 109–117
  types of contacts creating,
    determinants of ... 63

Nexus squads ... 171, 175

Nonbusiness income distinguished from
  business income ... 6–9

North Carolina
  consolidated returns in ... 33
  nexus of LLC in ... 74

North Dakota, water's-edge
  combination in ... 35

Nowhere sales ... 13

O

Ohio
  gross receipts tax replacing
    franchise tax in ... 1
  LLC taxation in ... 72
  partnership taxation in ... 62
  S corporation taxation in ... 55
  taxpayer approval of sampling
    methodology for sales and use tax
    audit in ... 143

Oregon, conditions applicable to unitary
  business in ... 47–48

P

Partnership interest owned by
  nondomiciliary corporation, nexus
  created by ... 110

Partnerships
  apportionment of income of ... 64–67
  check-the-box regulations for ... 59–60

composite returns by ... 67–68
federal tax treatment of ... 59
LLCs treated as ... 69, 74
nexus standards for ... 59, 63–64, 67
state conformity to federal pass-through
treatment of ... 59–60
states imposing entity-level
taxes on ... 60–63
tax year of ... 77–78
taxation of individual partners of ... 67
withholding requirements for nonresident
partners of ... 68

Pass-through entities ... 51–78. *See also*
Limited liability companies (LLCs),
Partnerships, *and* **S corporations**

Payroll factor of apportionment
defined ... 15
distortion in worldwide combined
reporting of ... 34
for partnership income ... 65
in three-factor formula ... 10–11

Penalties for taxpayers discovered in
nexus process ... 174

Pennsylvania
franchise tax in ... 84
LLC taxation in ... 72
partner-level taxation in ... 67
S corporation taxation in ... 55

Permanent establishment provision of
tax treaties ... 114–115

Personal service corporations (PSCs)
defined ... 76
flat tax rate for income of ... 77
tax year of ... 77–78

Physical presence standard
applied to foreign corporations ... 115
for income tax nexus, proposed ... 108
for sales and use tax ... 169

Physical presence test of constitutional
nexus ... 80, 82–85
bright-line ... 82, 88
for electronic commerce ... 115
landmark cases regarding ... 2–3, 82–83,
88–89, 105–106, 107, 112–113

Piggybacking federal tax base for
computing state taxable income ... 5

Pollution control exemption for
abatement-related equipment,
supplies, and facilities ... 186–188

Printer
as manufacturer versus service provider for
use tax exemption ... 193–194
ownership of raw materials or finished
goods at unrelated in-state ... 109

Privilege tax, sales tax in form of ... 119

Production machinery, exemption from
sales and use tax by most states for
... 182–183, 193

Property factor of apportionment
defined ... 14
distortion in worldwide combined r
eporting of ... 34
MTC regulations for ... 14
owned versus rented property for,
accounting for ... 26
for partnership income ... 65
in three-factor formula ... 10–11

Public Law 86–272
de minimis exception to nonsolicitation
activities under ... 87–89
enactment in 1959 of ... 3, 83
income tax safe harbor for net income
under ... 83, 85
independent contractor's
activities under ... 100–101
limitations of, for multistate
business taxes ... 84–85
meaning of solicitation of orders under
Wrigley for ... 85–87
MTC statement regarding proper
application of ... 90, 92, 100–101
nonancillary services
not protected by ... 93–94
protected activities under ... 91–92, 103–104,
113, 169
state income tax imposition under ... 3–4,
63, 74
unprotected activities under ... 90–91, 114

Publications, sales taxability of ... 123

Purchaser, determining tax
status of ... 159

Q

Qualification to do business, income
or franchise tax return
required upon ... 112–113

Qualified Subchapter S subsidiary (QSSS),
reporting on parent's return for ... 52

Quasi-tangible personal
property fixtures ... 180

Questionnaires completed by taxpayer
for auditor for sales and use
tax audit ... 149–150, 169
nexus ... 169–171

R

Raw materials or finished goods at
unrelated in-state printer,
ownership of ... 109

Real property
application or adaptation of item to
purpose of ... 178
physical annexation of item to ... 178, 179
tangible personal property
distinguished from ... 176

**Rebates applied to taxable sales price,
treatment of ... 133**

**Record retention issues for tax and
financial information ... 167–168**

**Recovery of lost refunds following sales
and use tax audit ... 153.** *See also*
Reverse audits

Referral audits ... 174

Refund claim for overpaid tax
following reverse audit ... 163–165
following self-audit ... 156, 159
outside consultants to manage ... 166

**Regressivity in tax system,
reducing ... 121**

Repair charges
exemption by some states of
separately stated ... 135
warranty for ... 129

**Repairs performed by construction
contractors ... 177–178, 180–181**

Resale, goods purchased for ... 131

Returns refunding purchase price ... 134

Reverse audits
billing errors identified in ... 159
improper application of sales tax
detected in ... 160
incorrect tax rate reviewed in ... 160, 162–163
key to success in ... 161
object of ... 159
overpayments on purchases in, steps
for detecting ... 161
overview of ... 159
payment of wrong state's tax
found in ... 162–163
refund claim procedures following ... 163–165
tax exclusions reviewed in ... 162
tax status of purchaser or
transactions in ... 159–160

**Royalty payments for intangible property
... 9, ˙3, 24, 25**

S

S corporation shareholders
nonresident, returns and
withholding for ... 57–58
state taxation of ... 56–57

S corporations
eligibility for electing status as ... 52
federal tax treatment of ... 51–52

state conformity to federal pass-through
treatment of ... 52
states imposing entity-level taxes on ... 53–56
tax year of ... 77–78

Sales and use tax nexus ... 79–80

Sales and use taxes ... 119–135. *See also*
Sales tax *and* **Use tax**
application to Internet sales of ... 115–117
exemptions from ... 131–132, 161
expansion into service sector increasingly
included for ... 126
on manufacturers ... 182–196
overview of ... 119–120
sales price for imposing ... 133–135
state audits of. *See* Audits, sales and use tax
states' rates for ... 120
transactions subject to ... 125–129

Sales factor of apportionment
assigning sales to ... 24
defined ... 12
for partnership income ... 65
in three-factor formula ... 10–11
MTC regulations for ... 13–14
in UDITPA ... 12–14

Sales-only formula of apportionment ... 11

Sales price, determining ... 133–135

Sales tax. *See also* **Sales and use taxes**
application to property and
services of ... 126–129
basis for deficiency assessed by
state for ... 151–153
differences among states' rules for,
list of ... 135
exclusions from ... 121–122
imposed on retail sales of tangible personal
property and selected services ... 119
improper application of ... 160
items subject to ... 121–125
local, power to levy ... 119, 120
return to customer of refunded ... 160

Sales throwback rule
avoiding application of ... 23, 89
consequence of states not applying ... 23–24

**Samples of merchandise, use tax
on free ... 131**

Sampling methodology
for auditor's use,
suggesting alternative ... 141–142, 143
for self-audits ... 154, 157–158

Scheduling of sales and use tax audit
allowing time to resolve issues in ... 139
duration of audit considered in ... 138–139
factors to consider in ... 140
by out-of-state auditor ... 140

Self-assessments
reporting ... 156–157
transactions covered by ... 158, 162

Self-audit process. *See also*
   Reverse audits
   compliance in ... 174
   exemption certificates in ... 154, 155
   focus of ... 157
   missed transactions in ... 156–157
   overview of ... 154
   for purchases ... 156
   review of last self-audit in ... 156
   sample period for ... 155
   sampling for ... 154, 157–158
   self-audit list for taxpayer
      completion in ... 174
   summarizing and maintaining results of ... 157

Self-constructed machinery
   analyzing costs associated with ... 190
   common exemptions from use tax for ... 188
   compliance procedures for ... 190
   labor costs in construction of ... 189
   overhead charges in valuation of ... 189
   use tax base for ... 188–190

Separate-company returns
   mandatory ... 16–17
   opportunity to shift income to low- or no-
      tax states for affiliates using ... 25–26
   permission to change from consolidated
      returns to ... 27

**Shipping aids to facilitate transfer of
   products ... 184–185**

**Shipping and handling charges, sales and
   use taxation of ... 126, 134, 195–196**

Shipping containers
   items constituting ... 183–184
   misapplied treatment of shipping aids as
      ... 184
   repair and maintenance of ... 185
   returnable ... 185

Shipping supplies, sales taxability of ... 123

**Single member limited liability company
   (SMLLC), converting unprofitable
   affiliate into ... 26**

**Solicitation of orders by multistate
   corporations ... 85–87**
   de minimis exception to ... 87–89
   protected activities for ... 3, 91–92
   unprotected activities not protected as ...
      4, 90–91, 104

**Solicitation of sales through
   advertisements, nexus squad's
   review of ... 171–172**

**South Dakota, corporate income tax not
   levied in ... 1**

**Southeastern States Compact,
   information sharing by ... 172**

**State filing options for combined unitary
   reporting ... 16**

**State modifications to federal
   taxable income ... 6**

State not imposing sales and use tax ... 119

**State sales tax rules, list of common
   differences among ... 135**

State tax base
   determining corporate ... 65–66
   effects of electronic commerce on ... 115–117

**States imposing taxation, selecting
   preferable ... 22–23**

**States not imposing corporate
   income tax ... 1**

**States not imposing individual
   income tax ... 56, 67, 75**

**States not imposing sales and
   use taxes ... 125**

Statute of limitations for audit period
   commencement of ... 174
   waiving ... 142–143, 151–153

Streamlined Sales Tax (SST) Agreement
   amnesty for sales tax under ... 175–176
   categories of clothing for ... 124
   filing process for ... 121
   glossary of uniform definitions for
      tax base of ... 123–125
   goals of ... 116–117
   member states for collection and
      administration of ... 116
   website of ... 117

Structure planning techniques ... 25–26

Subpoena powers of auditors ... 148

T

Tangible personal property
   to construct pollution control facility ... 187
   consumed or destroyed in manufacturing
      process ... 192
   real property distinguished from ... 178
   repairs of ... 180
   resale of ... 179, 193

**Tax-exempt entities or organizations,
   contracts performed for ... 179–180**

**Tax-exempt status, allowance of pass-
   through of ... 180**

**Tax exemptions for sales tax, maximizing
   opportunities for ... 124**

**Tax-planning strategies,
   basic multistate ... 22–27**

Tax positions, providing evidence for ... 145

**Tax registrations by taxpayers,
   inconsistent ... 171**

**Tax year of pass-through entities,
   restrictions on ... 77–78**

Taxable income, state,
computation of ... 5–9

Telecommunications, sales taxation of
intrastate and interstate ... 128–129

Tennessee
franchise tax in ... 84
LLC taxation in ... 72
partnership taxation in ... 62
S corporation taxation in ... 55

Texas
LLC taxation in ... 72–73
margin tax in ... 2, 48, 62
partnership taxation in ... 62
S corporation taxation in ... 55–56
unitary business defined in ... 48

Three-unities test of
unitary business ... 20, 37, 40–41

Throwback exception to
destination test ... 13

Trade shows, exemption from creating nexus
for employees attending ... 109–110

Trademark licensing by holding
companies ... 24–25, 105–108

Transactional test of business income ... 9

Trucks, creation of nexus using
company-owned versus
common carrier ... 103–104

True object test to determine sales taxability
of mixed transaction ... 127, 132

U

Uniform Division of Income for Tax
Purposes Act (UDITPA)
business and nonbusiness income under
... 6, 8–9
payroll factor in ... 15
petition for relief for application of state
apportionment formulas under ... 12
property factor in ... 14
sales factor in ... 12–14

Unitary business
bright-line test for ... 43
factors in concept of ... 36
state judicial interpretations of ... 36–48
statutory definitions of ... 39

Unitary business group
approaches to computing tax on combined
basis for ... 33–35
concept of ... 19–21
determination of ... 36

Unitary business principle
for apportionability in state
income taxation ... 7, 29
development of ... 29

Unitary business test for inclusion in
combined report ... 18, 31

Unitary group. *See* Unitary business group

Unitary relationship between partner and
partnership ... 66–67

U.S. Model Treaty of 2006 ... 114–115

Use tax. *See also* Sales and use taxes
broad interpretations of ... 130–131
exemptions from ... 131–132
imposed on use or consumption of tangible
personal property and
selected services ... 119
on inventory transfers ... 191–192
local ... 120
storage of items triggering ... 130, 131
on taxable item subject to sales tax in
another state ... 129–130
valuation of self-constructed
machinery for ... 188–190
voluntary remittance
(self-assessment) of ... 125, 132

Use tax base for self-constructed
machinery ... 188–190

Utah, water's-edge combination in ... 35

Utilities used in manufacturing ... 194

V

Valuation
for inventory transfers ... 192
of self-constructed machinery ... 188–190

Vehicles, leased ... 110–111

Vertically integrated business treated as
unitary ... 20, 36

Voluntary disclosure agreement for sales
and use tax liability ... 174–175

W

Waiver of statute of limitations for
audit period ... 142–143, 151–153

Warranty contracts for equipment
and repairs ... 129

Washington State
business and occupations tax
imposed in ... 1, 84
corporate income tax not levied in ... 1
LLC taxation in ... 73
partnership taxation in ... 63
S corporation taxation in ... 56

Water's-edge combination, combined
report for ... 33–34, 35

West Virginia
LLC taxation in ... 73
partnership taxation in ... 63

S corporation taxation in ... 56
worldwide combined reporting
  election in ... 35
Withholding of tax
obligation created by agent for ... 101
for out-of-state LLC members ... 75

for out-of-state state partners ... 68
**Worldwide combination, combined
  report for ... 18–19, 33, 34–35**
**Wyoming, corporate income tax
  not levied in ... 1**

MULTISTATE CORPORATE TAX COURSE (2009 EDITION)

CPE Quizzer Instructions

The CPE Quizzer is divided into two Modules. There is a processing fee for each Quizzer Module submitted for grading. Successful completion of Module 1 is recommended for **6 CPE Credits.*** Successful completion of Module 2 is recommended for **8 CPE Credits.*** You can complete and submit one Module at a time or all Modules at once for a total of **14 CPE Credits.***

To obtain CPE credit, return your completed Answer Sheet for each Quizzer Module to **CCH Continuing Education Department, 4025 W. Peterson Ave., Chicago, IL 60646**, or fax it to (773) 866-3084. Each Quizzer Answer Sheet will be graded and a CPE Certificate of Completion awarded for achieving a grade of 70 percent or greater. The Quizzer Answer Sheets are located after the Quizzer questions for this Course.

Express Grading: Processing time for your Answer Sheet is generally 8-12 business days. If you are trying to meet a reporting deadline, our Express Grading Service is available for an additional $19 per Module. To use this service, please check the "Express Grading" box on your Answer Sheet and provide your CCH account or credit card number **and your fax number.** CCH will fax your results and a Certificate of Completion (upon achieving a passing grade) to you by 5:00 p.m. the business day following our receipt of your Answer Sheet. **If you mail your Answer Sheet for Express Grading, please write "ATTN: CPE OVERNIGHT" on the envelope.** NOTE: CCH will not Federal Express Quizzer results under any circumstances.

NEW ONLINE GRADING gives you immediate 24/7 grading with instant results and no Express Grading Fee.

The **CCH Testing Center** website gives you and others in your firm easy, free access to CCH print Courses and allows you to complete your CPE Quizzers online for immediate results. Plus, the **My Courses** feature provides convenient storage for your CPE Course Certificates and completed Quizzers.

Go to **www.cchtestingcenter.com** to complete your Quizzer online.

---

* Recommended CPE credit is based on a 50-minute hour. Participants earning credits for states that require self-study to be based on a 100-minute hour will receive ½ the CPE credits for successful completion of this course. Because CPE requirements vary from state to state and among different licensing agencies, please contact your CPE governing body for information on your CPE requirements and the applicability of a particular course for your requirements.

Date of Completion: The date of completion on your Certificate will be the date that you put on your Answer Sheet. However, you must submit your Answer Sheet to CCH for grading within two weeks of completing it.

Expiration Date: December 31, 2009

Evaluation: To help us provide you with the best possible products, please take a moment to fill out the Course Evaluation located at the back of this Course and return it with your Quizzer Answer Sheets.

CCH is registered with the National Association of State Boards of Accountancy (NASBA) as a sponsor of continuing professional education on the National Registry of CPE Sponsors. State boards of accountancy have final authority on the acceptance of individual courses for CPE credit. Complaints regarding registered sponsors may be addressed to the National Registry of CPE Sponsors, 150 Fourth Avenue North, Suite 700, Nashville, TN 37219-2417. Web site: www.nasba.org.

CCH is registered with the National Association of State Boards of Accountancy (NASBA) as a Quality Assurance Service (QAS) sponsor of continuing professional education. State boards of accountancy have final authority on the acceptance of individual courses for CPE credit. Complaints regarding registered sponsors may be addressed to NASBA, 150 Fourth Avenue North, Suite 700, Nashville, TN 37219-2417. Web site: www.nasba.org.

CCH has been approved by the California Tax Education Council to offer courses that provide federal and state credit towards the annual "continuing education" requirement imposed by the State of California. A listing of additional requirements to register as a tax preparer may be obtained by contacting CTEC at P.O. Box 2890, Sacramento, CA, 95812-2890, toll-free by phone at (877) 850-2832, or on the Internet at www.ctec.org.

Processing Fee:
$72.00 for Module 1
$96.00 for Module 2
$168.00 for all Modules

Recommended CPE:
6 hours for Module 1
8 hours for Module 2
14 hours for all Modules

CTEC Course Number:
1075-CE-7183 for Module 1
1075-CE-7193 for Module 2

CTEC Federal Hours:
N/A hours for Module 1
N/A hours for Module 2
N/A hours for all Modules

CTEC California Hours:
3 hours for Module 1
4 hours for Module 2
7 hours for all Modules

One **complimentary copy** of this Course is provided with copies of selected CCH Tax titles. Additional copies of this Course may be ordered for $29.00 each by calling 1-800-248-3248 (ask for product 0-0981-200).

MULTISTATE CORPORATE TAX COURSE (2009 EDITION)
Quizzer Questions: Module 1

1. The most recent landmark case on constitutional nexus is:

   a. *National Bellas Hess, Inc. v. Department of Revenue*
   b. *Quill Corp. v. North Dakota*
   c. *Wisconsin Department of Revenue v. William Wrigley, Jr., Co.*
   d. None of the above

2. In which of the following cases did the Supreme Court define the phrase *solicitation of orders*?

   a. *National Bellas Hess, Inc. v. Department of Revenue*
   b. *Quill Corp. v. North Dakota*
   c. *Wisconsin Department of Revenue v. William Wrigley, Jr., Co.*
   d. None of the above

3. Income arising from transactions and activity in the regular course of the taxpayer's trade or business comprises the ___ test in determining whether an item of income is business or nonbusiness.

   a. Classification
   b. Functional
   c. Transactional
   d. None of the above

4. Which of the following states does not use an apportionment formula that includes only a sales factor?

   a. Pennsylvania
   b. Oregon
   c. Nebraska
   d. Illinois

5. Which of the following is *not* an advantage of filing a consolidated return?

   a. Ability to offset the losses of one affiliate against the profits of other affiliates
   b. Allows a taxpayer to create legal structures to shift income from affiliates in high-tax states to affiliates in low-tax states
   c. Deferral of gains on intercompany transactions
   d. Use of credits that would otherwise be denied because of a lack of income

6. Which test for determining the existence of a unitary business looks to functional integration, centralization of management, and economies of scale?

    a. Three-unities test
    b. Contribution or dependency test
    c. Flow-of-value test
    d. Factors-of-probability test

7. To acquire the right to apportion its income, the corporation generally must have nexus in at least one state other than its state of domicile. In such cases, whether a corporation's activities or contacts in another state are considered adequate to justify apportionment is generally determined by:

    a. Reference to the tax laws of the domicile state
    b. Reference to the tax laws of states other than the domicile state
    c. Reference to the tax laws of all states
    d. None of the above

8. Creating nexus in a state can be beneficial in which of the following situations?

    a. The corporation wants to include loss affiliates in the consolidated return of another state
    b. The corporation currently does not have the right to apportion its income
    c. The corporation wants to avoid the application of a sales throwback rule
    d. All of the above

9. Diversity among the states' apportionment formulas can result in more than 100 percent of a corporation's income being subject to state taxation. *True or False?*

10. States that impose income taxes but do not tie the computation of taxable income directly to a corporation's federal tax return typically do not adopt the majority of the federal provisions governing items of gross income and deduction in defining the state tax base. *True or False?*

11. Which of the following statements is **not** true?

    a. The unitary business principle reflects the practical business reality that different affiliates often function as a single economic entity.

    b. The unitary business principle allows states to require a commonly controlled group of corporations engaged in a unitary business to compute their state taxable income on a combined basis.

    c. The *unitary business* test is a requirement for inclusion in an elective consolidated return.

    d. Membership in a combined unitary report generally requires more than 50 percent ownership.

12. Which one of the following states does **not** require members of a unitary business group to compute their taxable income on a combined basis?

    a. California

    b. Illinois

    c. Michigan

    d. None of the above

13. The constitutionality of requiring a corporation to compute its state taxable income on a worldwide combined basis has:

    a. Been questioned but *not* resolved

    b. Been firmly established

    c. *Not* been questioned

    d. Been ruled invalid

14. Which of the following statements is **not** true?

    a. Indiana may require commonly controlled corporations to file a combined return.

    b. New Jersey permits an affiliated group to elect to file a consolidated return.

    c. New York requires related corporations to file a combined report if they engage in substantial intercorporate transactions.

    d. All of the above are true.

15. The Supreme Court articulated the three-unities test in which case?

   a. *Edison Cal. Stores*
   b. *Container Corp. of America*
   c. *Butler Bros.*
   d. *Allied-Signal*

16. Which of the following is *not* a test developed by the courts for determining the existence of a unitary business?

   a. The flow-of-goods test
   b. The three-unities test
   c. The contribution or dependency test
   d. The flow-of-value test

17. Which state attempts to provide a *bright-line test* for the existence of a *unitary business?*

   a. Colorado
   b. Illinois
   c. Michigan
   d. Texas

18. Which one of the following states generally allows commonly controlled corporations to file separate-company returns, but also requires or permits a combined unitary report if certain conditions are satisfied?

   a. California
   b. Kansas
   c. Minnesota
   d. North Carolina

19. Because of the many judicial interpretations of a unitary business, it is *not* always clear which of the available tests should be applied. *True or False?*

20. In California, if the unitary group includes operations conducted in foreign countries, a worldwide combination is *always* required. *True or False?*

21. If a portion of an S corporation shareholder's pro rata share of income is subject to tax in two states:

a. The shareholder is subject to double taxation.
b. The state of residence usually allows the individual to claim a credit for income taxes paid to the other state.
c. The taxing state in which the shareholder does *not* reside usually allows the individual to claim a credit for income taxes paid to the state of residence.
d. None of the above.

22. The federal government taxes earnings of a regular corporation _____, but of an S corporation _____.

a. Once, twice
b. Once, three times
c. Twice, once
d. Twice, three times

23. States generally conform to the federal pass-through treatment of S corporations, but only if:

a. The corporation has filed a valid S corporation election for state tax purposes.
b. The corporation has filed a valid S corporation election for federal tax purposes.
c. The corporation has two classes of stock.
d. The corporation has more than 100 shareholders.

24. Which of the following statements is *not* true?

a. States generally conform to the federal pass-through treatment of S corporations.
b. Most states provide that the filing of a federal S corporation election automatically qualifies the corporation as an S corporation for state tax purposes.
c. A handful of states require taxpayers to comply with special procedures in addition to federal procedures in order to make a valid S corporation election.
d. All of the above are true.

25. In a _____ partnership, every partner can participate in the management of the partnership.

a. General
b. Limited
c. Both a and b
d. None of the above

26. The issue of whether a state has jurisdiction to tax a nondomiciliary corporation whose only contact with the state is through a limited partnership interest has been litigated in a number of cases, with the taxpayer prevailing in *all* of the cases. ***True or False?***

27. Based on _____, most states take the position that mere ownership of a partnership interest is sufficient to create constitutional nexus for an out-of-state corporate partner.

    a. The U.S. Constitution
    b. Public Law 86-272
    c. The aggregate theory
    d. None of the above

28. If the activities of the corporate partner and the partnership constitute a unitary business, which of the following is true?

    a. Partner-level apportionment must *always* be used.
    b. Partnership-level apportionment must *always* be used.
    c. Whether the partner and the partnership constitute a unitary business *never* impacts whether partner-level or partnership-level apportionment should be used.
    d. In *some* states, whether the partner and the partnership constitute a unitary business affects whether partner-level or partnership level apportionment should be used.

29. What is the default classification for an LLC organized in a foreign country, assuming *all* the members have limited liability?

    a. Partnership
    b. Sole Proprietorship
    c. S Corporation
    d. Corporation

30. The extent to which nexus principles that apply to general partnerships also apply to nonresident corporate members of a multi-member LLC has been addressed in a comprehensive fashion by the states. ***True or False?***

31. The federal income tax treatment of a partnership or LLC is determined by an elective system of entity classification known as check-the-box. ***True or False?***

32. Which of the following statements is *not* true?

    a. Many states require some form of withholding with respect to nonresident partners.

    b. Many states permit partners who are individuals and meet certain other requirements to file a composite return.

    c. The physical presence of any partnership assets within a state is imputed to the partners.

    d. If partnership-level apportionment is used, a corporate partner is allowed factor relief with respect to the inclusion of the entire distributive share of partnership income in the partner's apportionable income tax base.

33. A natural business year is one in which at least ___ _____ of the taxpayer's gross receipts are received in the last two months of the 12-month period.

    a. 10 percent

    b. 25 percent

    c. 33 percent

    d. 50 percent

34. In the case of an LLC with two or more members, states in which an individual member does *not* reside but in which the LLC has nexus generally tax:

    a. Only that portion of the nonresident member's distributive share of income that is attributable to sources within the state

    b. None of a nonresident member's distributive share of LLC income

    c. The entire amount of a nonresident member's distributive share of LLC income

    d. None of the above

35. Under a Code Sec. 444 election, a personal service corporation with calendar-year shareholders may elect any of the following year-ends *except*:

    a. August 31

    b. September 30

    c. October 31

    d. November 30

MULTISTATE CORPORATE TAX COURSE (2009 EDITION)

Quizzer Questions: Module 2

36. Which of the following is true?

    a. P.L. 86-272 applies only to a sales or use tax.

    b. P.L. 86-272 protects only sales of services.

    c. For businesses that send employees into other states to sell tangible personal property, P.L. 86-272 applies *only* if those employees limit their in-state activities to the solicitation of orders that are approved out-of-state and are filled by a shipment or delivery from a point outside the state.

    d. None of the above.

37. Which of the following activities, if not *de minimis*, would create nexus with a state for income tax purposes?

    a. Installation

    b. Solicitation of orders

    c. Recruiting and training sales personnel

    d. None of the above

38. Which of the following activities is considered "protected" under a statement adopted by the MTC?

    a. Maintaining a display room for two weeks at a location in the state

    b. Providing maintenance in the state for previously sold property

    c. A salesperson in the state conducting order approval

    d. None of the above

39. Which of the following states have enacted affiliate nexus statutes?

    a. Alabama

    b. Arkansas

    c. Minnesota

    d. All of the above

40. In which of the following cases did the Florida Supreme Court uphold a district court's *insufficient nexus* decision?

   a. *National Geographic Society*
   b. *Dell Catalog Sales*
   c. *National Bellas Hess*
   d. *Share International Inc.*

41. In which case did a state Supreme Court rule that the activity of making deliveries in company-owned trucks is protected under P.L. 86-272?

   a. *National Private Truck Council*
   b. *Asher Inc.*
   c. *Geoffrey Inc.*
   d. *Bandag Licensing Corp.*

42. Which of the following is *not* a true statement?

   a. Texas has a statute that requires a corporation to file a franchise tax return and pay tax if the corporation has the authority to do business in the state.
   b. Treaty permanent establishment provisions are binding for state nexus purposes.
   c. California has a statute that provides a nexus exemption in certain situations where an employee attends an in-state trade show or convention.
   d. It is possible for a foreign corporation to have nexus for state tax purposes but not federal income tax purposes.

43. Which of the following statements is *not* true regarding leased property?

   a. Factors that help to support nexus include the negotiation or execution of the lease agreement in the state or the receipt of the rental payments in the state.
   b. In the case of immobile property, the lessor typically is considered to have established nexus with each state where the leased property is located.
   c. In the case of leased property that is immobile, the creation of nexus generally is difficult to identify.
   d. For leased mobile property, many states provide that an isolated landing or trip through the state will not create nexus.

44. In which case did the Massachusetts Supreme Judicial Court hold that various warranty claims activities performed in the state created nexus?

   a. *Tyson Foods*
   b. *Dell Catalog Sales*
   c. *Alcoa Building Products*
   d. *Amgen*

45. Which of the following activities is considered "unprotected" under a statement adopted by the MTC?

   a. Providing an automobile to a salesperson for use in conducting protected activities
   b. Providing a personal computer for use in conducting protected activities
   c. Maintaining a display room for two weeks at one location within the state
   d. Repossessing property

46. Which of the following activities is included in the definition of *permanent establishment*?

   a. Using facilities solely for the purpose of storing, displaying or delivering inventory belonging to the taxpayer
   b. Maintaining inventory belonging to the taxpayer solely for the purpose of storage, display or delivery, or processing by another enterprise
   c. Maintaining a fixed place of business solely for the purpose of purchasing goods or collecting information for the taxpayer
   d. Employing individuals in the United States who conclude contracts that are binding on the foreign corporation

47. Which of the following is *not* a potential solution for the issues encountered in the state tax arena because of electronic commerce?

   a. Federal legislation
   b. State legislation
   c. The Streamlined Sales Tax Project
   d. All of the above are potential solutions for the problems

48. Which of the following is an in-state activity by independent contractors that is *not* protected by P.L. 86-272?

   a. Soliciting sales
   b. Replacing damaged property
   c. Making sales
   d. Maintaining an office

49. For nexus purposes, the U.S. Supreme Court has held that there is a critical distinction between the duties of an employee and an agent engaging in solicitation. ***True or False?***

   a. True
   b. False

50. Under an economic nexus standard, taxpayers would be required to collect sales tax on *all* sales, regardless of whether they are physically present in a state. ***True or False?***

   a. True
   b. False

51. Which of the following is true?

   a. At the local level, jurisdictions that impose a local sales tax *always* enact a local use tax.
   b. All states impose identical rates for state sales tax and use tax.
   c. All states and the District of Columbia impose a sales tax on retail sales of tangible personal property and selected services.
   d. None of the above.

52. Which of the following is typically the key in determining whether an item is subject to sales or use tax?

   a. The transaction itself
   b. Whether it involves manufacturing equipment
   c. The true object of the sale
   d. Whether it is an item sold at a grocery store

53. Which of the following has *not* been defined by the Streamlined Sales Tax (SST)?

   a. Four mutually exclusive categories of clothing
   b. Purchase price
   c. Tangible personal property
   d. None of the above

54. Which of the following is *not* one of the four broad categories into which exemptions usually fall?

   a. Use of the product
   b. Nature of the transaction
   c. Character of the item sold
   d. Location of the purchaser

55. When a transaction involves the provision of nontaxable services in connection with a taxable sale, the charge for the nontaxable services may *not* be subject to tax if separately stated. **True or False?**

56. Which one of the following statements is *not* true?

   a. While auditors have a great deal of authority regarding the timing of an audit, taxpayers have rights too.
   b. When scheduling an audit, prior audit experience with the state should be considered.
   c. If attempting to reduce the scope of an audit when time constraints exist, a taxpayer should identify transactions that may be excluded from review and propose the exclusions to the auditor.
   d. In scheduling an audit with an out-of-state auditor, the taxpayer should *not* consider whether the auditor is under a time constraint.

57. A _____ audit refers to an approach where the taxpayer performs some of the audit work, subject to auditor review.

   a. Field
   b. Sampling
   c. Managed
   d. None of the above

58. If a nexus questionnaire is mailed to a taxpayer and it appears that the taxpayer has been targeted for specific reasons, the taxpayer should do which of the following?

   a. Respond in writing to the request
   b. Attempt to contact the state via telephone to discuss the questionnaire before responding
   c. Not respond, *unless* there is follow-up from the state
   d. Not respond, *even* if there is follow-up from the state

59. Which of the following statements is *not* true?

    a. On the phone, taxpayers should go *no* further than providing some assurances that a sample is an acceptable audit methodology, subject to a formal review of the state's sampling techniques.

    b. To reduce the scope of the audit when time constraints exist, a taxpayer should use less sampling.

    c. Taxpayers should discourage the auditing of transactions they feel may be unnecessary.

    d. Taxpayers should refuse to allow the auditor to audit the books or transactions of entities without nexus.

60. Audit confirmation letters usually contain all of the following information **except:**

    a. The period under review

    b. Items to be included in the nexus questionnaire

    c. The taxes under review

    d. Any agreements previously reached regarding the scope of the audit

61. When a jeopardy assessment is made:

    a. The states tend to err on the low side when making assessments.

    b. The burden of proof rests with the state.

    c. The auditor and taxpayer must agree on the amount.

    d. The state can base the assessment on the best available information.

62. Which of the following statements is true of a self-audit?

    a. It is performed to identify and correct *underpayment* errors before the auditor reviews the books.

    b. It is performed to identify and correct *overpayment* errors before the auditor reviews the books.

    c. It is performed to find errors that will generate a refund.

    d. It is performed to correct inefficiencies.

63. If a taxpayer has *never* filed a return, which of the following is true?

    a. The taxpayer is open to assessment as far back as the state can establish a connection between the taxpayer and the state.

    b. The taxpayer is open to assessment for a maximum of 10 years.

    c. The taxpayer is *only* open to assessment until the state's statute of limitations has run.

    d. None of the above

64. Which of the following is the object of a reverse audit?

    a. To identify and correct underpayment errors before the auditor reviews the books

    b. To identify and correct underpayment errors when filing an amended return

    c. To recover tax incorrectly paid to a taxing jurisdiction

    d. To recover tax incorrectly paid to a vendor

65. The greatest opportunities for refunds are related to:

    a. Purchases by a taxpayer

    b. Incorrect tax status of a customer

    c. Incorrect tax status applied to items sold

    d. Errors made by the taxing jurisdiction

66. Which of the following documentation should *not* be included with a refund claim?

    a. A copy of the invoice from the seller on which the tax was billed

    b. A copy of the check that shows that payment was made to the seller

    c. An explanation as to why the transaction in question is *not* subject to tax

    d. None of the above

67. A voluntary disclosure agreement benefits which of the following?

    a. *Neither* the taxpayer nor the state

    b. *Both* the taxpayer and the state

    c. The taxpayer *only*

    d. The state *only*

68. Negotiations with the auditor should *only* take place in the latter stages of audit fieldwork. *True or False?*

69. Some states allow taxpayers to estimate their tax liability through sampling, using state-approved sampling procedures. *True or False?*

70. Records should *always* be discarded once the statute of limitations has been reached. *True or False?*

71. In most jurisdictions, the key to understanding the treatment of a construction contractor is to understand:

   a. Whether the contractor is a retailer or consumer

   b. The distinction made between *real* and *tangible* personal property

   c. The treatment of labor associated with *real* and *tangible* personal property

   d. The type of contract involved

72. Which of the following would *not* be exempt from sales and use tax in most states?

   a. The cost of materials incorporated into a contractor's real estate repair project

   b. Labor performed by a contractor to repair real estate

   c. Parts consumed in the repair of tangible personal property by a contractor

   d. Labor performed by a contractor to repair tangible personal property for a tax-exempt customer

73. Which of the following is a requirement most states impose for production machinery equipment to be exempt from sales tax?

   a. It must be used indirectly in the manufacturing process.

   b. It must be used directly in the manufacturing process, but often with a *de minimis* exception.

   c. It must be used at least 40 percent in the manufacturing process.

   d. It must be used at least 25 percent in the manufacturing process.

74. Which of the following statements is *not* true?

   a. Many states have special provisions exempting from sales tax the sale of equipment and materials to taxpayers engaged in farming.

   b. Many states impose tax on returnable shipping containers but not nonreturnable shipping containers.

   c. Generally, production machinery and equipment are exempt from tax if certain requirements are met.

   d. Sales to manufacturers and processors are usually subject to sales tax if the property purchased becomes or is made a part of a product that is to be sold by the manufacturer.

75. Manufacturing activities that generally fall within a state's manufacturing or processing exemption and are *not* considered marginal activities include:

    a. Shipping and receiving
    b. Research and development
    c. Machine handling in the step-by-step process
    d. All of the above

76. In states that provide a manufacturing exemption, equipment and tools used to manufacture self-constructed production equipment:

    a. Are covered by the state's manufacturing exemption
    b. Are *not* covered by the state's manufacturing exemption
    c. May or may not be covered by the state's manufacturing exemption
    d. Are covered under the state's *use-on-use* exemption that is part of every state's manufacturing machinery and equipment exemption

77. Which of the following statements is true?

    a. The burden of proof rests on the state that a taxpayer is *not* qualified to claim an exemption.
    b. Applied overhead charges are ordinarily included in the tax base for machinery that is purchased and modified for another use.
    c. Whether the cost of materials for the repair and maintenance of taxable shipping containers is subject to tax is unrelated to the treatment of labor to repair tangible personal property.
    d. It appears that judicial bodies are moving toward broader interpretations of the scope of exemptions.

78. Which one of the following statements is *not* true?

    a. States offering production machinery exemptions often include printers in their definition of manufacturers qualifying for the exemption.
    b. When the printer acts as a manufacturer, it is selling tangible personal property and is *never* required to collect sales tax on the transaction.
    c. Printers function as manufacturers when they produce a printed document from raw materials.
    d. When the printer acts as a service provider, it may or may not have an obligation to collect the tax, depending on whether the state taxes the services performed by the printer.

79. In some states, the material exemption is expanded to include property that is used and either consumed or destroyed in the manufacturing process. *True or False?*

80. Under the *Integrated Plant Doctrine*, each manufacturing task is viewed as part of a synchronized system that is engaged in manufacturing. *True or False?*

MULTISTATE CORPORATE TAX COURSE (2009 EDITION)   (0718-3)

Module 1: Answer Sheet

NAME _____

COMPANY NAME _____

STREET _____

CITY, STATE, & ZIP CODE _____

BUSINESS PHONE NUMBER _____

E-MAIL ADDRESS _____

DATE OF COMPLETION _____

CFP REGISTRANT ID (for Certified Financial Planners) _____

CRTP ID (for CTEC Credit only) _____ (CTEC Course # 1075-CE-7183)

On the next page, please answer the Multiple Choice questions by indicating the appropriate letter next to the corresponding number. Please answer the True/False questions by marking "T" or "F" next to the corresponding number.

A $72.00 processing fee wil be charged for each user submitting Module 1 for grading.

Please remove both pages of the Answer Sheet from this book and return them with your completed Evaluation Form to CCH at the address below. You may also fax your Answer Sheet to CCH at 773-866-3084.

You may also go to **www.cchtestingcenter.com** to complete your Quizzer online.

METHOD OF PAYMENT:

☐ Check Enclosed   ☐ Visa   ☐ Master Card   ☐ AmEx

☐ Discover   ☐ CCH Account* _____

Card No. _____ Exp. Date _____

Signature _____

* Must provide CCH account number for this payment option

EXPRESS GRADING: Please fax my Course results to me by 5:00 p.m. the business day following your receipt of this Answer Sheet. By checking this box I authorize CCH to charge $19.00 for this service.

☐ Express Grading $19.00   Fax No. _____

⬤.CCH
a Wolters Kluwer business

Mail or fax to:
CCH Continuing Education Department
4025 W. Peterson Ave.
Chicago, IL 60646-6085
1-800-248-3248
Fax: 773-866-3084

MULTISTATE CORPORATE TAX COURSE (2009 EDITION)   (0718-3)

Module 1: Answer Sheet

Please answer the Multiple Choice questions by indicating the appropriate letter next to the corresponding number. Please answer the True/False questions by marking "T" or "F" next to the corresponding number.

1. ——	10. ——	19. ——	28. ——
2. ——	11. ——	20. ——	29. ——
3. ——	12. ——	21. ——	30. ——
4. ——	13. ——	22. ——	31. ——
5. ——	14. ——	23. ——	32. ——
6. ——	15. ——	24. ——	33. ——
7. ——	16. ——	25. ——	34. ——
8. ——	17. ——	26. ——	35. ——
9. ——	18. ——	27. ——	

Please complete the Evaluation Form (located after the Module 2 Answer Sheet) and return it with this Quizzer Answer Sheet to CCH at the address on the previous page. Thank you.

MULTISTATE CORPORATE TAX COURSE (2009 EDITION)   (0719-3)

Module 2: Answer Sheet

NAME _____

COMPANY NAME _____

STREET _____

CITY, STATE, & ZIP CODE _____

BUSINESS PHONE NUMBER _____

E-MAIL ADDRESS _____

DATE OF COMPLETION _____

CFP REGISTRANT ID (for Certified Financial Planners) _____

CRTP ID (for CTEC Credit only) _____ (CTEC Course # 1075-CE-7193)

On the next page, please answer the Multiple Choice questions by indicating the appropriate letter next to the corresponding number. Please answer the True/False questions by marking "T" or "F" next to the corresponding number.

A $96.00 processing fee wil be charged for each user submitting Module 2 for grading.

Please remove both pages of the Answer Sheet from this book and return them with your completed Evaluation Form to CCH at the address below. You may also fax your Answer Sheet to CCH at 773-866-3084.

You may also go to **www.cchtestingcenter.com** to complete your exam online.

METHOD OF PAYMENT:

☐ Check Enclosed   ☐ Visa   ☐ Master Card   ☐ AmEx

☐ Discover   ☐ CCH Account* _____

Card No. _____ Exp. Date _____

Signature _____

* Must provide CCH account number for this payment option

EXPRESS GRADING: Please fax my Course results to me by 5:00 p.m. the business day following your receipt of this Answer Sheet. By checking this box I authorize CCH to charge $19.00 for this service.

☐ Express Grading $19.00   Fax No. _____

CCH
a Wolters Kluwer business

Mail or fax to:
CCH Continuing Education Department
4025 W. Peterson Ave.
Chicago, IL 60646-6085
1-800-248-3248
Fax: 773-866-3084

MULTISTATE CORPORATE TAX COURSE (2009 EDITION)   (0719-3)

Module 2: Answer Sheet

Please answer the Multiple Choice questions by indicating the appropriate letter next to the corresponding number. Please answer the True/False questions by marking "T" or "F" next to the corresponding number.

36. ___	47. ___	58. ___	69. ___
37. ___	48. ___	59. ___	70. ___
38. ___	49. ___	60. ___	71. ___
39. ___	50. ___	61. ___	72. ___
40. ___	51. ___	62. ___	73. ___
41. ___	52. ___	63. ___	74. ___
42. ___	53. ___	64. ___	75. ___
43. ___	54. ___	65. ___	76. ___
44. ___	55. ___	66. ___	77. ___
45. ___	56. ___	67. ___	78. ___
46. ___	57. ___	68. ___	79. ___
			80. ___

Please complete the Evaluation Form (located after the Module 2 Answer Sheet) and return it with this Quizzer Answer Sheet to CCH at the address on the previous page. Thank you.

MULTISTATE CORPORATE TAX COURSE (2009 EDITION)   (0981-2)

Evaluation Form

Please take a few moments to fill out and mail or fax this evaluation to CCH so that we can better provide you with the type of self-study programs you want and need. Thank you.

About This Program

1. Please circle the number that best reflects the extent of your agreement with the following statements:

	Strongly Agree				Strongly Disagree
a. The Course objectives were met.	5	4	3	2	1
b. This Course was comprehensive and organized.	5	4	3	2	1
c. The content was current and technically accurate.	5	4	3	2	1
d. This Course was timely and relevant.	5	4	3	2	1
e. The prerequisite requirements were appropriate.	5	4	3	2	1
f. This Course was a valuable learning experience.	5	4	3	2	1
g. The Course completion time was appropriate.	5	4	3	2	1

2. This Course was most valuable to me because of:

    ____ Continuing Education credit   ____ Convenience of format
    ____ Relevance to my practice/   ____ Timeliness of subject matter
    employment   ____ Reputation of author
    ____ Price
    ____ Other (please specify) _____

3. How long did it take to complete this Course? (Please include the total time spent reading or studying reference materials and completing CPE Quizzer).

    Module 1 ____   Module 2 ____

4. What do you consider to be the strong points of this Course?

5. What improvements can we make to this Course?

MULTISTATE CORPORATE TAX COURSE (2009 EDITION)   (0981-2)

Evaluation Form *cont'd*

General Interests

1. Preferred method of self-study instruction:
   ____ Text ____ Audio ____ Computer-based/Multimedia ____ Video

2. What specific topics would you like CCH to develop as self-study CPE programs? ____

   _____

   _____

   _____

3. Please list other topics of interest to you _____

   _____

   _____

About You

1. Your profession:

   ____ CPA   ____ Enrolled Agent
   ____ Attorney   ____ Tax Preparer
   ____ Financial Planner   ____ Other (please specify)

   _____

2. Your employment:

   ____ Self-employed   ____ Public Accounting Firm
   ____ Service Industry   ____ Non-Service Industry
   ____ Banking/Finance   ____ Government
   ____ Education   ____ Other _____

3. Size of firm/corporation:

   ____ 1 ____ 2-5 ____ 6-10 ____ 11-20 ____ 21-50 ____ 51+

4. Your Name _____
   _Firm/Company Name _____
   Address _____
   City, State, Zip Code _____
   E-mail Address _____

THANK YOU FOR TAKING THE TIME TO COMPLETE THIS SURVEY!